BACK OF THE HOUSE

"Forgive the unappetizing metaphor, but Scott Haas is a fly on the wall at Craigie on Main. He sees all, hears all, tells all. Did the wonderful chef Tony Maws know he revealed so much?"

—Alan Richman, *GQ* Food and Wine Critic

"Haas is that rare breed of writer: part investigative reporter, part father confessor, wrapped up in the poetry of culinary genius and served with a twist of humor."

—Amanda Foreman, author of *A World on Fire* and *Georgiana*

"Scott Haas provides an insider's perspective that truly takes you into the belly of the restaurant-industry beast."

—Drew Nieporent, restaurateur (Tribeca Grill, Nobu, Corton)

"Reading *Back of the House* is like reading my own autobiography about my life in the kitchen. Scott brings out an uncensored, unbiased reality to the restaurant industry. Every young cook should sink their teeth into it." —Marc Vetri, chef and restaurant owner

"I look to Scott for digging deep to uncover what really motivates and inspires us. He is one of those rare food writers who brings an intelligence and understanding from beyond the kitchen to his culinary reporting."

—Daniel Boulud, chef and ~~~~ ~~~~ ~~~~ ~rants

"I have been waiting to read ~~~~ ~~~~ ~~~~ ghts about restaurant kitchens are al ~~~~ ~~~~ ~~~~ ain-ing. His views on chefs surpris ~~~~ ~~~~

—Thomas Keller, chef and restaurateur

BACK OF THE HOUSE

THE SECRET LIFE OF A RESTAURANT

Scott Haas

BERKLEY BOOKS, NEW YORK

THE BERKLEY PUBLISHING GROUP
Published by the Penguin Group
Penguin Group (USA) Inc.
375 Hudson Street, New York, New York 10014, USA
Penguin Group (Canada), 90 Eglinton Avenue East, Suite 700, Toronto, Ontario M4P 2Y3, Canada
(a division of Pearson Penguin Canada Inc.) • Penguin Books Ltd., 80 Strand, London WC2R 0RL,
England • Penguin Ireland, 25 St. Stephen's Green, Dublin 2, Ireland (a division of Penguin
Books Ltd.) • Penguin Group (Australia), 707 Collins Street, Melbourne, Victoria 3008, Australia
(a division of Pearson Australia Group Pty. Ltd.) • Penguin Books India Pvt. Ltd., 11 Community
Centre, Panchsheel Park, New Delhi—110 017, India • Penguin Group (NZ), 67 Apollo Drive,
Rosedale, Auckland 0632, New Zealand (a division of Pearson New Zealand Ltd.) • Penguin Books (South
Africa), Rosebank Office Park, 181 Jan Smuts Avenue, Parktown North 2193, South Africa • Penguin
China, B7 Jiaming Center, 27 East Third Ring Road North, Chaoyang District, Beijing 100020, China

Penguin Books Ltd., Registered Offices: 80 Strand, London WC2R 0RL, England

BACK OF THE HOUSE

The publisher does not have any control over and does not assume
any responsibility for author or third-party websites or their content.

PUBLISHING HISTORY
Berkley trade paperback edition / February 2013

ISBN: 978-0-425-25610-7

An application to register this book for cataloging has been submitted to the Library of Congress.

PRINTED IN THE UNITED STATES OF AMERICA

10 9 8 7 6 5 4 3 2 1

For Madeline and Nicholas

Like my mother used to tell me—if you're good at something, never do it for free.

▪ CONTENTS ▪

UNLIKE MOST OF THEIR COLLEAGUES IN OTHER CITIES, TOWNS, AND VIL-
lages throughout the world, the chefs of Boston and Cambridge, inspired in part by the great Spanish chef Ferran Adrià, are more celebrated for creativity than their devotion to or refinement of a specific cuisine, and Tony Maws, at Craigie on Main, is the most imaginative of them all. When the restaurant first opened in West Cambridge, the name had been Craigie Street Bistrot (Tony had insisted on what he viewed as the French spelling), and although it was within walking distance from my home, I had never eaten there.

The restaurant had been located in the basement of an apartment building in a posh neighborhood of West Cambridge, with views from its tables of shrubs and car bumpers, and it was unlike bistros in France, which typically serve moderately priced and simple, classic dishes.

Craigie Street Bistrot had a clientele with extremely deep pockets and served long, expensive dinners. Too rich for my blood, I thought; and, why would I eat in a basement?

The establishment also seemed to be limited by an ever-changing daily menu, posted outside its entrance, that when I read it, which I often did when walking my dogs, suggested a lack of focus and an inability to use a few ingredients to create flavor. I could not see a culinary tradition that might provide structure to what was being served.

The critics, local and national, however, were unvarying in their praise for Tony's inventiveness and appreciation of both the food and financial markets. He shopped locally and altered his menu based on what he found from farmers and purveyors. Although he refused to carry any American wines—all his wines are still from Europe, predominantly France—his food was inspired by the New England region, by what was available locally.

I was intrigued when the restaurant relocated to Main Street in Central Square. The neighborhood is one of Cambridge's liveliest. Increasingly, it combines the city's tradition of political radicalism with very cool, crazy-hip restaurants, cafés, and bars. Across the street from the new Craigie you find a Pentecostal church, a cookie factory, and a fire station. Down the street is a huge public housing project. Around the corner: another Pentecostal church and a Puerto Rican restaurant called Izzy's. Young and old, white folks and people of color, student and suburban, local and foreign, straight and gay and transgender can mingle without being hassled. It is a vibe I embrace. So I stopped in one night with my wife.

The restaurant was at street level; had a full bar, compared to just wine and beer at the old place; and, with its big, open kitchen and capacious dining room, seemed to be an effort to shift gears and be part of a happening area rather than exclusive. I figured that the food cooked and served at the new Craigie might reflect its setting, that the strain of purely upscale dining would be lessened. Open to the influences of passersby, no longer on a street of mansions, as the old Craigie had been, the new restaurant might be just the sort of place where people could stop by and eat good food without pretense or fuss. I was curious, too: After all these years that I had been avoiding it, what was Tony Maws cooking at Craigie? It was one thing to read about it. How did his food taste?

"I can't eat anything here," I said to Laura after looking over the menu that had been handed us by the amiable waiter. "I don't recognize half the food that's here, and what is familiar seems goofy."

My wife suggested I have a salad, but I wondered if it might not be better to have drinks, go home, order a pizza, and watch a rental.

Something resembling a discussion followed, and then, just as I shifted in my seat and got up to leave, Tony stopped by to say hello. We had not met before, but I had interviewed him by phone for a piece I had done for *Gastronomica* on sous vide cooking. He had seen my name on the night's guest list. I had been impressed during our phone interview by his wit, knowledge, intelligence, and honesty.

"Hey, how's it going?" he said.

We shook hands. He has small, delicate hands.

"Good, good, great," I said.

"Decided?" he asked.

"I'm having the oysters and then the swordfish," said Laura, with a barely noticeable so-there glance in my direction.

"Excellent choices," said Tony. He took her menu and cocked his head to look at me with a grin.

"Ah, I don't know," I said. "Pig's tails?"

"Got to have the tails," said Tony. "And for your main course?"

It was early in the restaurant's evolution, only a few months since its move to Central Square, and there were no burgers or pasta on the menu yet. The menu seemed to be a hodgepodge of surefire hits like beef and weird courses like a ragu of pork hearts and *uni*. Tony did not seem sure of what he wanted the new place to be. This indecision was reflected by what was on the page, I felt, and being there was unlike being in a good Italian, French, Chinese, or Japanese restaurant where the personality or character of the chef, how he or she felt and thought, mattered far less or not at all in comparison to what was on the plate. The menu here seemed more ego-driven than many places where I had dined, but unlike the egoistic restaurants of Keller, Boulud, Ripert, Pasternack, Batali, or Carmellini, here I saw a lack of focus and a cry for help.

"Why don't you decide?" I said pleasantly, handing the menu back to him.

Tony took the menus, smiled broadly, and bounded back to the kitchen.

"This is ridiculous," I said to Laura. "This place is ridiculous."

We were seated in the bar area, which had filled up with happy, healthy-looking people, well dressed, drinking cocktails, untroubled by what I believed to be a troublesome menu. By their relaxed postures and the spontaneity of the thundering laughter, it was evident that I was the problem here.

"You need to relax," said Laura, taking my hand, pretending as usual to be unaware of the gravity with which I regard food and dining.

"I *am* relaxed," I said. "This is relaxed."

I thought about it: Why be incurious?

Laura was right, of course, as usual. I needed to absorb what was happening rather than distance myself from it by being analytical, which was a feature of my day job. I have worked as a clinical psychologist, chiefly in communities of color and locked, inpatient units of mental hospitals, for decades. Besides, what was there to analyze? I had not eaten anything!

I have to admit that I don't like people to cook for me. I don't like most restaurants; they usually seem fussy and overpriced and, like most artists, 95 percent of chefs are not good at creating memorable experiences. Dining out seems to me to be a colossal waste of time and money, unless it's done right, a righteous distraction from more pressing needs.

Which is why, when I meet a great chef, it is transcendent. Many others feel that way, too, of course: Great food for the very lucky is the new privilege, almost a religious prerogative, a way to position ourselves in relationship to nature.

As I started to unwind, the first course arrived.

"Ah," I said.

The tails.

The tails came on an egg-shaped plate in a thick, dark sauce topped with little ringlets of fried onions, and to say that they were delicious does not do them justice. I am sure that the same effect could have been achieved with oxtails, but I respected the chef for wanting to put his stamp on the food. They were extraordinary.

Raw oysters, swordfish, and striped bass: Each had a depth of surprising flavor, unanticipated due to an inability to place the dishes in a geography or a style. Not European, Asian, South American, or North American per se, not presented with some recognizable plating, just flat-out terrific.

When the evening wound down, I thought of Lupa, on Thompson Street in the West Village: gutsy flavors, and here at Craigie unencumbered by the need to conform to a rigid set of traditions or guidelines that apply to Italian cooking and are even mandated in some instances by the European Union.

"Wow," I said to my wife.

"See?" Laura said.

What struck me that night, and on subsequent visits, was the freedom of the cooking. Principled food, driven by technique and informed by a global pantry; I saw in Tony's dishes a kind of personal statement that relied on strains of the world's flavors but did not muddy them or try to dazzle.

Tony had been to Asia once to cook for a week at an event in Singapore. Twenty years ago, he had been to Italy for a total of seven days, traveling by train from the northwest border with

France down to the heel. He had traveled to London and Paris (multiple times), Mexico (three times), and Spain (four times). During his adolescence and twenties, he had once visited Morocco, Belgium, Ireland, Switzerland, the Netherlands, Greece, and Israel. His direct experience with French gastronomy came solely from living with a family more than two decades ago for two weeks in Champagne, working for six months in a restaurant near Lyon, and cooking with a French chef who had moved to San Francisco. He did not have a culinary tradition. Rather what Tony cooked was, gloriously, Mawsian.

The best restaurants are, in addition to the food being cooked and served, the ones in which the chef tells you his or her story. The emotions that inspire their cooking are felt in the dining room and on the plate, and it was obvious to me that night that Tony's story was unique.

While the story of each restaurant varies, there are three common ones:

First, there is the restaurant where the chef tries to re-create the joy and sensuality of a childhood kitchen. Safe, warm, fun, spontaneous, and nurturing, these restaurants—Daniel and Jean-Georges are good examples—convey the love of a childhood spent with mothers and grannies while the men were outside working in the fields or conducting business. These restaurants are about pleasure and sexuality.

Second, there is the restaurant that conveys the child's fantasy— The French Laundry, Robuchon, The Inn at Little Washington, and Le Bernardin come to mind—of rooms where finesse, anticipatory service, and calm define the experience. Here the chef tries to create the type of kitchen he wished he had known as a child. It is an idealized view that has little to do with the reality of the chef's upbringing.

Finally, there is the restaurant that is extremely personal, such as Momofuku Ko or Craigie on Main. At these idiosyncratic places, the food and presentation are usually unfamiliar to customers. Unless you tell the kitchen you have an allergy to what is served on the tasting menus, the chef expects you to trust him, eat what is on your plate, and love the food. If you do not like it, go somewhere else. The defiance of early failure—letting down their families—is evident in this third type of restaurant.

At Craigie on Main, the food has no definable roots in a recognizable cuisine, nor in techniques, flavors, or ingredients specific to a region or tradition. This is cooking with refinement, but without many rules. It is an ironic reversal of what customers experience in most high-end restaurants, which is why Chef Maws's story is so compelling. The food is *him*.

"My food, my way of doing things, my menus," Tony would tell me later.

The danger here is *goofy cuisine*, which is an extension of fusion cuisine, in which lots of ingredients from all over the world are piled onto a plate. Tony's food required restraint. If you do not know when to stop, you should not attempt his type of cooking. Better to learn to make a good tomato sauce, where there is a clear beginning, middle, and end. With Tony's cooking, he stopped when he achieved what he believed to be just the right taste.

What sets Tony apart, along with the few others like him, is his unwillingness to compromise on his creativity to conform to the paternalistic tradition of a specific cuisine. Like David Chang, another chef from the upper middle class with an extremely complicated relationship with his dad, Tony refused to cook a certain way because the rules of a culinary tradition demanded it. These men do not want to cook the food of their fathers.

It takes enormous nerve to cook with creativity, lead teams, and satisfy the hunger of strangers. As a result, chefs suffer terrible doubts about themselves and their work. I am at once drawn to

chefs' spellbinding mix of nerve and despair and moved by the sacrifices they make to take care of others. That predicament—feeling
powerful and yet dependent on others for validation—makes them
artists: creative, no matter what, but in need of an audience. The
bad-boy mentality, being outlaws, the histrionic nature of their
work? These are also very appealing to me.

Chefs are ecstatic when a night of service goes well, and devastated and humiliated when things have gone wrong. Their highs and
lows are extreme. The restaurant slang for falling behind and risk-
ing failure says it all: *in the weeds.* Feeling lost, adrift, unable to reach
solid ground, overwhelmed, but somehow embracing the struggle to
restore order.

The men and women who choose to be chefs have transformed
self-doubt into consistent hard work, dedication to service, and creativity. Chefs are the opposite of the mentally ill whose passivity
and repetition of past failures dooms their relationships, productiv-
ity, and sense of well-being. Still, I see the roots of what drives chefs
and where the restlessness lies in them. I am drawn to the turmoil
of chefs and their narrative of feeling incomplete. They work hard
to feel better about themselves, obviously, and when they succeed in
that endeavor, they feel pride and satisfaction for a while.

I feel protective of them, and I admire their resilience.

WHAT FOLLOWS IS THE TRUEST ACCOUNT OF WHAT HAPPENED WITH TONY
Maws after spending a year and a half in his restaurant to find out
what motivates him and how he leads those in the back of the house
and throughout the restaurant.

I.

NOT HIS FATHER'S FOOD

ONE

We'll Head Them Off at the Pass

FOR FUCK'S SAKE!" SAID TONY.

Creative acts begin with anxiety. Scared or uneasy? Build a fire, write a ghost story like *The Shining*, compose a song like Coltrane's "Alabama," cook a nine-course meal to show love. One difference between the artist or performer and a person who suffers from anxiety and is disabled by it is that the creative individual manages more routinely to use the worrying to inspire action.

I was thinking about anxiety and creativity as I watched Tony at the pass where the food is looked over, and corrected if necessary, before being brought to tables by servers. It was my first night of observation.

I had e-mailed Tony a few weeks after my first visit to see if we could meet up in the restaurant. I asked him if I could shadow him and learn what inspired his remarkably personal culinary approach, and then in thirty minutes, with a handshake, he had agreed to let me in. I was stunned by the speed of his trust and confidence. He applied no rules or conditions to my visits or my writing: I could come and go as I liked, talk to whomever I liked, and he did not demand or ask to see what I had written until after it was published. That philosophy or outlook applied to his style of cooking: Spontaneous, sure of himself, implicitly asking the person he trusted to believe in him and show him comparable respect.

As the chef-proprietor of Craigie on Main, widely regarded by national critics as one of the country's best restaurants, Tony stood at the pass of his open kitchen looking like a bundle of energy, a vortex.

"Ordering eight tastings! Five three-way porks! Two *hiramasa*! One pig's head!" he said.

Cooks recited back: "Ordering eight tastings! Five three-way porks! Two *hiramasa*! One pig's head!"

The ticker tape of fresh orders, known as tickets, came in. Tony glanced down.

"For fuck's sake," he said.

His face glowered. He looked as if he had been called a bad name. He was still as a statue, seething.

He was looking at a fifth order for a burger, medium rare. Tony did not become a chef in order to fry burgers. When he opened Craigie on Main, he knew he would have to have a bar menu, so he created the burger. Like many upscale restaurants, from the lounge at Daniel to the bar at Harvest in Harvard Square, chefs cater to people on the go, dining solo, or eager to eat good food without fuss.

As he explained the basics of what it took to make the burger, Drew Romanos, one of his three general managers, came closer to coax him into whispered, confidential communication. Drew was tall, lean, and so graceful in his movements that he inspired calm in those around him. Tony leaned in and Drew spoke into his ear.

"Chef, VIP four-top, any suggestions on what to send out?"

Tony looked at the guest list for the evening. Each name had to its right a brief description of the occasion being marked in the restaurant or some notes about preferences, such as: *Hyun: Daughter's birthday. Duerler: Wedding anniversary. Horton: Comes in weekly, no pork. Goldman: With State Department.*

"Look at this," Tony said. "People used to go to L'Espalier for special occasions. Now they're coming here!"

Craigie on Main was more expensive than L'Espalier, one of Boston's top restaurants, described on its website as serving "New England–French" food: The average tab for two at Craigie was well over $200 ($63 per person for three courses, exclusive of tax, cocktails, wine, and tip) and could easily be as much as $350 or more if the customers ordered tasting menus ($115 per person for eight courses; $95 for six courses, exclusive of tax, cocktails, wine, and tip)—but it was informal and inviting. High-end dining without the formality, with a waitstaff in jeans, aprons, and black shirts. Wooden floors, simple flatware. With the restaurant's low-key atmosphere, the food was the emphasis.

Which is why Tony was disappointed about the burger and decided that, as of Tuesday, he would serve them only in the bar. "No more burgers in the main dining room!"

It would be a challenge to move burgers into the bar only. Especially following the burger's debut on the cover of *Bon Appetit* in September 2010, customers were coming for the sole purpose of having a Craigie on Main burger.

"We can move the guests to the bar area if they insist on having the burger," he said. "It may be a problem at first."

"Chef?" said Drew.

Drew's bushy eyebrows went up and down. He had been waiting for Tony to tell him what to send out as a comped or free dish to the VIP customers.

"Send them a terrine," Tony said.

Drew conferred with one of the sous chefs, and Tony returned to the tickets that by now were coming in fast. Meanwhile, behind him, the pace was picking up. He had two cooks, a man and a woman, both medium height and slender, at garde manger who were assembling sets for the burgers. Four cooks, all men with the bony bodies of runners, were on two sides of an enormous contraption that held a salamander oven, a long and rectangular griddle, and four burners. To his immediate left: a sous chef slicing fish, another cook getting chickens ready for extended roasting.

Below us, in the basement, was the prep area where Tony's second sous chef commandeered the prep crew: all hard-core, built like boxers with attitudes to match, most Spanish-speaking, most tat-covered. It was here that the restaurant's engine was kept powered from four A.M. until one A.M.

Back at the pass, Tony was the epitome of calm among all the commotion: guests being led to tables, servers dropping off orders, the GM handling a disputed bill, the line cooks moving like bees. At five feet, eight inches tall, in his early forties, with a slight beard that resembled Ben Affleck's look in *The Town*, he has a canny grin, a looped gold earring, and a lean appearance.

"How do you do it?"

"I love it," he said. "It's what I've always wanted to do."

"You always knew you wanted to be a chef?"

"Absolutely," he said. "Getting things accomplished. Feeding people, making them happy. The pace. The setting: staying up late and being in the restaurant world that is so different from the world others outside of it live in."

"From what age?"

"Oh, since I was a child," he said.

I was skeptical.

Tony grew up in an upper-middle-class Jewish American household, in Newton, a well-off Boston suburb, with no ties to the restaurant industry. He was raised by two highly successful parents who believed in the power of education, and he attended Belmont Hill School, an exclusive, all-boys, private day school, and then he had gone to the University of Michigan, where he studied psychology. While his parents encouraged his interests, they certainly never intended to send him to elite schools in order for him to become a cook. A dream to be a chef rooted in childhood fantasy and experience was unlikely.

I sensed that another narrative existed alongside it. Everyone has a public persona that is often utterly different from who he or she is once you acquire trust through intimacy. Generally, what we express to others, especially those we do not particularly know well, is part of that public narrative. Meanwhile, so obviously that it may not be worth stating, there is what we keep to ourselves. That is a huge part of the pleasure of deep relationships, whether as a parent, a spouse, a child, a close friend, or even a shrink: getting to know the person who is overshadowed by the demands of reality.

I knew there was something else that drove Tony to work in professional kitchens. And if I could discover his motivation for becoming a chef, I knew I might understand how he created the highly personal story of his restaurant and inspired his staff. Whatever motivated him was what he considered critical in leading others.

"I've always thought about food," he said.

"Me, too."

"So you know what I'm talking about," he said.

He smiled. He has a remarkable smile, a memorable one; with his small teeth and thin lips, his mouth is wider than expected and seems, through its exposure, to inspire. It is one of those genuine smiles that the wearer can use to persuade others to be happy around him so that he might acquire some of that pleasure from outside himself, as there is not enough within. It is the smile of a shy person trying to be bold.

"Yes, but thinking about food and running a restaurant are not the same thing. So, no, I don't know. I don't think about food 24/7 the way you do."

"You think I don't know that?" he said.

He spoke like a guy who had gotten a tat talking to another guy who was *thinking* of getting one.

We were approaching eight o' clock on a Thursday night, and the tickets were flying in even faster than before. Jazz played louder over the restaurant's speakers: Bill Evans competed with the din and laughter of hungry customers. It felt like a scene, a sophisticated private party, a place to be, better than a quiet dinner at home or a romantic evening quelled by small talk.

Waitstaff had a crisp look as they went to tables holding plates of food, but when they reached Tony at the pass, a few appeared to be discombobulated. Some were more professional or experienced, but others were scared. They were clearly the recent hires.

"Chef, three people at my four-top finished their entrées," said Billy, a gangly guy who looked like he played guitar when he wasn't serving. It was an effort for him to stand up straight. He would last only a few months at the restaurant and then leave, like many others in the restaurant industry, to parts unknown. "Should I wait to bring out dessert menus?"

"How the fuck should I know?" said Tony.

The waiter looked as if he were going to burst into tears. Tony ignored this. He did not even look up. He crossed off orders that had been completed. He had a job to do; this was not the time or the place for the waiter to indulge in emotions. It was typical restaurant hierarchy: The chef was entitled to say whatever he liked, but those over whom he had authority had to do what they were told. It was not a discussion; it was about following the chef's orders.

Nor was it a TV food show where tantrums took place unrealistically in order to entertain viewers. It was unusual for guests to overhear anything coming out of the kitchen above the sizzling, the clanging of pots and pans, and the typical restaurant noise. Depending on where people sat and what night it was, one might hear blasts of profanity. Tonight, as with most nights, Tony spoke with firmness in his voice, rather than with pure, undiluted rage. He did not quite yell. He hardly raised his voice—*most* of the time. He would occasionally scream, and he never threw a physical tantrum. With floor staff, he might swear or at times speak with derision. With cooks, he literally got inches away from them periodically—"You have to get in their face," he had told me—and with language familiar to a Marine drill sergeant, sometimes with the barking, he told them *what the fuck* they were doing wrong.

For the job to get done, the staff had to tamp down emotions from their work and absorb the emotional blows—in some ways, it was in part what made the job deeply frustrating and stressful: What was pent up did not go away until after work, when everything that had been bottled up could lead to all kinds of trouble.

TONY FINALLY LOOKED UP AND SAID TO BILLY, "OKAY, WAIT. WAIT UNTIL the fourth cover is done."

He shook his head and crossed off a completed order on a ticket.

"This is my life. No one can make a simple fucking decision without coming to me," Tony said. "They don't take ownership. They don't figure things out for themselves. Pisses me off! That's why I have to be here all the time. No time off."

Tony had a sous chef, but he didn't have an executive chef who could run things for him, which I did not understand. Most chefs at his level have someone to turn to routinely so that they can take time off.

"Did you ever have someone? In the nine years since you opened your first place?"

"Nope," he said.

"Hmm."

"'Hmm?" he said with a big smile. "What's that mean?"

"It just makes me wonder what dynamic you've created here," I said, writing to keep up with our conversation. "You're in charge, you want at times to get away, but you can't delegate your authority."

"It's a real problem," Tony said. "I'm not making this up."

The action swirled around him. He looked as if he had been caught up in the surf and that rather than worrying about whether he would topple over, he was thriving on the undertow. He seemed to love the stress.

"Chef?"

Danny, one of his sous chefs, was at his side. He was shorter than Tony, incapable of standing still, and wiry. He kept touching his face, flexing his arms, and moving his head from side to side. He showed Tony a small plate on which he had placed a fillet of sea bass.

"Wrong," said Tony. "All wrong. Fuck!"

It *was* wrong, too. Even I could see that. The idea was to slice the rectangle of fish into paper-thin slices that would then be put on a bed of watermelon radish wafers after which a yuzu-infused oil would be sprinkled over everything. For crunch, little fried bits of shashito pepper. This was a perfect idea for a dish: plenty of umami, beautiful presentation, ingredient driven, with a relatively simple technique required to create and assemble it. There was only one catch.

"Nobody knows how to cut fish in my kitchen," said Tony.

This was a surprising and honest admission, especially considering the high prices charged for the fish, but Tony explained as he went to the cutting board to show Danny how to do it right.

"This is why," Tony said, leaning in, putting the right amount of pressure on his knife so that it glided in, "I am"—moving with the blade—"here"—and now pulling back—"every night."

Danny stood by his side. It was clear that he knew what was required of him, equally clear that his efforts were inconsistent, and evident that this predicament was a source of tension between the two men.

"C'mon, Danny," said Tony. "C'mon. Got to stay focused, get your head out of your ass!"

He spoke like a frustrated older brother to a younger sibling whom he loved, but who also kept dropping the easy pop fly. The anger in his voice was powerful, but again, he was motionless. The economy of movement that was needed to cook efficiently applied to nearly everything in the restaurant.

I had to wonder how a fancy restaurant like Craigie could operate consistently when the cooks clearly did not have the skills needed to get the job done on a day-to-day basis.

"Some of them have the skills," Tony said, "but they just don't use them without me teaching them constantly. Plan B: From now on, I cut all the fish. Nobody else will cut the fucking fish. Done!"

"Why not just drop everything and do the burgers? That's something your crew can do. They would fly out the door. You'd be able to spend more time with your wife and son. Less stress, more fun."

"Because we should aspire to do more," Tony said. He had a steely look that made me think of Max Payne from the popular video game. Defined by the task, on a mission. It was flat-out inspiring to see and hear, especially when I knew that so many people go through life searching for an activity to bring meaning. Tony had found that and, though it may sound corny, I saw this in his face. "When my crew is on, we're the best in the city. No compromise!" As I watched the cooks struggle to keep up with orders, their focus and speed had become more intense with every minute as the room was filling up. Watching these men and women, in the open kitchen, was fascinating as it provided a sense of the purpose that cooking brought to their lives.

"When you're working the line, you can feel rhythm and speed," Tony said. "One reason it's hard to relax after work. It takes discipline to establish focus, maintain it, and then find ways at the end of the night to let it go."

"Sex and drugs and rock and roll."

"Exactly. Back in the day," said Tony. "Old school. Sure, that was the way it used to be."

"Not anymore?"

"No, man," he said. "Can't." Big smile. "Can't. We've got work to do. We're the best. Craigie is the best. We can't play around with that."

Tony admitted that part of the attraction of becoming a chef, at the very beginning, *was* the sex, the drugs, and the rock and roll. But he also talked about how it was much, much, much more than that. "It was the feeling of getting something done. Even if it was just washing a sink full of dishes. When the job was done, the results were immediate."

Tony compared the high one gets from line cooking to the feeling of being in the zone that athletes talk about when the work takes over and they enter a transcendent consciousness that alters time. I knew what he was talking about. I had been a line cook and loved feeling that nothing mattered outside the dish I was working on. The sense of accomplishment from that immediacy was great. Little else yields results so quickly outside of sex or competitive sports.

"I mean, look at Timmy," Tony said.

He pointed out a stocky, tattoo-covered cook with biceps as thick as a python. He was stirring a small pot of sauce, frying up baby brussels sprouts, and grilling buttered buns for the burgers.

The delicate nature of his movements contrasted with his appearance. He looked like a roadie or biker. Cooking was clearly Timmy's way of letting go and, whether he realized it or not, a way to stay true to being a tough guy while nurturing others.

"My cooks have to keep up with the orders," said Tony. "It's my job to make the guests happy."

The great chefs are capable of responding to and anticipating the hunger and expectations of their customers. It is hardly a secret that they have a heightened sense of the same feelings as the people who come to eat their food. I have dined with chefs outside their restaurants, and they ordered just about everything on the menu until the table teemed with plates. Chefs are hungry all the time. Their insight into the emotions created by cooking and good food is deeper than that of most people they serve in their restaurants.

I looked back at Timmy, who was focused as he moved his stubby fingers like a watchmaker. I remember losing track of what I was doing when I line cooked and how I couldn't keep up with the orders.

"That's a skill," said Tony. "Everything we do here involves learning new skills. Here. Watch this. Timmy, what are you working on?"

"Sauce for the veal, sprouts on the chicken, buns on burgers," said Timmy, without looking up. "Waiting on the order to fire the onion rings for the pig's tails."

"Psychologically, I think that many people who enter the profession of cooking have trouble paying attention. ADHD, whatever," said Tony. He still retained an interest in his college major. "You're the shrink, I don't know what to call it. Michigan was psychoanalytic and I didn't get past the *DSM*-III."

The *DSM*, developed by psychiatrists, is the *Diagnostic and Statistical Manual* used by mental health clinicians. There are even more disorders now in the *DSM*-IV than in its predecessor and more still in the latest edition in 2013. A new disorder for every day. It's like adding holidays.

"How about ADHD?" Tony asked. "Have you seen it?"

"Sure, I've seen it. It exists in nature. Overdiagnosed, but sure, it's there, and I can see why you feel that your cooks are inattentive and how line cooking suits them."

"Working in a kitchen gives them the structure they need to get focused," he said.

"Do they take that strength and apply it to other parts of their life?"

"I do," he said.

WITHIN THE PAST SIX MONTHS, TONY HAD BEEN WRITTEN UP IN *GQ*, THE *New York Times*, and *Bon Appetit* and had been named a James Beard finalist for Best Chef in the Northeast. People were coming in these days with higher expectations. He was no longer the chef at the cozy basement bistro he had opened nine years ago with two cooks. The Craigie on Main that customers had come to know about now had ten cooks, twelve waitstaff, and three general managers. On weeknights it averaged about 115 covers, and on weekends it averaged 130 to 140. They were seeing walk-ins at the bar area and at least two seatings.

"I was always ambitious," Tony said, looking over another set of tickets that had just come in. Scratching off dishes completed, looking over his shoulder at the cooks, plating a beautiful-looking dish of veal three ways that his crew had cooked and handed to him. Watching Tony was like viewing an athlete who can adroitly perform many tasks at the same time. At one point I hung back, near Danny's station, so that our conversation would not interfere with Tony's efforts to expedite orders. He motioned me back.

"You don't mind?"

"No," Tony said. He laughed. "I like talking. I mean, you see what goes on here. Nobody talks to me! Not a rock star among them."

"No one?"

"No one," he said. "Not yet. Maybe Jess. We'll see."

Jess was Tony's pastry chef. A bio major at Stanford, she decided against applying to medical school and chose instead to pursue a passion for baking. Hair pulled back, pale blue eyes, a ready smile, agile, and moving like a person who chose to respond or not, she had great social confidence. She fit in, but she also conveyed a mature perspective that made others around her try to gain her favor and respect.

Until Jess arrived at Craigie, Tony concocted all the dessert recipes, keeping the list small, and had his cooks execute them. Jess stood apart from Danny, who, like James Brown, was the Hardest Working Man in the Business but lacked a desire to invent, and from Lydia, another sous chef who wanted to pursue her own interests. Jess understood Tony's outlook—creativity over tradition.

Watching the cooks at the five stations of the open kitchen, I could see how their exuberance trumped their finesse. Tony needed to step in often to correct their mistakes. He shook his head frequently in exasperation.

"Can't you hire cooks with greater ability? Or teach them what they need to know?"

"It's complicated," Tony said. "The short answer? No."

Craigie was unlike any other high-end kitchen I had been in. At other renowned establishments where I had spent time in the kitchens, the cooks worked with consistent, high-level abilities, and there was usually an executive chef in charge. The executive chef does not primarily create, but rather orchestrates the menu of the chef. It is like the difference between being a composer and being a conductor.

Craigie, it seemed, was a work in progress. Did that mean that Tony was a work in progress, too? Perhaps, despite his complaints, did he enjoy feeling indispensable?

"So what's your plan?"

"I'm trying to get Danny to do what I do so that once a week I can get a night off," Tony said.

Danny heard us and looked over. He smiled and then bent in, shoulders caved, to season the huge, beautiful Vermont chicken that had been cooking, sous vide, for hours and was now ready for final, high-temperature roasting. The aroma of the bird was so intense that I closed my eyes and could readily imagine how good it would taste.

"Danny," said Tony. "Take over."

Danny stopped what he was doing, wiped his hands on his apron, and took Tony's place at the pass. Danny always had on a game face: wildly impressive energy that benefited most from a coach telling him which play to make rather than to decide what to do on his own.

"Let me show you around," Tony said.

As we walked through the open kitchen to the narrow staircase leading to the Civil War–era stone-and-dirt basement, Lydia brought Tony a plate of Portuguese sardines to see if they had the right texture.

Tony took a bite. She stood before him, plate in her palm, expressionless.

"Fucking awesome," he said.

"Thanks, Chef," Lydia said. She said it with diffidence, not needing his praise to feel better about herself but pleased to have done the job properly. It meant that she now had time to do the next thing on her long list of tasks.

Little in the restaurant was intended to have emotion attached to it, which is really what made it functional. The focus was on the food, not on the person making it. Emotion had no part in the execution of the dishes by the cooks. The only person allowed to express feelings was Tony.

He led us through the commotion of the basement prep area, where a half-dozen prep cooks and line cooks were grinding meat, making stock, breaking down fish and pork and chicken, cutting up squid, and stirring sauces. The vibe was outlaw, as it often is in restaurants, with beards, tats, profanity, dark comedy, and threats. I had to wonder if the copping of the identities came from well-thumbed copies of Tony Bourdain's classic, *Kitchen Confidential*, or if the bad-boy and bad-girl mentality was a true reflection of the cooks around me.

Watching them in action, I realized it was both. For sure, most of these cooks were incapable of fitting into a nine-to-five setting where they had to act normal. Their poor eye contact, limited social skills, unique verbal styles, and general unwillingness to take it easy meant that this crew, like so many restaurant workers, saw life very differently from most people. Their intensity set them apart.

On top of that, they embraced their isolation, the love and commitment that kept them up day and night cooking, cutting meat, making stocks, and so on. If they were banned from the straight world, well then: Good-bye, straight world!

Beyond the prep area was Tony's office, which resembled a cave. It had a low ceiling. The only light came from a small lamp on a long wooden worktable. Then we reached a tiny room that was next to the wine cellar. Here a recent culinary school graduate handed Tony a plate of uncooked pasta made in-house.

The kid was only a few years out of high school. He tried to look Tony in the eye but was intimidated by him. Tony was about twice his age, a well-known chef, a man that the boy dreamed of becoming one day. Maybe, maybe not.

The pasta was to be a new dish for the bar and an item, if Tony felt like it worked, on the tasting menu.

Tony had bought a sleek pasta machine from Italy and placed it in this back room. He rolled a tubular item between his thumb and index finger.

"What do we call it, Chef?" asked the cook.

"I don't know," said Tony. "Penne? Pennette? Rigatoni?"

"Garganelli?" I asked.

"Maybe," said Tony.

This restaurant, it was becoming apparent, was based on spontaneity. The chef made up many things as he went along.

"At our first location," Tony explained, "when I first opened, I changed the menu literally every day. No limits!"

This made no sense to me based on what I had observed for decades in other restaurants with other chefs whose aim was consistency. Most chefs I knew wanted their crews to cook food with precision and repetition. I did not understand why anyone would not want to learn to cook a dozen or even fewer dishes perfectly and would rather indulge in experimentation.

Unlike a French, Italian, or Japanese restaurant, where what is served is driven by the rules of the cuisine, family kitchens, and regions or *terroir*, where the chef is the interpreter or intermediary, Craigie on Main is a restaurant where the chef decides *everything*. There was a menu at Craigie with items that stayed the same for weeks and even months, but a huge part of the restaurant was the chef's six- or eight-course tasting menus, which often changed nightly, even hourly, and were called, accurately, "Chef's whim." For example, a pork heart sausage panino? Why not? Swordfish wrapped in guanciale? Sure! Slow-cooked Spanish sea eel? Of course!

I could see where this would lead to problems with cooks who did not share Tony's vision, could not execute his ambitious designs, and were unable to keep up with his drive. I wondered why he would invite these problems. Tony had said that he did not have a crew with the prerequisite skills. But he refused to create a menu that matched the skills of his cooks; the cooks had to match his demands of the menu.

It made me think of something Duke Ellington had said: that he wrote tunes based on the talents of his bands. Long sax solos for Johnny Hodges, percussive triumphs for Sonny Greer.

Likewise, wouldn't it be simpler and less stressful to serve food that a crew was capable of cooking? Or was running Craigie an outlet for Tony's anger and frustration that would be completely out of place in a nine-to-five job?

"How do you explain this to your cooks?" I asked.

"Explain what?" he asked.

"Each new dish."

"Part of my job."

"Frustrating."

"True dat," he said.

"You know, Tony, one reason why many chefs focus on creating a well-defined, relatively unchanging menu is because that's what their cooks are capable of doing."

"Right," he said. "Of course. But I believe we can take it to the next level at Craigie."

"Have you come close to reaching that level? In the nine years since you've been a chef-owner?"

"No," he said.

"You keep trying."

"I do."

"Maybe you enjoy being angry and frustrated."

"No," he said, shaking his head. He positioned the fingers of his right hand onto his chin, narrowed his eyes, and grinned. The appealing pose was just like a PR shot he had on the restaurant's website!

"What I'd love to do is have a restaurant without menus. You sit down, you eat what I cook," he said.

This was not the first time I had heard this—I knew many other chefs who felt exactly the same way: Thomas Keller and Daniel Humm ran restaurants based on that principle.

"Yeah," said Tony. "If people would just let us do what we do best, they would have a better overall dining experience."

"Many people feel that deciding what to eat for themselves is part of the dining experience."

"You don't drill your own teeth, do you?" he said. "You don't repair your car engine. Why should eating in a restaurant be any different?"

"Many people feel it's a control issue. They struggle with the kitchen. They fight with the chef." I laughed. "That's part of the fun of dining out for them."

He made a thumbs-up for the still-unnamed pasta and took me back to the prep area. The culinary kid nodded and scurried away. I heard, "Whew," as he took a deep breath.

At prep, vision met chore. We were knee deep among plastic trays holding squid, peeled potatoes no bigger than casino dice, and the nightmarish, residual, unidentifiable by-products of creatures that, not too long ago, had probably been given organic feed while roaming free range until the moment they were separated from their sustainable herd or school and slaughtered humanely.

"You got the burger rolls under control?" Tony asked Dakota, one of his cooks.

Dakota had a mischievous look; he seemed almost feral, as if he were a fox come to life. Long hair, sometimes up in a samurai bun, other times on the sides and parted, cultivating a Depp look. Always grinning, always looking as if he might let you in on a private joke if he thought you were cool enough. He made people around him want to act cool.

"Yes, Chef," said Dakota.

"The burger is driving me fucking nuts," said Tony.

"Why not take it off the menu?" I asked.

"Too late," he said. "It's too popular. Look, it's a start by taking it out of the dining room. Soon I'll make it so that I only have enough burgers to sell eighteen a night. When the eighteen are sold, the burger will be gone for the night, eighty-sixed."

It was ironic that a chef devoted to improvisation had wound up with a cheeseburger. Here was a man who had trained in high-end kitchens, including Clio (Boston) and Coyote Cafe (Santa Fe), whose oeuvre was the multiple-course, tiny-portioned cuisine synonymous with upscale dining. Yet the dish that many knew him for was a burger the size of a Buick with a side of French fries.

"I want to talk to you about that burger later," I said, turning a page in my notebook. I thought of an artist who wanted to paint in oils but whose claim to fame was a clever and humorous Hallmark card. "I'm curious to know how it reflects your personality."

Tony shrugged. "My personality?" he said. "There's more to what we do at Craigie than the burger. That's the point."

I realized later that Tony was absolutely right: The burger had nothing to do with his personality. Sometimes a burger is just a burger. It was a delicious part of a smart business plan. At $21 (with bacon), each one was making him great money. His inclusion of the burger was no different than the sides sold with beef at steak houses. Ben Benson, owner of the eponymous restaurant in New York City, told me that years ago: The profit does not come from the steak, but from the double-digit-priced sides of baked potatoes, vegetables, and salads. The burger was Tony's version of a side to his "real" menu. It was not his fault that critics and 30 percent of Craigie's covers fell for the burger when the source of his pride in being a chef was in his far pricier and elaborate tasting menus.

▪ ▪ ▪

"BEAUTIFUL *TAOTOG*," SAID MATT, WHO WAS ONE OF THE PREP COOKS.

"Blackfish," Tony explained to me.

Matt, a tall, bearded man with a loopy grin, had on a pillbox hat that kept his long hair from falling into the food. Using a pair of tweezers to extract tiny bones from the fish, while supervised by Tony, he was not having an easy time of it.

"Here, look, let me show you again," said Tony. He sighed, running low on patience, as he held the fillet in place and swiftly pulled out tiny bones that were as thin as dental floss. "See?"

"I got it, Chef," said Matt.

"I've got to work with Matt on this fish," said Tony. "It's an ongoing problem."

Matt worked on the fish. After a few minutes, he presented the finished product again to Tony. Matt's brow furrowed. He stood back with his hands bent in at his hips.

"For every bone I find," Tony said to Matt, "you give me ten push-ups. Okay?"

"I nearly got it last time," Matt pleaded with him. "Just one bone."

"One bone is one bone too many," said Tony. Anger turned his face red. "Fuck!"

"Yes, Chef," said Matt. He sighed and returned to the task. Tony watched him intently and then examined the fish, which Matt said he had finished deboning: tiny bones still apparent.

"I'm . . . going . . . to show you . . . *again*," said Tony. He shook his head and pursed his lips, then stepped up to where Matt had been and began the extractions. Swiftly, within moments, little bones were lined up alongside the fish. "That's how you do it, Matt. Okay?"

I could not get over this: We were in the middle of dinner service and the fish needed upstairs still was not ready. No wonder

Tony was upset. Why didn't his cook know what to do? Was it a combination of Tony's difficulty in teaching him properly and Matt's inability to absorb his lessons?

"Yes, Chef," said Matt.

Danny had come downstairs. "Chef?" He had a spoonful of stock for Tony to taste.

Tony tasted the stock. Danny stared at the spoon and rubbed his chin.

"It's missing something," said Tony. "I'll give you two guesses. You have to guess; I'm not going to tell you."

Not a word from Danny. This went on for longer than Tony thought to be necessary. The frustration showed on his face. He rolled his eyes. I thought: How could he subject himself to this every night? Unless he found it appealing.

"Okay," said Tony angrily. "We need something to cut the bitterness. Maybe a little honey. What do *you* think?"

"Honey, Chef," said Danny. "Right away!"

"See what I mean?" said Tony. "They can't figure out these things on their own."

I nodded.

"They need you," I said.

"Right," said Tony. "My job is to motivate my crew. Keep them focused. Help them understand that I'm not going to praise them just for showing up. These millennials! This whole Generation Y, man, it's like they think everyone loves them. It's all they heard at home and in school. You can't be critical because it hurts their self-esteem. What a fucking pain in the ass!"

"You do love them," I said.

He laughed.

"Oh, I love them," he said, "but I also want to see them working without their heads up their butts. That's why I have a daily *kaizen* for them."

Tony sounded like a teacher frustrated with students who need to have the same lessons repeated to them, but who has difficulty in seeing how his teaching style had contributed to that problem.

"What do you need to work on today?" Tony said. "What needs improvement? What's your *kaizen* right now?"

He went from one prep area to the next.

"James, what's your *kaizen* today?"

James, one of the line cooks, looked startled. Like most of the other cooks, he was in his twenties. Lanky, a man of few words, and clean shaven, he moved with an intentionality that suggested it was best to steer clear of him. He looked like a fragile, angry man who moved rigidly in order to keep from exploding. It was apparent that James had been elsewhere in his thoughts.

"My *kaizen*?" he said.

"James!" shouted Tony.

James did not look sad or upset, not even preoccupied or distracted, just lost. He had the sort of look that likely worried others around him but was of no concern to him. He looked blank.

"Right proportions for the pig face, better Peking pancakes, work on the texture for the boudin noir–hoisin sauce," James said, finally. His voice was robotic.

What James and Tony were referring to was the confit and roasted milk-fed pig's head (for two) with Peking pancakes, spicy cucumber sambal, and boudin noir–hoisin sauce, for $60.

"We sell about four or five of these every night," Tony said, pointing to the pink half-face of what had once been a pig. "It's delicious."

Who ordered the pig, I wondered. I imagined frat boys doing it on a dare, bored people who thought of themselves as adventurous eaters, or IT engineers.

"No, man," Tony said, "we get repeat orders."

"Some people," said Matt, joining us happily, "got to have their pig's head, man."

He and Tony laughed, and then Tony told me to follow him while Matt went back to the *taotog*. He led me to a stocky man, short in stature, with thick black hair, a pocked face, and a thin mustache, who was working at a meat grinder, not saying a word.

"I want you to meet Santos," Tony said. Santos had been with Tony from the beginning, which is how he introduced him. He came from El Salvador, where he served in the army and where he had been shot in combat, Tony thought, though he wasn't sure. One day, Santos walked into the old Craigie looking for a job. "Started out as a dishwasher and now he does all our butchering. Dude's chill."

Santos was grinding meat for the notorious burger: deboned short ribs, hanger steak, brisket, and beef cheeks. To which he then added kidney fat and powdered miso the color of clay. He took chunks of meat from a rectangular metal tray and dropped them into the spout of a tall, churning, silver-colored grinder. The meat came out in long strands from a filter with many holes and then fell into a large stainless-steel bowl.

"How long does this take?" I asked him.

"Hours," Santos said.

He spoke with a slight accent and stutter, averted his eyes, and showed little emotion.

"You do this every day?" I asked.

"Except Monday," Santos said. Then he smiled. "Monday we're closed."

"Hard work," I said.

"Good that everything has to be perfect," he said.

We left Santos with the meat and walked upstairs.

Tony's parting words for the night were, "I'd like a sidekick.

Someone I could bounce ideas off of, someone who is at my level in cooking. There's no one like that at the moment here."

He returned to the pass, where he would stand alone.

On the way out, I waved good night to Tony. He had open, on the huge cutting board that stood at the pass, a book called *Encyclopedia of Pasta*, by Oretta Zanini de Vita. Like an expectant parent, he was leafing through it to find a name for his pasta.

The second seating had started. Tickets were streaming in, but Tony did not looked stressed. I could see it now, even at the outset of our relationship, that forgetting, each night, his own troubles and focusing on the needs of others was a grand distraction for him.

"We'll talk about taking care of people the next time you're in," Tony said without looking up, scratching off a ticket that had been completed, tasting a spoonful of jus from Danny, ordering two chickens and four more burgers (with a wince). "Tomorrow?"

"Tomorrow, Chef," I said, and then I left him at the pass to reckon with the hungry crowd who needed more answers than I did.

TWO

Baba Hannah

MORE COFFEE?" ASKED TONY.

It was early afternoon. Lights blazing before service, soon to be dimmed to seductive level when the doors opened. Hip-hop keeping everyone energetic. That would change at night, when jazz played.

Tony was in the outfit he wore each day when he was not on display at the pass during service: Cargo shorts, a T-shirt, and sandals. A few staff in the front of the house were polishing glasses, vacuuming, and setting tables. Prep was going on downstairs; the upstairs kitchen was gleaming, empty, and quiet.

"Oh, sure," I said. I slid my cup toward Tony. It was an ordinary white ceramic cup, nothing fancy. All of the flatware and crockery were plain white. Tony poured. "Thanks."

Chefs occupy a celebrated position in our culture. We admire them for many reasons, chiefly because of the unique flavors they create. Their food alters our moods. Ultimately, they stir up feelings we had when we were younger and ate meals prepared for us by our parents and grandparents. As a result, people develop an unconscious relationship with them. We expect chefs to take care of us emotionally, which is a powerful anticipation.

The best chefs recognize the unconscious relationship that their customers have with them and use it to ensure a steady, trusting clientele. When we are satisfied with what they feed us, we regard chefs with feelings of intimacy. When they disappoint us, the letdown can be intensified as it is displaced emotion from earlier relationships, and distrust is then the consequence.

Some people avoid restaurants for that reason.

My grandmother hated eating outside her home. A joke my mother told me when I was a child summed it up: An old woman walks into a drugstore with a lunch counter and asks: "Do you do urinalysis here?" The counter man says, "Of course we do!" The woman replies, "Well, then go wash your hands and make me a malted!"

"I thought it would be a good idea for you to come to Craigie during the day," Tony said. "That way I can show you what's involved in the early prep."

It was my second week at the restaurant. My routine was to be in the kitchen and on the floor two to three afternoons or nights each week, before and during service, attending front-of-the-house meetings and meetings with the cooks, interviewing anyone I chose at almost any time. There were times when I talked to wait staff when they were about to pick up an order. Times when I stood next to a cook working at his or her station. As he had promised, Tony allowed me complete access to everyone.

We were seated at the corner table of the empty dining room: white tablecloths, sparkling glassware; a few shadowy staff cleaning the plate glass, doorknobs, and counter spaces.

"What's your earliest memory of food?" I asked him.

"My grandmother Hannah," he said without hesitating. Her photograph was high up on the wall, just to the left of the pass.

"My mother's mother. Baba Hannah loved to cook. My mother? She's a good cook, but being in the kitchen wasn't central to her life. She started a consulting business. She was outside the house as much as she was in it. Not so for Baba Hannah. If you look at my menu, you can see that my ideas and recipes are shared by about ninety percent of the world's grandmothers."

I had both the dining room and bar menus out before me. *Hiramasa* sashimi? Monkfish cheeks? What did these dishes have to do with grandmothers? And what did it have to do with *his* grandmother?

As is the case for many grandmothers, having grown up before globalization and refrigeration helped define how we live and what we eat, Tony's Baba Hannah always cooked what was in season. She went to local farms and family-owned butcher shops. And she made gutsy, filling, fatty peasant dishes and used ingredients that reflected historical impoverishment: flanken, schmaltz, kreplach, kasha, tongue, and livers. Her kitchen was driven by the legacy of social exclusion, no access to markets more than a few miles from the rural areas of her ancestors, and the need to feed big families. Few people from the tradition of her class background ate in restaurants or knew the first thing about how food tasted outside their culture or religion.

"'Nothing should be wasted!'" Tony quoted his grandmother. "We're talking 'nose to tail' cooking before the hype."

Talking about his grandmother's cooking lifted Tony's spirits as her food must have when he was a child.

"Baba's food *created* memories," said Tony. "That's what I'm after in my restaurant, too."

Cooks were arriving through the open door in the bar area.

They waved and went downstairs to change out of street clothes. A few remained in the prep area below. Others came back up to the main floor and began cooking sauces and placing chickens in the low-heat oven in the open kitchen.

"Baba Hannah was more than a cook," Tony said. "She was the person that brought people together with her food. Her food got conversation going: strong views, loud voices, fabulous energy."

As Tony recalled memories of his grandmother, I noticed the blue diamond-pattern tribal tattoo that rounded his right bicep. I could picture him with his earring, slight beard, and attitude along with his edgy crew as young boys and girls in her kitchen.

"You may cook like Baba Hannah, but you don't act like her. How did you go from being innocent to being tough?"

"You wouldn't say that if you met Baba Hannah," said Tony. "Tough? She wrote the book."

Maybe, I thought. More so, I realized that when Tony spoke of his grandmother being tough, he meant she was tough enough to protect *him*. It was the love she brought to his life that kept him going, and it was her love that gave him permission to be as offbeat as he liked. Tony was obviously offbeat: his decision to serve pig's head and other odd ingredients like lamb's tongue and pig's tail, his choice to become a cook instead of pursuing psychology, his quirky sense of humor, his desire to make everything from scratch (except his breads). All of this demonstrated a guy who was bushwhacking his way through life.

"Who loves you more than your grandmother?" he said.

Tony's grandmother loved him no matter what he did and no matter what anyone said about him. No wonder Tony wanted to cook like Baba Hannah.

"I have to see what my cooks are up to."

We got up and went from station to station. The aroma of leeks sautéing in butter hit us. We smelled pork belly frying. We were hit by the scents of cumin, anise, and sesame seeds. We watched Matt make venison sausages. I held the menu and took notes while Tony tasted sauces, stocks, and butters.

On the menu, I found tzimmes, barley, couscous, grilled tongue, and a brunch item of a bagel with salmon and smoked bluefish, house-brined corned beef, and horseradish cream that went with a potato galette.

"It goes beyond the ingredients, too," said Tony when he returned. "I try to think like Baba Hannah. What would she do when cooking or tasting a dish?" Baba Hannah would taste and taste a dish until she felt it achieved perfection. Tony had learned how to tell when something was done by watching her cook without recipes. These days when Tony seasons a dish, the right amount is enough.

He sipped a spoonful of *pistou*-dashi broth brought to him by Dakota, who was a tall, very thin cook who worked garde manger but was learning to be a saucier.

"Delicious, man," said Tony.

"Needs more salt," said Dakota. He was bouncing up and down on his heels.

"No, it's good," said Tony. He grinned. "The miso we're adding later will take care of that."

"Thanks, Chef," said Dakota. He spun off.

I wondered whether if Tony had his grandmother's food today, it would taste as good as he remembers. Other chefs have told me how they idolized their grandmothers, just like Tony, but admitted that when they returned as adults to these kitchens, the food did not taste as good as they remembered.

The best example? André Soltner craving his mom's noodles and cheese and returning home to Alsace only to discover it was very ordinary.

Let's face it: There is no reality to the taste of food that we ate decades ago. It is the memory of whom we were with and who we were that matters more than the recollected supposed taste of the food; the taste restores to us the narratives. The food is the Mac-Guffin.

As we headed downstairs to see what the prep cooks had been up to all morning, Tony made it clear that he does not cook memories.

How could he? Tony took a foundation of memories of the food—the ingredients—and combined flavors in ways that were startlingly original.

Downstairs, in the hubbub, Matt, Timmy, Danny, Lydia, James, and a couple of others were working hard. In their aprons and caps, sleeves rolled up, they resembled people in the service. As with men and women in the military, the cooks' individual personalities are flattened by their identical outfits, extremely limited opportunity to improvise behavior, and the virtual impossibility of being able to show spontaneity, emotion, or behavior in reaction to the environment they are in.

Here beneath the earth's surface, illuminated by bulbs suspended on long, narrow wires, their look was one of fatigue tempered by devotion to a task that took them outside the turmoil of everyday life.

Tony went from one to the next.

"You ready to go?"

"I have to finish the dressing and taste it," said Matt.

"Ready to go?"

"Working on the miso and the greens," said James.

"No way," said Tony. "What do you miss every day?"

"What do I miss?" asked James.

"What do you miss?" said Tony.

James stopped stirring the broth. The other cooks stayed on task. Danny ran over to answer for him: "Razors, clams, crabs."

"Right," said James.

"C'mon, man," said Tony. "Get it fucking right!"

I took Tony aside. I wondered if he was worried about James, who usually seemed off-kilter.

"You mean, will he work out at Craigie?" Tony said. "I'm not worried, I'm pissed off! He's been here two months and he still doesn't get it."

James was in his own world, so limited in his responses to what people said that often directives had to be spoken to him twice, which was deeply irritating to the chef as well as grossly inefficient. He kept making the same silly mistakes.

"He can be offbeat, I don't care. A lot of my guys are offbeat, but they cook. James isn't cooking."

Danny brought Tony a long list of dishes that would be served that night: skirt steak, swordfish, pork, chicken, tongue, sweetbreads, salmon tail, and boudin noir.

"This is good," said Tony. "Are you on it?"

"I'm on it, Chef," said Danny. "I'm very excited!"

"Are we all good to go?" Tony asked the assembly of cooks, who, without looking up, shouted back: "Yes, Chef!"

We headed back upstairs to look over the reservations, to see who was VIP, what special occasions needed to be acknowledged by the kitchen and waitstaff.

"I couldn't do this in Boston," said Tony.

"Tony, that's less than a mile away, just across the bridge," I said, "C'mon."

"It's different here," he said. "Cambridge isn't Boston."

Cambridge, with its students, biotech industry, global consultants, and left-wing legacy, has an aura that does not quite match its reality. Tony, like many people, still thought of Cambridge as kind of a cool place when, in fact, its racial and economic diversity had nearly vanished with the end of rent control decades ago. It was now more of an enclave for well-off (median income $69,000) white people (62 percent).

The real reason why Cambridge was the perfect setting for Craigie had nothing to do with food. The real reason was that the city had plenty of rich people with time to kill; 40 percent of the residents were single, and you did not have to walk more than ten feet before bumping into a trust fund recipient or hedge fund manager.

"You don't think you could cook like Baba Hannah in Boston?" I asked.

"This setting is more intimate," he said.

"More like a home."

Tony lived down the street in a small, simple house with his wife, Karolyn, and young son, Charlie. All his money had gone into the restaurant. Karolyn had met Tony when he was cooking at Clio and she was tending bar. They had been together ten years and married for seven; Karolyn had worked the floor at the old Craigie and done whatever was needed. On special occasions, she continued to help out, though her day job now was as a kindergarten teacher at Buckingham Browne & Nichols, a fancy private day school. It was the perfect job for the wife of a chef who runs an upscale restaurant; both Tony and Karolyn were in the business of taking care of people who felt entitled to the best. Only Karolyn had to be calm and patient about it, which was a skill I imagined she brought to her relationship with Tony. Karolyn sometimes brought Charlie in before service. While Charlie sat on the expediting table, Tony fed his toddler son food such as bits of pickled mushrooms and pig tails.

Even though Tony had a young family at home, his bearish presence was in the restaurant from early in the morning until the last customer was served. He told me that he missed being with his wife and his son, who was turning three in June. It was just that the demands of being the owner and the chef meant that Tony was in Craigie no fewer than ninety hours a week.

"I'm here just about every night. I walk to work. I spend more time here than anywhere else. This *is* my home!"

THREE

Show Some Emotion

KNEW WHEN I WALKED INTO CRAIGIE ON MAIN THAT TONY WANTED TO BE seen as a maverick: a chef who was fearless in his ability to improvise, cook animal parts not typically seen in expensive restaurants, dazzle customers with his sophistication, and supervise a knowing staff who saw their role as educating customers nearly as much as serving them.

Tony was aiming to be a great chef, better than most, but his uncertainties and limitations were as much a part of his story as the nerve. His difficulties defined him and contributed to high staff turnover.

Since I had been at Craigie, within three months, a sous chef, a cook, two hostesses, and a bartender had left. Lydia would be the first to go. She had found a job at a restaurant–bookstore–record shop in Jamaica Plain, a rather hip, transitional, sort of Hispanic, kind of old Irish and German neighborhood of Boston. It was a place that once the working and poor people were kicked out, the folks who replaced them would gripe about their loss over delicious croissant and cold pressed coffee. Being in J.P. would allow Lydia to live closer to home, but I wondered if it wasn't a step backward for someone whom I had observed as having greater ambition.

"Working here is hard. I know that," Tony said. "I know I can be a fucking pain in the ass to work for. Either you love the hard work or you don't."

Lydia was capable of working hard, times ten, but unfortunately for Tony, who saw her potential, she apparently did not love working for him enough to stay longer.

Early on I had asked Tony what turnover was like. He singled out Danny, who had been with him for almost five years, and then pointed to how easily people come and go—front of the house and in the kitchen.

"It's the business," Tony insisted.

But it wasn't, I thought, not in top restaurants where I knew cooks and chefs. There was longevity in these great establishments: loyalty, a sense of purpose, a feeling of being part of the team, the knowledge that one was essential to the restaurant's success. When a sous chef did leave from these other places, it was often to open his or her own restaurant or travel or do a stage, which is kind of like a brief internship, at a restaurant in Napa, New York, France, Spain, Italy, or Tokyo, and then return. What about the environment Tony created in his restaurant added to Lydia's decision to leave and work in a simple neighborhood establishment?

Tony held daily meetings outdoors, unless it was raining, in late afternoon with the sous chefs and cooks. Here the cooks went over the work they had completed and what still needed to be done before service each night. This was typical for any good restaurant; this was what the meetings were about each and every day: review, preparation, a back-and-forth dialogue.

As in every other restaurant where I had spent massive amounts of time working, such as Da Silvano in the West Village, there were no manuals, few recipes, and almost nothing written down. So dialogue, a verbal exchange between chef and cooks, was essential. The best restaurants have the best lines of communication in place.

Tony explained to the cooks the types of ingredients he was using and why he had chosen to have them cooked in certain combinations. He talked about the seasons, his choice of purveyors, the differences between types of oysters, how kitchen equipment worked, and how to create balance in a dish. Throughout the time that they met, the cooks handed him tiny white plastic spoons to taste the food. It was a hushed atmosphere punctuated by nervous laughter.

The cooks, all of whom were fifteen to twenty years younger than Tony, were in awe of him, and for good reason. They were years away from acquiring his knowledge and might never be able to do so.

As is true with most restaurant crews, these men and women were so young that many of them did not know who they were yet. They felt one way today and another way the next. They were still their parents' children and talked often to me about their moms and dads. Their personalities were mostly what they imagined that they would one day do or be. Like many of us were in our twenties, they were more passionate than informed.

The meeting was run by Danny and Lydia. Tony hung back and talked to me while they went through the lists of prep items that still needed to be done. No one was asked for his or her ideas or suggestions; they were there to follow directions, not to deviate from the plans, and to cook exactly the way they had been shown countless times by Tony and the sous chefs.

"I want everyone to read this," said Danny.

Danny passed around the daily quiz.

"I like to keep my cooks mentally stimulated," Tony whispered to me.

Tony had photocopied a page from *Setting the Table*, restaurateur Danny Meyer's book on hospitality, and added to it: *Failure, Learning, Confidence. Please connect these three words and discuss the relationship between them. Talk about the relationship with respect to our food and service philosophy at Craigie on Main. You may use personal examples, but do not have to—it is more important to connect them to our work, overall.*

"Due in a week," said Tony.

Tony did not grade the papers and simply used them as a tool to get his team to think about what they were doing in the kitchen. It was his way of keeping them motivated and focused. No different than any other good chef.

"I understand that many of my crew have difficult emotional lives that I have to deal with when training them," Tony said to me, as the meeting continued.

"Do you think that a good chef has to be emotional?" I asked.

"If by emotional, you mean passionate, yes," he said, "but the best chefs are the ones with the greatest focus."

Moods brightened, postures became more formal, people stopped slouching.

Then Tony asked the cooks what projects they were working on for service that night.

"Working on the *pistou*-dashi broth," said Dakota. "Again!"

Timmy: "Shallots for oysters."

"James?" asked Tony.

"Fine," said James.

"Fine?" said Tony. His mouth opened in wonderment. "Fine? What the fuck? I mean: What do you have left to do?"

"Boudin noir sauce," said James.

"That it?" asked Tony.

"Yes," James said.

He looked at his feet.

James had seemed odd before, preoccupied, and now he was even more aloof. He did not share the interests of his fellow cooks. He was not approachable.

"Okay, then," said Tony. "Good."

After Tony had spoken to everyone and was satisfied that they had prepared as best they could for the night of service ahead, he said, "Let us rock tonight!"

"Yes, Chef!"

"Got it, Chef!"

"We'll get to it, Chef!"

To succeed, all the crew needed to do was straighten up, work hard, and do what they were told. Unlike home cooking or being a chef, working the line was all about speed, repetition, and surrendering your will to the act and the directives of the chef in charge. Many cooks did not know this when they began their careers or went to culinary school. They had thought that being a cook is creative; on the contrary, few jobs are as deeply unimaginative. Ironically, that is where redemption lies: in the act of repetition. Stop thinking and cook. Get it right again and again and again and again.

James's personal life might have been chaotic, but if he could allow the repetition to give it meaning he would be all set. It was like saying the same prayer every day and night. For now, however, I saw him sinking deeper into himself.

Tony was ending the meeting when he saw that a conflict had started between Danny and one of the two bakers.

"We need the cake batter by five P.M.," said Danny.

"I don't have a mixer," said Paul.

"You don't have a mixer?" said Danny. He laughed angrily. "Tell me you don't have a mixer."

"I don't have a mixer," said Paul angrily.

"How can a baker not have a mixer?" asked Danny. His voice

took on the inflections of his home: Cranston, Rhode Island. "How is that possible? Am I dreaming?"

Dakota laughed.

Paul put his head down. Shaggy-dog look, have pity, don't get mad at me please.

Danny asked: "What are we gonna do, Paul? How are we gonna solve this fucking problem?"

"I'll find a mixer," said Paul.

"You'll find a mixer?" said Danny. "Where the fuck are you gonna find a mixer today?"

"Hold on," said Tony. "You're a baker and you don't have a fucking mixer?"

"There's a story," said Paul.

"Uh-huh," said Tony. His eyebrows went up and he grinned. "Yes?"

"I gave it to my girlfriend," said Paul.

Tony asked: "Break-up gift?"

"Right," said Paul.

Paul looked as if he were trying to decide whether smiling was worth the effort.

"Okay, man," said Tony. "Danny, don't worry about it. Paul?"

"Yes, Chef?"

"I'll get you a mixer," Tony said.

AFTER THE MEETING ENDED, WE RETURNED TO THE KITCHEN.

"Is it better perhaps to have kids just out of culinary school or who've never had a restaurant job?" I asked.

Tony was tasting all sorts of things as we talked: soups, stocks, slivers of fish, beans, powders.

"Not necessarily," he said. He used his fingers to pick up pieces of fried oyster that a cook had handed him on a plate. He pulled off the coating. He sniffed the oyster. He rubbed it with his index and middle fingers. Then he took a bite. "Mmmm, good."

"Thanks, Chef," said Mary. Then she returned to her station to work on some house-smoked bacon that needed to be sliced up.

Mary was from Indiana, working in both garde manger and pastry, as the kitchen was short-staffed, and although she was delicate in how she moved, she had great intensity in her mien and posture: out to win, get out of the way.

"I like to have a staff with advanced skills," said Tony. "The thing, too, with culinary school? Look, I tell my crew here, cooks who think of leaving and going to culinary school: *This* is your culinary school. *This* is where you'll learn to cook."

"You have that much to teach them?" I asked.

"Not me alone," he said. "It's the process of cooking—being here every night, prepping all day, working from scratch, doing it the hard way. Cooking well comes from doing. This isn't something you learn in a classroom or at home."

Tony pointed out who was who in the open kitchen, where more noise came from slicing, chopping, and sizzling than from conversation.

"Matt Foley worked for Michael Schlow at Radius downtown," Tony said. "Kyle was at Bouley."

"What do they bring to Craigie from the restaurants where they worked?"

"Commitment," said Tony. "A professional outlook. Show up, cook, clean up. You've got to be super organized to work here. My guys who worked with other chefs know how to do that."

"Right, Chef," said Danny.

Even without a task at hand, as he stood beside Tony, Danny's eyes blinked, his neck moved side to side, and one shoulder shot up. He rarely spoke, and when he did it was with terrific, comical profanity.

"I also expect speed, ability to work with others, agility," said Tony. "Passion. Willingness to take criticism."

"Works in progress," I said.

"Exactly," said Tony.

"What *are* you doing here?"

"It's more than team building," he said, gesturing warmly and expansively with open arms. "We're not playing sports. I played hockey in high school. I know the difference between that kind of team building and what I'm doing here. This, is more like starting a family, but . . ."

"But?"

"But it's not," he said. "It's not the same. I have Karolyn and I have Charlie. The people who work for me at Craigie aren't my wife and kid."

"Yet you've said that this is the place where you spend more time than anyplace else. You're with people here far more hours than you are with your wife and son."

"Right," he said. "So I don't think about them the same way, I certainly don't *feel* about them the same way, but . . ."

"But de facto they are your family."

"Maybe," he said, and then he went back to tasting more dollops, forkfuls, spoonfuls, and little bits of the food that were to be served that night.

"So what exactly has the psychology you learned at Michigan got to do with it?"

"I think my background in psychology helps me understand who's working for me," he said. "To know them as individuals. Not just as cooks."

"Doesn't always work."

"No," Tony said, "but at least I'm trying!"

FOUR

The Chef Leaves Town

THROUGHOUT THE YEAR, TONY HAD NO MORE THAN TEN CONSECUTIVE days off. He regularly went away in the summer with his wife and son to stay with his mom at her place in Menemsha on the Vineyard. For him to take any more time away from his restaurant, it had to be related to his work as a chef.

This year he would be returning to Manhattan as a Best Chef Northeast James Beard Award finalist, as he had done the two preceding years. To be recognized by peers was a great honor, but it had been disappointing to *remain* a nominee; the trains there and back, two nights at a hotel, and the $425 ticket for Karolyn to be admitted to the awards ceremony were also big expenses. To make it worthwhile, Tony wanted to win. He had also accepted an offer to cook at a Beard event in San Francisco, followed by a Meals on Wheels benefit dinner at Rockefeller Center. He would be away a total of about four days.

Danny, put in charge, ran the daily meeting for cooks and, although it was sweltering, they met, as usual, in a tiny spot outside the restaurant on cement benches and beneath spindly sumac and locust trees. The noise was deafening as tractor-trailers drove by hauling, horns blasted, and radios played hip-hop from passing cars.

Immediately, the vibe was different. Like Tony, Danny ran the meeting with authority, but unlike him, he needed to remind the cooks that he was in charge. It was just like being in a classroom with a substitute teacher. Half the time is spent getting the kids to take you seriously; the other half you spend trying to take yourself seriously.

"Okay, Bobby," you're up," Danny said. He was going from cook to cook to see what they still had left to do before the start of service. "Bobby, you listening?"

Bobby, whose real name was Thomas, which was never used by anyone in the restaurant, looked like he had stepped out of a Norman Rockwell painting. He had a sweet-as-sugar personality, a gentle smile, and an easygoing manner. He moved calmly, as if he were on the beach, resting during a long hike, or just waking up from a nap.

Bobby didn't address Danny as *Chef*, the way he referred to Tony, but launched in: "Finish up the lamb sausages, sharpen my knives."

"Right," said Danny. "Good. Dakota?"

"Yes?" said Dakota.

Dakota picked up his notepad and stood as if to run back to the kitchen.

"We're not done yet," said Danny. "Please sit down."

Dakota sat down and grinned at the other cooks. He was pleased to have challenged Danny. Oddly enough, Danny grinned, too. He was uncomfortable with authority, and I had to wonder what lay in store for him as he got older and might want to own his own place.

"One of my struggles," Danny told me later that night, "is running things when Tony's not here. This is only the sixth or seventh time I've done it."

Danny had been with Tony for four and a half years.

"Without Tony, it gets a little lax around here," he said. "I noticed that last summer. It's my own need for greater maturity. I'm not going to let things get lax again. He keeps people on edge."

The restaurant was fifteen minutes from doors opening. Customers were lining up outside. The kitchen was humming: cooks in motion, but sillier and more talkative than when Tony was there.

A crew witnesses and feels the chef's willingness to endure pain and confusion and the intense, pure concentration often seen in the most successful people. By becoming what they do, chefs overcome ordinary life, which makes them leaders. The chefs' leadership, night after night, separates them from cooks. Lacking the ability to lead, many talented cooks never own restaurants, end up with physical injuries from working on the line past their prime, cook for caterers, teach in culinary schools, or give up the profession and start over at a job that has little or nothing to do with cooking. A real chef is a grown-up who is more than just willing to sacrifice: A chef is *eager* to sacrifice. Sacrifice provides the rush.

"Do you want to be like him?" I asked.

"I don't think I'll ever get the same level of respect as Tony," Danny said. "My relationship to the cooks is just different. There's a word for what Tony gets the guys to feel here. Not anxiety . . . not worried . . . not on edge," he said.

Danny looked thoughtful as he looked over the menu, tasted stock brought to him in the tiny white plastic spoons by several cooks, answered questions regarding VIPs asked by the managers, and dialed a supplier to order more eel.

"*Angst!*" he said triumphantly. "That's what he gets the cooks to feel."

"Isn't that the same as fear?"

"No, it's different," Danny said. "Look, we're like dogs." He put out his arms and looked around the kitchen. "See?"

I saw what he meant. Somebody had to direct the crew. The cooks were laughing, fooling around, and engaging in horseplay. Without a chef, the crew would do as they wished or follow the example set by one of the cooks.

"I have to address any fuckup right away. Otherwise they'll think it's okay some of the time," Danny said. He revealed that the last time he ran Craigie, he did a bad job as a leader and everyone got too relaxed. As he took out a long, wet, gray stone and began to sharpen magnificent Japanese knives, he admitted that he let it go on purpose.

"Everyone needs a break from Tony now and then," he said.

Not with resentment, jealousy, or anger, but as a simple fact.

"Opening up the doors!" shouted Meredith, who was one of the general managers—statuesque, charming, and as polite as a suburban Girl Scout awkwardly selling cookies at her grandfather's country club, knowing that allowing the old men to flirt with her meant more money for the troop. "Opening up!"

With the doors open and the restaurant gradually filling up, Tony's mother, Marjorie Maws, had found a spot at the bar to dine alone: oil-poached halibut, a glass of wine, and *The New Yorker*, folded in half, to a piece about Nabokov's letters.

"It's a little bit more mellow here without Tony," Marjorie said in response to my question about life at Craigie without him. "And we keep the numbers down when he's not here. It's what the cooks and Danny can handle without him . . . We stagger the reservations, and we have fifteen to twenty percent fewer customers."

Excitement in the rooms, but Marjorie was the epitome of calm. Eating Tony's food without him being there enabled her to create an ideal picture of her son.

As the evening progressed, Danny was aided by Matt. Matt was the sort of person I would want by my side if cast away on a deserted island. He did not move in subtle ways, but what he lacked in finesse he made up for with a powerful sense of humor and the culinary equivalent of not just the willingness, but the desire to climb the tallest trees to get the best coconuts. After Lydia had left, Matt had been promoted to the line and then swiftly to sous chef.

Both men had grown up in New England—Matt in Hyde Park, Massachusetts. Both had attended prestigious culinary schools: Danny at the Culinary Institute of America (CIA) and Matt at Johnson & Wales.

"A big part of why most Boston restaurants are so terrible," Tony had told me weeks before, "is that most talented cooks gravitate to much better food cities. Finding cooks from this area means that maybe they'll want to stick around to be close to their families and friends. For sure that's why I came back after working on the West Coast."

Unlike Danny, who is a cook's cook, someone for whom cooking has its own enchantments, Matt talked about chefs and restaurants like a so-called foodie. It is what differentiated him from the other cooks in Tony's kitchen and what distracted him periodically from the work. He was philosophical.

Both Matt and Danny were directing teams in the kitchen rather than working with their hands, which gave them ample opportunity to talk about why they did what they did. The first customers had been seated. Besides ordering the cooks around, Danny and Matt were tasting food.

It was cold out, and people came in grumpy, but as the first plates arrived at their tables, the behavior changed, at first almost imperceptibly through posture, and then through raised voices, rapid speech, and happy topics of conversation. It was that first-date method of operation: Even couples who had been together a long time, or business associates, were eager to please because the food they were eating had elevated their moods.

"Look at that," said Danny, beaming at the expediting table, looking over tickets as they clicked in electronically. "Instant gratification! We don't have to wait to find out if someone likes something. We see it right away!"

Matt, who was at garde manger, managing three cooks, chimed in.

"I love belonging to the restaurant community," Matt said. "That's what makes me happy . . . Working in a restaurant I feel like I'm part of this family, here at Craigie, but part of a bigger family, too. Like when I was eating at Corton, in Tribeca? The waiter took me into the kitchen when I told him I worked in a restaurant."

"Did you feel at home?" I asked.

"Yeah," Matt said. He paused. "To be honest? Yes and no. I mean the chef there, Paul Liebrandt, he's probably a good person, but he got real adamant when I tried to buy the cooks a round of beers. 'No way,' he said. I mean, I was just trying to be friendly."

The kitchen was heating up. Plenty of six-course tasting menus, eight-course tasting menus, a few à la carte dishes, and nearly a dozen burgers at the bar. Butter and shallots, vinegar being reduced, clouds of cumin-scented vapor rising, cream, and savory olive oil. Kyle and Bobby, the two young cooks at the grill station under Danny, were working at the same speed as they had when they first came in, but now it appeared that they were in slow motion. In contrast, Danny and the rest of the team looked as if they were being paid to move by the second. It was purposeful, and beautiful to watch. Outside the kitchen, life might not make sense, but here everything had meaning. That Kyle and Bobby did not quite share that feeling infuriated Danny.

"Put your cap on, Bobby," said Danny.

Bobby came over to him. He put his cap on.

"Get the fuck back to your station," Danny said.

Bobby turned around silently.

"Get back here," said Danny. He glanced up from the tickets he was writing on. "What the fuck?"

Bobby's apron was on backward.

"What the fuck, Bobby," Danny said.

"The other side got stained," Bobby said. He spoke blandly, as if not quite sure why what did not bother him was upsetting to someone else. He could not see outside himself. He was that young.

"Go the fuck downstairs and get another apron, for fuck's sake, Bobby."

Danny shook his head and called Matt over.

"Taste the *hiramasa*," Danny said to Matt. Danny can handle fish, but if he eats it, he has a severe allergic reaction.

"Tastes good," said Matt. He grinned.

"Good to go," said Danny.

He instructed Kyle to plate the fish, which then was brought over to the expediting table, where a server and then Meredith rearranged it and mopped the edges of the plate with a napkin. Three people stood over the plate, turning it, examining its contents, looking at it, thinking things over.

"I need a runner," the manager said.

"Got it," said Bunny, who was being cross-trained to be waitstaff as well as work the door. She had tiny freckles, an innocent smile, and little eyes. She looked like a quiet person who was actually no Miss Goody Two Shoes. Bunny was majoring in library science and along with an amazing head for numbers, the ability to arrange diagrams of tables where people were seated, and an extraordinary memory, her instincts included goofing off. Her laugh got others going. I had the sense that she was the one in high school whom all the parents trusted, but also the person who got her brother to buy the keg for the party. Instantly likable.

"Thirty-seven," said Meredith, referring to the table awaiting the fish, before returning to the hostess lectern by the door.

Two Southern men arrived and swaggered over to her.

"The concierge at The Sheraton Commander reserved a table for us," said the tall, thin, gray-haired man of the pair. He seemed to think his hotel had cachet when, truth be told, its glory days took place during Prohibition. "Name's Griffin."

"Why, yes," said Meredith, catching his vibe effortlessly, "we'll show you right to your table."

The table was by the window, raised up, and the men were asked to sit on stools.

Then Meredith returned quickly to the door, where I stood, to take care of three customers who had just walked in looking like they were at a wake. I could see she had to attend to them immediately, but I also saw that the two Southerners were unhappy about where they had been seated. They began to fidget and look around the room.

"Hi, good evening, welcome to Craigie on Main," said Meredith to The Unhappy Trio at the door.

Meredith was twenty-four, inexperienced, but as comfortable with authority as an officer. Her bearing was serious and unyielding. Her posture was correct. She seemed at first to be an odd choice for hostess, but then I realized that the favors she granted customers felt to them even more special because when Meredith paid attention to customers, it was like having a star take time out from her day. Acting special rubbed off on them.

As Meredith granted their wishes, she also made it clear that this was something she *wanted* to do rather than something she *had* to do. Hospitality was not a job for Meredith; it was a vocation, something she had been born to do better than most people. It was, ultimately, a way to show who was in charge.

She was in charge.

The trio she was greeting were an older couple and a man, in his forties, who looked like he was their son. The younger man looked exhausted: bent over, poor eye contact, restlessly touching his face, hair sticking out, button-up shirt, and tee visible at his neck.

"So happy to see you," Meredith continued. She was from North Carolina, she had told me, and had been taught proper manners. "I'll show you right to your table!"

They followed her, shoulders slumped, into the dark dining room. When she returned, I asked, "Did you know them?"

"Nope," Meredith said, "they've never been here before, but I could tell they needed cheering up right away."

Meredith did not tolerate unhappiness in customers. Unacceptable! Simply unacceptable! She saw their discomfort, but it was as if she had decided that if she tried hard enough she could cheer anyone up. Meredith was not particularly empathic, and because of that she made certain that people coming in to dine would not be subjected to scrutiny. She was not interested in what made them unhappy, only concerned with what could cheer them up. When she said, "Welcome!" you had better show the love back. Now. She meant it.

She walked over to the expediting table.

"Sixes on eights," Meredith said to Danny.

Six orders had been placed, and as there were eight customers in the restaurant, two people had not yet decided what to eat.

Looking confident, pleased with herself, Meredith returned to the door to look through the list of VIPs coming in that night. It was not an impressive list: no celebrities, no high rollers, nobody from the restaurant industry. Instead, regulars with preferred tables, birthdays, anniversaries, and businesspeople with clients from out of town.

Certainly one of the key elements of a successful, expensive, and relatively exclusive restaurant is its VIP list. I have seen the most famous chefs, men who no longer cook, study the roster of VIPs with devotion, as they know that making these people happy is the essence of what they do.

It is a difficult balance to strike: how to get the VIP steak to the table without the customer at the next table noticing that *his* steak, well, honestly, it's just not as juicy, not as big, and not covered with as many morels.

Meredith, at the door, started this process of welcoming the VIPs, greeting them at the door with the right level of effusion and respect without other customers feeling slighted.

One particular challenge, which was about to take place, was the customer who is not a VIP but wants to be treated like one.

"Excuse me? Miss?"

Meredith looked up.

The tall, Southern gentleman she had seated was back.

"I don't like the table," Mr. Griffin said. "It's high off the ground, the stools are uncomfortable, and my feet dangle. We would like to be moved to another table."

"Ah, yes," Meredith said, sounding combative for fleeting seconds but then excited by the challenge. She went to the computer screen showing the layout of tables. It looked like the game Battleship. She stayed chipper. "Let's see what I can do!"

If she could solve the problem, she could make a complete stranger happy! Immediately! Most people do not have jobs like that. The great thing about hospitality is the immediacy of the experience and the goal being so focused: Make someone happy! Make them forget about their tough day at work, the arguments in their relationships, the memories that kept popping up—at the oddest times—of unhappiness they had experienced long ago.

"I don't have any tables available right at this moment," said Meredith, "but I do see something here that might interest you. Would you like to sit at the chef's counter?"

"And what is that?" asked the man, who was by now suspicious. "I mean, either you have a table or you don't."

"I really don't, I'm sorry," said Meredith. "I told the concierge that when she made your booking . . . *this morning*."

Edge had crept into her voice, but then was gone as quickly as it had appeared. What upset Meredith was the nerve of a customer who was far from a VIP asking her to devote time to a problem that should not have been one and who was not interested in her proposal.

"The concierge didn't say anything about a high table and stools," he said.

"The chef's counter offers a wonderful pair of seats," Meredith said. "You'll have the chance to watch the kitchen in action. People love it. Want to give it a try?"

Meredith widened her eyes and gave him her biggest smile. She had small, beautiful, very white teeth. He would be crazy to say no to her. She was the kind of person who inspired trust and got others to do what she wanted.

The best restaurants establish trust with their customers on the phone, at the door, and throughout the meal. The ways that great restaurants make their customers feel welcome based on that trust are so different from the homes most people grew up in, where trust was inconsistent. The struggle to trust the restaurant and the chef is why customers will often squabble over tables, food, wine, and prices, and why they will spend large sums of money to eat out.

"I'll try it," said Mr. Griffin.

Meredith walked him back to the table to collect his friend and then led the two men to the chef's counter: four tall stools and a marble top facing garde manger and within a few feet of the grill, the stovetop, two prep areas, and the expediting table. The height was the same as the table they had left, and the counter was more narrow.

"I did tell the concierge about the stools," she said to me when she returned.

"I believe you," I said.

I walked into the kitchen to watch Danny, at the pass, looking over tickets and trying to get the cooks to focus.

"What the fuck, Bobby," said Danny. He looked like a bantamweight boxer between rounds: red-faced, exasperated, eager to deliver the knockout punch. "C'mon, Bobby!"

"What?"

"Cook! Cook, Bobby! Stop hanging the fuck around!"

"But, Danny," said Bobby.

Danny glared at him.

"Believe me, Bobby, if I wanted to hear you talk, I'd ask you."

Bobby stepped closer to him to apologize for not working fast enough.

"Bobby!" said Danny. "What the fuck, Bobby! Stop standing so close to me!"

"But, Danny . . ."

"Stop looking at me!"

"But, Danny . . ."

"Welcome to the big time, Bobby! Now shut up and cook!"

Bobby smiled, turned his back, and returned to his station.

"And, listen, Bobby," said Danny over his shoulder, "if you're gonna fuck with me, it's downstairs with Santos for you!"

"Okay, Danny!" Bobby said with a grin. "Got it!"

"I swear to God," Danny muttered.

Bobby, whose complexion was now pink from blushing after being chastised, had been at Craigie only a couple of months and, despite the harsh reprimands, didn't appear to be sad or rattled by Danny's tirade.

Just the opposite.

Bobby thought that if Danny did not believe in him and was not convinced that he had the potential to cook faster and with greater focus, he would have ignored him.

Bobby thought he was the star in the kitchen. He thought that he was being groomed for a promotion.

Danny yelled out: "I have couth and none of you do! You're a bunch of uncouth bastards!"

Danny turned to the counter behind the pass to take out a small metal tray.

"Look at these," he said to me, lifting up a paper towel.

He took out three glistening, nearly translucent scallops, and as he sliced them paper thin, small bubbles rose from each.

"For a chef's tasting," Danny said, handing them to Jill in garde manger who would plate them to look like art: microgreens, squirts of sauce, pickled mango, salt.

Tony had told me about Jill: "Maybe another future rock star! She totally gets it!"

Jill had joined Craigie only a few weeks before. Robust, powerful, and the polar opposite of dainty, she had grown up in Brooklyn, worked in restaurants from age fourteen, and completed Johnson & Wales only weeks ago. Jill had the perfect combination of attributes needed to work in a restaurant kitchen: early passion (that word *again*!), solid experience, and an apparent willingness to sacrifice everything to succeed in the business. Plus, she was very young, just having turned twenty-two, with the physical and mental energy to work as many as ninety hours a week.

I loved being with Jill most of all because she was what she did: not just defined by her social class, education, skin color, or gender, but by her work. She could prioritize what was going on around her and in doing so brought profound focus to the kitchen.

Danny shouted orders to the cooks. To see the kitchen move now, at high speed, made the rest of the world appear dull by comparison. Here was alacrity, concentration, and . . . but what was that? Why was Dakota dancing?

Dakota, his long hair bundled up, long tattooed arms fluttering, was jumping in place as he worked hard to keep up with orders.

Danny started laughing.

"Hey, Dakota," he said, "hang in there, Dakota! Counting on you, buddy!"

"What's up with him?" I asked.

Danny grinned.

"Dakota," Danny said, "has to go to the bathroom. In the middle of service. But Dakota knows that if he walks away from his station, we will fall behind and I will kill him."

"Danny, please!" shouted Dakota.

"Shut the fuck up, Dakota, and keep cooking!" said Danny. He began to laugh. "Cook, Dakota, cook!"

Dakota, now also laughing at his discomfort and predicament, flew into action. It is rare to see anyone move so fast and with such finesse. He kind of looked like Harold Lloyd covered in tattoos.

"Okay, Danny? Okay?" he yelled.

"Okay, Dakota," said Danny. "Go, Dakota! Go and get your ass back here pronto!"

Dakota tore off his apron and, shouting, "Behind you, behind you," he ran downstairs and past the cooks.

"Matt, cover for Dakota, please," said Danny.

"Sure thing," said Matt.

"That's what I'm talking about," said Danny. "Getting the fucking job done. Is that too much to fucking ask?"

"No," I said. "It is not."

I nodded my head in the direction of the two Southerners at the chef's counter and explained to Danny why they had been seated there.

"Think they'll have a good time?" I asked. "This doesn't look like their kind of restaurant."

"Yeah, I see that," said Danny. "Not formal. Not predictable. Unfamiliar menu. But I bet they have a *great* time! I'm gonna make sure of that. *That* is my challenge tonight!"

No ties, but buttoned up, the pair kept looking around the room and fidgeting. Having been moved from a table, not receiving the attention they had felt they had deserved, and now only a few feet away from a dancing cook and a swearing sous chef, they needed a sign that they mattered to the restaurant.

Older and stiff-jointed, one man was large and the other long-limbed. The stools were designed to provide "foodies" with a ring-side view of the kitchen. These men looked as if they could not care less about food. It was hard for them to find a comfortable position, and it seemed that in a few minutes they might chuck it all and leave in search of a good steak or lobster.

A waiter brought them menus and filled their water glasses, but I could see the frowns from where I stood twenty feet away.

Meredith came over and said, "E.C.," to Danny.

"Understood," he said. He crossed off a couple of recently completed tickets.

"E.C.?" I asked.

"Extra care," he said. "Got to make these guys extra happy."

"When we first opened here, we called them D.B.s," said Timmy.

"Douchebags," explained Danny. "But that isn't nice."

"And we wouldn't want a customer to hear a waitress say someone's a D.B., and then have to explain what D.B. meant," said Timmy.

"Although maybe they shouldn't have been D.B.s to begin with,"

Danny said. He added, ironically, "We want to make people happy. That's our job!"

"We're in the hospitality industry," said Matt with a big grin.

"It's what we do," said Danny.

"That's the challenge," Dakota chimed in, "of the E.C."

"We like a challenge," said Matt.

The E.C. men had ordered a bottle of expensive French wine. It was poured, the tall man tasted and approved, and now he and his companion were swirling red wine in big glasses, sniffing the aroma, and savoring the taste.

"Wow," I said to Danny, "they look like they know their way around wine. I had thought from their conservative clothing and hairstyles that they'd order cocktails."

"They're gonna love it here," Danny said. "Love it! Wait and see."

A few minutes passed by and then the men's tickets came in. Danny grabbed the orders and turned to the cooks to shout: "Two clams, a halibut, and pork three ways!"

Bobby nodded his head to show he had heard, but that wasn't enough.

"Bobby, what'd I say?"

Bobby strolled over to Danny.

"Two clams, a halibut, pork three ways," Bobby said.

"Good, Bobby, good," said Danny. He shook his head again. "Cook, Bobby, cook!"

"Yes?" said Bobby. He looked puzzled.

"Why the fuck are you still here?!" said Danny. "Go and start the fucking orders!"

"These guys," said Danny, stretching out his arms, cracking his knuckles, scowling at Bobby, and then laughing, "are going to leave happy. Or else."

Later that night, when the plates of the two men had been brought to the back of the kitchen, I saw that they had eaten everything.

"See?" said Danny. He nodded in the direction of the cooks and then the front of the house. "We did it."

I had been at Craigie for four months, and that was the first time I saw Danny behave like a chef.

FIVE

Dinner Without Tony

'LL BE A CUSTOMER," I SAID.

Tony had been away a couple of days.

"We don't say *customer* at Craigie," said Danny. "We say *guest*. It's more consistent with the idea of hospitality. Tony and Meredith like the word *guest*."

It is a unique word choice nonetheless, since people eating out are paying customers. A guest does not pay.

Danny smiled and put his face back into the bowl of stewed leftovers that was staff or family meal. He had gotten a crewcut and kept a slight beard. In his white uniform, hunched over the long plank of the bar, he looked like a man serving time.

I had booked a table for Friday, a few days ahead, and asked to be seated in the bar area rather than the dining room. The bar is darker, noisier, and livelier than the restaurant's dining room. Perfect for someone who prefers to observe people rather than join in.

My wife, Laura, and I had been to Craigie a few times since our initial visit. But I had mostly tasted the food in the kitchen with the cooks. Laura was out of town, so it seemed opportune to take our adult daughter. Madeline has a generous appreciation of food, a good palate, and limited economic resources, so a meal in an expensive restaurant is more of a treat for her than it is for me.

Madeline was tentative. "Are you sure you want to do this? It might be expensive."

"Hey, I'm working," I said. "It's work." From the outset, I had told Tony to charge me, but he laughed. He said that he would not charge me for *my* food, but that he might charge me for the food that people I brought in would be eating.

"Does Mom know you're taking me to Craigie?" she asked.

"She might know."

Friday afternoon I arrived to continue to observe staff and conduct interviews. It was my fourth month in the restaurant. Some familiar faces were gone, new crew in the kitchen and on the floor, and still the mainstays.

Except for one waiter, Chuck, who looked like he was in his late forties, everyone was in their twenties or very early thirties. Chuck, who used to run a travel agency, had a clear sense of his skills.

"When the agency closed," Chuck said, "I realized I had one great talent that would be perfect for being a waiter. Can you guess what that was?"

"A great palate?" I said.

"Nope," he said. "I can sell. I'm great at selling!"

That made sense. A waiter is a salesperson. It might as well be bicycles, computers, or cars. In a restaurant, the waitstaff's goal is to increase the bill. Sell the tasting menus! Sell the sides! Sell the pricier wine! Sell the after-dinner drinks!

"I often win the weekly contests," Chuck said, "to sell the most expensive wines."

Chuck had gray hair, a small gap between his two top front teeth, and a ready smile. He looked like a second cousin in the Kennedy clan, but instead of being a risk-taking, bungee-jumping downhill skier like the famous men he so closely resembled, Chuck had become a waiter to pay for his daughter's college tuition. Working at Craigie could be that lucrative, because it was so good and the experience of dining there so distinct. The menu had Flintstone-sized bones, sliced in half, roasted to allow access to thick troughs of marrow that could be spread onto toasted baguette. Other than cheeseburgers, pig's heads, and pig's tails, it had refined dishes, too, like *assiette* of house-made terrines and *côte du boeuf.* Everything I had eaten there was, without exception, delicious, and when I sent friends and colleagues, who dined anonymously, they reported having great experiences.

That most of the dishes could not readily be found elsewhere, that it was a pure expression of Tony's palate, added to the allure. People came to Craigie to eat Tony's food. This was no different from the way many other chefs operated: *The Daniel Boulud Show, The Mario Batali Show, The Emeril Lagasse Show.*

At Craigie on Main, it was *The Tony Maws Show,* and when customers or guests came into the restaurant, they often looked into the open kitchen: Was Tony there? Where was he? Would he return later that evening? If not, they expressed disappointment. (Too bad about that open kitchen! Transparency has its drawbacks.)

Like all so-called celebrity chefs, Tony encouraged the fascination. He signed birthday and anniversary cards nightly, stopped by the tables of regulars and VIPs, and made clear through interviews with media that his food did not conform to any cuisine, but that it was *his* food, a highly personal expression of *his* taste, *his* training, and *his* growing up with a grandmother whose kitchen boasted of big flavors created by chicken or beef fat, bones, and organs.

No wonder Tony felt that he had to be in the restaurant every night. It was not that the food was not delicious in his absence. It was. It was not just the missteps of cooks who were often lost without his leadership. It was that Tony was as defined by the food as the food was defined by him. He needed the restaurant to make him who he was. When he was away from Craigie, he suffered a loss of identity. He was most aware of being Tony Maws when he stood at the pass.

Being synonymous with his food deeply complicated the efforts of his cooks. They could never quite create his identity through the food without him there to tell them exactly how to do it. They also lacked the confidence to cook his food because they knew he did not trust them completely to do it without his being in the restaurant.

In conversations with Tony, he sometimes compared being a chef to being a musician: He refused to do covers of other people's songs, and his work did not represent any specific genre—meaning that he had little interest in perfecting classics through technique or the use of rare ingredients, and no desire to serve as an interpreter of a specific tradition or cuisine. His approach to food was comparable to Louis Armstrong's wonderful quote: "There is two kinds of music. The good and bad. I play the good kind."

Tony felt that the dishes he created must express his personality. He cared more, too, about being prolific—coming up with new dishes—than consistency.

What concerned me was what might be diminished by replacing repetition with a highly personal and inventive style of cooking.

Without a tradition, cooks create an immediacy that can destroy flavor combinations that have worked for centuries. It is harder to roast a chicken perfectly or make a perfect omelet than it is to cook something that has no comparison.

Of all the dishes Tony served, how many would last? And what about all the other chefs who went about inventing?

The talk of signature dishes, in many restaurants, is smoke and mirrors and has next to nothing to do with what the food of great chefs is about. I thought of what Chef Gary Danko had said to me in an interview. I had asked him: "Of all the signature dishes throughout the world, how many will last more than ten years? I'd guess five percent, but what do you think?" Danko replied, "I think you're being generous."

Tony agreed with Danko when I brought the opinion to his attention, but what was he doing about it? And what did he gain from improvisation?

"We might stumble on a great dish," Tony had said. "You never know what you'll find. You can't keep doing the same thing."

He had paused and reflected.

"It also keeps the cooks sharp," Tony had said. "It helps them discover what they are capable of doing."

But this would work only if the cooks understood what he wanted them to do and were given the same rules each night, and when the new dishes being created had deeper, more soulful, and better flavors than what had preceded them.

"My crew works harder here than in most restaurants," Tony had said. "We don't do things the easy way. At Craigie we don't have a simple roast chicken, as much as I respect that dish, or bluefish fillet, or whatever. The cooks who will succeed at Craigie are willing to learn what I have to teach them. I had a guy here who had worked at Daniel."

He was referring to Chef Daniel Boulud, who is one of the five best French born chefs with restaurants in the United States; his eponymously named restaurant is a top-rated three-star Michelin and has a top rating of four stars from the *New York Times*.

"He kept insisting on doing things his way. 'This is how we were taught at Daniel.' Didn't work out."

"What if what he was doing was technically correct?" I had asked.

"I think that guy simply didn't want to do things *my* way," Tony had said. "If he really had something to offer, something original, I'd have been thrilled. Thing is: He was lazy. He didn't want to learn. He was here to learn to cook my food my way."

A strong and confident cook, ironically, might fail in a restaurant while someone who agrees to be shaped by the chef will succeed. To cook Tony's food, you had to think like him.

His approach was the same as that of other chefs in that he was the boss; it was different in that these were his rules, and they did not reflect a canon or a tradition like what is found in Alsace, Bangkok, Burgundy, Hokkaido, Lyons, Mumbai, New Orleans, New England, Paris, Provence, Rome, Shanghai, Singapore, Tokyo, or Tuscany.

The biggest difference, though, between how Tony did things and how other top chefs worked had to do with the extreme change-ability of Tony's kitchen: *The rules kept changing*; his desire for change was what he thought of as the pursuit of perfection, which meant that he was the only fleet-footed one and that his cooks had to keep up with him.

My daughter arrived at eight. I was in the kitchen, at the pass, finishing an interview with Matt. After I introduced Madeline to the cooks, we were shown to a wide corner table near the bar.

"Wow," Madeline said, "thanks for inviting me!"

The room was filling up. From behind the bar, outlandishly mustachioed Ted Gallagher, laughing and looking a lot like a guy in an old barbershop quartet, poured and mixed drinks and made sure his two sidekicks, Sally and John, kept pace.

Miles going strong on muted trumpet, Ray Garland melodic on the piano, Paul Chambers playing sturdily on bass: old school and extremely mellow. Music was everywhere in Craigie; it was all about finding a rhythm, which was the soundtrack for the dining experience. Everyone who came into the restaurant caught the vibe.

Our waiter, Dan, brought over menus. He had a dull smile, no oomph to it, but seemed reliable and capable of focus—tall, slightly bearded, and moving like a man with time on his hands. I had interviewed him only days before: A recent graduate of Boston University, which placed him or his family in the hole for $200,000, Dan had studied film and majored in screenwriting.

Dan was not the only artist among the group; there was Holly, who had also studied film, and Chuck, a painter. Being an extremely young person who idealizes what it means to be a true artist—unlike T. S. Eliot, who worked in a bank, or Chekov, who labored as a doctor, their day jobs seeping wonderfully into their art—Dan had found work that would not interfere with what he thought of preciously as art but what was really a desire to hold on to what remained of his youthful potential. "I'm not selling my soul," Dan had said. "I'm not stuck in a nine-to-five job. I can still stay true to my art and count on getting paid."

"Bottled water or tap?" Dan asked Madeline and me.

"Tap's fine," I said.

We ordered cocktails, and when they arrived we puzzled over the menus while sipping our drinks. The list, with the silly name *Libations*, was, like the food menu at Craigie, filled with deeply inventive flavor combinations. The *Ardoise* was described as: "Rain, sage, juniper, lime." I wondered what they would do during a drought. *The Improved Whisky Cocktail?* Rittenhouse, maraschino, Angostura, gomme syrup, absinthe. Like so much at Craigie, the drinks were a way to tell guests to shake things up.

And yet it *all* felt so grown up, which is what restaurants do, make people feel grown up, which is fine if you are but not fine if you still have unresolved issues about being grown up. My daughter and I, having grown up together, felt good about it.

"What's good?" Madeline asked. "Everything looks good."

"Everything *is* good," I said. "No kidding. That's one reason why I decided to write about this restaurant. It just depends on what you're in the mood for."

She mulled over the salad of bluefin tuna sashimi and the Vermont pork three ways but was unsure about leaving out the crispy fried clams and the stuffed chicken. So I suggested we order six-course tasting menus.

I love watching my daughter eat.

"Oh, what the heck," I said, when she worried about the cost.

"Besides, you're working," she said. "Right? That's what you'll tell Mom."

My notebook was on the table, and I had been writing since walking in the door hours earlier.

"Excellent choices," Dan said when we put in the orders, which included specific items we wanted in the tasting menus.

I had told Dan during our earlier interview how I was not a fan of that expression. Dan had shrugged, and then explained that Tony liked to congratulate guests on their choices.

While we waited for our food, I observed the room. Drew was patrolling the floor, positioning himself in a corner, crossing his arms, eyeing tables and front-of-the-house staff, making certain that the room kept up its rhythm. The manager directs the traffic, helps establish the pace, and reports back to the chef in the kitchen. It is the perfect job for a good social observer.

People were having a great time, that was obvious, and no more so than at a four-top to my left where the two couples were polishing off two burgers, a chicken entrée, and the striped bass.

Two back waiters arrived with our first course: a long white rectangular ceramic tray with three recesses in it. The first recess held tiny cubes of Armenian cucumbers resting on a red beet purée. The second had a thin slice of house-cured salmon. The third was citrus-cured halibut with a dollop of trout roe.

We each took a bite. "Wow," we both said at about the same time. I closed my eyes to try to make the sense of taste more pronounced. "Delicious."

"Really delicious!" said Madeline.

"How was it?" asked Dan when he returned to clear the plates.

We told him. Earlier, I had mentioned to Dan that this, too, was a request made by waitstaff I did not understand. I could not imagine doctors asking patients after a cardiac catheterization: "How was it?"

At the four-top next to us, the two couples were laughing and talking loudly. The great time did not appear to be due to alcohol but instead seemed to come from the food. They were savoring each bite, eating so rapidly that the talk between them was diminished by their efforts to chew.

"Great textures on the first course," said Madeline.

"I was thinking the same thing," I said.

"Just like sushi," she said.

"Except for one thing," I said. I lowered my voice.

"The fish was warm," I said. "Raw fish shouldn't be served warm."

"Are you going to say anything?" Madeline asked.

"Of course not," I said.

I did not want to criticize the cooks. Tony was not in the restaurant, and the cooks were feeling more vulnerable without him. Anyway, who was I to complain? I *never* complain in restaurants, honestly; it's a night out, people are working hard while I'm enjoying myself, and what's worse? My complaint or their feelings? It's just not worth it.

Dan arrived with the next course and explained that it was *hiramasa*, which is a fancy-pants word for farm-raised amberjack or kingfish. It was served with pickled mango and yuzu. The dish was spectacular: subtle heat, sweet but bracing, and flavors so well woven together that the result on the plate tasted as if it were something to be found in nature rather than assembled in the kitchen.

Dorade with tiny garbanzo beans and a faint brush of curry followed. Then rye-flour rigatoni with boudin noir in a spoonful of sauce topped with a few pieces of arugula that wilted from the heat as we ate them.

"Unbelievably tasty," I said. "Now we're talking."

Miles drifted in: "Blue in Green."

As we ate, my daughter and I were forming new ties inspired by the food. A great restaurant can do this for people, of course: help them feel their love for one another intensify. I imagined that this was also happening at the table next to ours, where four very clean white plates had been removed from a laughing quartet.

Things took a turn for the worse, though, when the check was presented to them. One couple looked down the list of charges. Then the two couples leaned in, lowered their heads and voices, and had a big discussion. One man called over their server, who came over, listened, nodded her head, and walked away. Then Drew showed up.

Drew listened: shoulders bent in, eyes averted, practically bowing, nodding his head, pouting. He looked sad. Wait, that was not sadness! That was shame.

"Well, have a great weekend!" Drew said as they got up, scraped their chairs, and made their way out.

I caught his eye.

"Drew?" I asked. "Drew, can I talk to you for a second?"

He came over. Now he looked uncannily like Bert from Sesame Street! Drew has a long face and a doleful personality such that apologies come as readily to him as song to a bird.

"What was that about?" I asked.

He nodded his head. He looked as if he felt personally responsible for the problem. "They thought it was too much to pay," he said.

"But the menus have prices, and they ate everything on their plates! I saw it! They enjoyed the food! I can understand if they sent the food back, but how can they complain about the costs when they knew in advance what they were and then ate everything?"

"I don't get it either," he said, "but it's not my job to get it. I'm here to make people happy." Drew had not charged them for one of the entrées in an effort to avoid having an argument. "It's the business." Drew shrugged and walked to the kitchen to see why several orders for the dining room were delayed.

Madeline and I were had two more courses to go. Two small plates of oxtail pastrami on heirloom carrots topped with what the kitchen had termed "a farm fresh egg" arrived at our table. This dish also proved to be delicious as well as visually appealing when the egg broke and the yolk flowed.

Then we had our final savory course: lamb's-neck sausage, which looked nothing like one might expect and instead resembled short ribs. It had the firm but juicy texture of the lamb and was stellar because of the play of salt and pepper and the extremely deep flavors that resonated with each bite.

Sally, because of slow traffic at her end of the bar, came by to clear our plates. Her left arm exposed a tattoo from shoulder to wrist. Combined with her haircut, which was a buzz cut on one side and long tresses on the other side, she proclaimed a toughness to the world—a willingness to endure pain and the ability to turn suffering into art. Très cool.

"How was everything?" Sally asked.

"Great," I said, more intent on satisfying her requirement to comment on the food than on any desire to do so. "Delicious."

Four new guests or customers sat down at the table that had

been left by the people who had complained. Menus were brought over to them and their water glasses were filled. The two new couples looked unhappy, but I figured that in time the kitchen could win them over.

Moments before our desserts arrived—amaretto ice cream, pistachio crumble, apricot tart, buttermilk ice cream—the four new guests or customers called the server over. After hearing their complaints, she left and then Drew appeared again.

"Nothing appealed to us on the menu," said one of the two men.

Drew bowed so low and so flexibly that he seemed to be made out of soft plastic.

"I'm so sorry," Drew said. "I am so sorry."

"Well, we'll just have our drinks and leave then," said the man.

His companions nodded in agreement.

"I am so sorry," said Drew again.

"Yeah, well," said the man.

Drew smiled hopefully.

"Well, I do hope you enjoy Boston," Drew said. "It's supposed to be a terrific weekend weatherwise!"

The man grunted.

"Table fifty-six," Drew said after I'd asked him to come over and tell me about what happened.

"What do you think was the problem?"

"Hard to say," he said.

"Sticker shock?"

"Maybe," said Drew. "It happens sometimes. We have a reputation for being a great restaurant, and people might come in not knowing what we do or about our food or what things cost. So these people tonight? They'll have drinks and then they'll eat someplace else and be angry at us for who knows what."

Not many people could do Drew's job, which requires a great deal of humility and self-control. When I praised him for this, he offered that he does the best he can, as he was trained by one of the best in the business: a huge Italian guy in South Beach who knew how to handle difficult guests.

KNOWING THAT PEOPLE EXPECTED THE FOOD NOT JUST TO TASTE GOOD but to make them happy is added stress for a chef. But a chef is attracted to the challenge. Nailing it means a room full of satisfied people looking to the chef as the power who is responsible for giving physical and emotional pleasure.

No wonder Tony had such a complex relationship with his restaurant and food. He was drawn to the intensity but made anxious by it, too. When friends who cook well at home talk about food the way people used to talk about their favorite family members, and say they think of one day opening their own restaurant, I think of Tony and others of his caliber: You want to be a chef? You think you have what it takes? The stamina, focus, creativity, and ability to lead? You wouldn't get beyond the first night.

SIX

The Chef Returns Home

WHAT DID IT MEAN FOR YOU TO WIN A BEARD?" I ASKED TONY WHEN he returned home from New York, and then San Francisco.

"It means I don't have to go down to New York," he said, "like I did twice before this happened, as a nominee, hoping to win only to come back home empty-handed. It means that we get calls and e-mails asking for reservations from people who follow this sort of stuff. It means that I get invited to PR events at restaurants owned by other chefs who won the Beard."

The recognition felt great, but it was not why he did the work, nor did it alter lives in positive ways only. Ironically, it had the potential to make things worse. Tony would have to face guests or customers who followed a trend without knowing his food.

He was wearing the same de rigueur University of Michigan T-shirt, a relic from his student days twenty years ago; knee-length drawstring shorts; and sandals, checking e-mail and messages on his cell phone. With him he had a copy of a book called *The Forager*, as well as a book about molecular cooking titled *The Modernist*. He would spend the rest of the morning calling suppliers, reviewing the guest list for the night, and looking at pictures of food while studying new cooking techniques.

"Fucking unbelievable," said Tony, when he learned that while he had been away one of his hostesses had told Chef Daniel Boulud's assistant that the restaurant was fully booked the night he had wanted to come in with his daughter Alix, who was graduating from Tufts.

"Can't happen again. I would have loved to cook for Daniel!"

Tony had contacted Daniel's office, but it was too late.

"We tried everything," Tony said in a raised voice. He glared at his computer screen. He sent a text message to his wife. He deleted a voice message. Whatever it took to distract him from what he saw as a missed opportunity to have shown one of the world's greatest chefs what he could do. And with Alix having finished Tufts, it was unlikely that Daniel would be in Boston ever again. "Fucked up! The front of the house fucked up. I need people at the phones to know who they're talking to. Fucked up! Totally fucked up!"

Tony had a right to be angry, but the way he expressed outrage was inappropriate outside a restaurant kitchen, military barracks, or locker room.

"My mother is fed up with my anger at this point," he admitted. "She doesn't like hearing me say *fuck* all the time."

THE ISSUE WAS THAT TONY WAS LOCKED INTO RUNNING CRAIGIE WITH anger, unmotivated to try new and more effective strategies, and unencumbered by negative consequences for his behavior. He could be angry in public, at his staff, without anyone challenging him, which was utterly luxurious.

"Lots went wrong while I was away," Tony said.

"I guess you heard about table fifty-six," I said.

He looked up from the list of names.

"No," he said, "I did not hear about table fifty-six."

He raised his eyebrows, smiled, and gestured with open palms.

"Oh, Drew was ace," I said, before going into the aggravated couples who did not want to pay for the dinners they had enjoyed and eaten. "First rate! He handled the situation beautifully. Didn't take any of it personally. Calmed them down, comped them a dinner. He's great. Really. That's not an easy job. A lot of people would have lost their cool."

Tony tapped a pen onto a pad of paper.

"Drew comped them a dinner?" he asked. "I didn't hear about that." Had Tony been in the restaurant that night, he would have gone to the table and smoothed things over. It was not the comp that bothered him. He had left Danny in charge, but handling customers or guests on the floor was not in his sous chef's repertoire of skills.

"He comped them one dinner or two?"

"One," I said.

"He comped them a dinner," he said.

"So, Tony, anyway, what do you think of the situation between Meredith and Ted?"

"That's been brewing for a while," he said. "It's the number one rule, and she's breaking it. My GM is breaking the rule. Look, things happen, but she should have known better than to sleep with someone she's supervising. She's his boss, for fuck's sakes!"

"It's better than if he was *her* boss," I said, trying to be helpful.

"That's for sure," Tony said, "but it's still not okay."

Since I had started coming into the restaurant and established a presence as a decent listener to the restaurant family, staff had confided in me. I did not tell Tony everything they said, but when asked, I acted as a go-between.

Tony lowered his voice. "Listen," he said, "I'm happy to talk to you about how totally and utterly fucked up it is for my general manager to be in a relationship with the bartender, but that's a conversation we should have outside the restaurant. Okay?"

"Okay."

Tony closed his laptop.

"Let's go downstairs," he said, "I want to show you something. Get my mind off how fucked up my life is."

We went down the narrow flight of steps. Then we turned left, where we saw sous vide equipment, a small oven, a large walk-in, a cooking station for making ice creams and pastry, and two long slabs that served as slaughterhouse surfaces used to break down the carcasses of mammals, birds, fish, and seafood. We walked past Jess, who was working on a dessert of dark chocolate, pistachios, and preserved cherries, and met up with Santos.

"Santos, you ready?" asked Tony.

"Ready, boss," said Santos. "Hey, boss?"

Santos wore his usual wry smile.

"Yes, Santos?" said Tony.

"It's my anniversary today," said Santos.

"Happy anniversary, Santos," said Tony.

They laughed.

It was one of Santos's running jokes. Every day was either his birthday or anniversary, or his girlfriend just had a baby, or he needed a medical leave of absence. It was how he related to Tony, especially, and the rest of the staff.

Santos was often the first one at the restaurant each morning: signing for deliveries, then making stock and butchering; working with fellow Salvadorans Gabby, Jose, Juan Francisco, and Alex, on their cleanup chores, which included all the pots, pans, utensils, plates, bowls, cups, saucers, and flatware plus every inch of cooking surface, the floors, the windows, and the bathrooms. He had a great work ethic, but he still loved to joke about a different Santos, the one who had something to celebrate every day, needed time off, or was due for a raise.

"How about it, Santos?" said Tony.

"On it, boss," he said.

Santos headed to the walk-in at the end of the prep area and returned with a very large, dead animal. He carried it with both arms, crooking the stiffened legs above his elbows, and placed the skinned and bloody carcass onto a white slab.

Thud!

"Goat," said Tony.

It looked like a dog. It was enough to make me want to stop eating meat.

"How do your vegetarian cooks, like Mary, deal with this?" I asked.

"They deal," Tony said. "You get used to it."

"It's just a goat," said Santos, but I could see from his expression, growing a little bit sadder, that he was beginning to see it as the living creature it had been.

"Okay, let's get to work," said Tony. "I'm going to do half of this, Santos. Please watch because I want you to do the rest."

"Got it," said Santos.

Tony reached for a long, steel Japanese blade, as sharp as a razor. He cut the goat open from its neck down to below the belly. He put his hands into the cavity and pulled out the lungs, heart, liver, and kidneys. I heard snapping and tearing. He cut around the shoulders and over the back and through the butt.

"We'll make sausages," said Tony. "We'll make a ragu for the pasta, we'll use the ribs, we'll use the organs, we'll cut the rump into little pieces and figure out what to do with them in a tasting menu."

This was why Tony had become a chef: to think creatively about ways to make delicious food. Conflicts on the floor, food sent back, cooks who didn't understand him? All that was secondary to the thrill of creating.

"Got it, Santos?" he said.

"Got it!" said Santos.

"Thanks, brother!" said Tony.

No anger, no questions, no problems. Whatever insurmountable difficulties had brought Santos to this kitchen from El Salvador gave him the strength to handle a boss like Tony. He had seen much worse.

"I love butchering," said Tony. "I honestly love everything about my job."

"Even the cooks?" I asked.

"Dude," Tony said, and laughed, "I love the cooks most of all!"

But unlike the best teachers, Tony could not focus on the potential and uniqueness of his cooks, who were essentially his students. He saw their flaws and what got in the way of their success. Identifying closely with them made it even worse. His anger was directed as much toward himself as toward them.

He told me, "I wouldn't make their mistakes! Why can't they do things the way I do them?"

Tony did not understand adequately that not one of his cooks was like him, that they had varied skills and weaknesses, and that it was his job to differentiate between them.

"You good, Santos?" he asked.

"Good," said Santos as he made his first cut.

"C'mon," Tony said to me.

He led us back upstairs and into the bar area where the daily meeting for front-of-the-house staff was under way. Servers and bartenders occupied the corner seats and benches, folding napkins and taking notes. Two GMs ran the meeting. The hostesses attended. Marjorie was there, too; she often was.

The meeting had many purposes: a review of culinary terms on the menu, discussions about problems from the night before, quizzes, tidbits about where staff had eaten, the listing of the VIPs expected in that night.

"Nicholas Gibson has a five-top on fifty-eight," said Meredith. "He becomes a regular tonight with his third visit, so we'll send out sorbets. Very serious reservation at twenty-seven. Four-top on the turn at twenty-one or twenty-two."

Stacks of napkins grew in height on the black wooden tables as the waitstaff listened in silence and folded. Shutters in the room let in a little bit of light. The meeting typically belonged to Drew and Meredith, but Tony would interject periodically and, before they broke up, go over the menu painstakingly with everyone.

Most meetings at Craigie had a frisson to them, but today's, which was among the first following Tony's return with a Beard, was surprisingly somber. In response to the mood, or perhaps having helped create it, Tony started talking.

"Things happened here last week when I was away," Tony said slowly. His voice was low and scary. "Things I find completely embarrassing." Pause. "I don't need to go over what I'm talking about. Do I?" Silence. "Okay?" Silence. "Okay. So let's go over tonight's menu. Bluefin sashimi, plum for watermelon. Six Duxbury oysters, not winter point. Tails, octo, terrines. Farro rigatoni with goat, not boudin. Squash and lettuce. It's sword for striper with the guanciale. Steak, bass, pork three ways—tonight it's confit, rib, belly—chicken, and veg. Pig's head, whole chicken. I've got four orders of beef at sixty dollars, prize to who sells the most. Tastings: *hiramasa*, cukes, scallops, squid noodles, Spanish eel, halibut, veal. Eights you can add in oxtail pastrami and then we'll see. Cheeses: Époisses, Due Latte, and Chèvre Mont." Pause. "Questions?"

"Tony?" Jess stood at his side. Throughout these meetings, the cooks came to Tony with tiny spoonfuls of food to taste. "Celery-apple sorbet with a little bit of Burrata and mascarpone as a bed," she said.

Tony tasted.

"Wow," he said. His mood brightened. He wasn't happy, but Jess's achievement for the moment contrasted with what he saw as broad failures in his staff from when he had been away. "This is great. Can you bring out a bowl and some spoons so that everyone can have a taste?"

"Sure," Jess said.

She spun on her heels, took strides to her prep area downstairs, and returned with a bowl of the dessert. As it was passed around, Chuck asked, "How do you want this scripted?"

"Celery-apple sorbet, burrata, mascarpone," said Tony.

"Tony?" Now Danny was at his side with a spoonful of almond butter. He moved from side to side and scratched the right side of his neck.

"Needs salt," said Tony, after a nibble.

"On it," said Danny, and returned to his station to work on the butter.

It was time for the daily quiz.

Each quiz was printed out and every staff member received a copy. Today's quiz had seven questions and one for extra credit. The quizzes were meant to inspire discussion, raise awareness of the menu, anticipate questions asked by guests or customers, and provide ways for staff to sell the food and wine.

Today's questions included the following:

Why are we serving bluefin tuna if it is on the "watch list"?

No one knew, so Tony told them that the bluefin had been line-caught in the Gulf of Mexico by small fishermen's collectives.

Describe two Italian reds at $90 or higher and how you would sell them.

In a smooth, deep voice, as if he were pitching a fully loaded Beamer to a customer in a showroom, Chuck said, "It tastes of wild cherries . . . it's kept ten years in the bottle . . . and it has *never* been sold until now."

The waitstaff cheered.

"Excellent!" said Tony.

"Nice," said Meredith.

Extra credit: *List a recent service experience outside work that blew you away and how we can adapt it to Craigie on Main.*

A lively discussion about tacos in East Boston and Somerville followed and then, just as the meeting was about to break up, the question of how to get the guest or customer to spend more came up again.

"We want to find the customer's inner wallet," Marjorie said.

"How can we figure out how much a customer is willing to spend on wine?" asked Dave.

Dave was new.

"I look at their shoes and watches," said Michael.

"Doesn't always work," said Tony. He gestured to himself. "Look at me: T-shirt, shorts, sandals, but I was out last week and bought a ninety-dollar bottle of wine."

"So what works?" asked Chuck.

"Cars," said Tony. "If they drive up, try to check out the car."

"Good point," said Chuck, noting it down. All the waitstaff had notepads.

"We don't want to undersell," said Marjorie. "We don't want to leave money on the table."

A few minutes later, when the meeting ended, Tony went into the kitchen to gather the cooks for their daily meeting.

"Let's go, let's go, let's go," he said. "Now! Stop what you're doing!"

Outside, the cooks took up places around Tony. I sat off to the right, next to Timmy, whose tattoo-covered arms included a big scaled fish.

"We have a bit of a situation," said Nate.

Nate had just shaved his head. He shaved his head every couple of months. No one knew why. He looked grave, pensive, and frightened.

"What kind of situation?" asked Tony.

"The sour cream," said Nate.

"What about the sour cream?" asked Tony.

"It went bad. I saw it. Just now I saw it," said Nate. He spoke like a man in a crisis. Short breaths, gulps of air, eyes cast down at his hands restlessly turning a pocket notebook in circles. "What are we gonna do?"

"Nate, are you asking me that in all seriousness?" said Tony.

Nate nervously pushed back his eyeglasses with his right index finger and then looked at his feet.

"Okay, Nate," said Tony. The other cooks began to giggle. "You see that alley across the street . . . So you get to go through that alley and go to Star Market and get sour cream."

"Now?" asked Nate.

"No, not now," said Tony. He laughed angrily. "When we're done. Fuck!"

"He could go to the food co-op down the street," said Dakota.

"Where's that?" asked Nate.

"Dude, down the street!" said Dakota. He slapped his knees twice. "Dude! Dude! Dude! Do you know anything?"

"I don't hang out in this neighborhood, okay?" said Nate.

Dakota, who enjoyed being the kitchen clown, was laughing hard now. "Dude, it's a right turn, keep walking, and about half a block down, there it is. Big sign. *FOOD COOPERATIVE.*"

"I don't know if I'd find it," said Nate. "I have a terrible sense of direction. Tony? Is Star Market closer?"

Timmy volunteered to get the sour cream.

"Thanks, man," Nate whispered to Timmy.

I had expected Tony to follow his usual routine next, but instead he said, "I understand that Scott dined with us last week."

All the cooks looked at me very attentively.

"Let's have your full report," Tony said with a big grin.

"My full report?" I asked.

"Full report," said Tony. "C'mon, everyone's waiting!"

"First of all, I enjoyed everything," I said. "Everything was delicious."

"Details!" said Tony. "Details!"

"Okay," I said, flipping through my black notebook. "Ah, here we are! Great textures on the cukes, subtle and smoky salmon, curry went well with the dorade, thought the rye-flour noodles were spectacular and wish you had more pasta on the menu."

"No more pasta," said Tony. "Fuck you. We're not an Italian restaurant."

"Just a thought," I said.

"Not a good one," said Tony. "Go on."

"You heard Chef," said Danny. "Go on!"

"Fine," I said, laughing, "sorry I said anything."

"You bet you're sorry," said Tony.

"Loved the egg and pastrami," I continued. "Lamb's-neck sausage: Great! Beautiful desserts, and I don't even care about sweets."

"So," he said, "a perfect dinner? No mistakes?"

"Well . . ."

"Yes?" said Tony.

"You asked, right?"

The cooks leaned in, their expressions unvarying, curious and respectful, not angry.

"The raw fish was warm," I said as fast as I could. It sounded as if I had said, "Theraw fishwararm."

Tony had a grateful look on his face that it took me several moments to understand. Yes, it was an error, a significant one, but it took place when he had not been there, which proved that *had* he been there it would not have happened! It fit his theory: Without him, no Craigie!

"Say more," Tony said.

"Raw fish should be served cold. At least that's how we think of raw fish like sashimi. You associate warm sashimi with fish that's been left out on a counter or isn't fresh and might have an increased risk of bacteria. I'm not saying it's true, but it's a perception."

"Valid," said Tony, nodding his head.

"Ever see a female sushi chef? You won't in Japan. This isn't what I believe, and I think it's a typically sexist move in male-dominated Japan. I mean, is there a more sexist country on earth? One cabinet position goes to a woman and that's the Family and Child Ministry or something like that."

"Sushi, Scott, sushi," said Tony. "Focus!"

But I was nervous; it didn't seem fair to the cooks who had made so much effort.

"Dude, get to the point," said Dakota. "Dude!"

"Well, in Japan," I continued, "the men in charge are convinced that women's body temperatures are higher than men's and if they handle the raw fish, it will get warm and be ruined. I don't think it's true, but I do think that they're right about raw fish: Don't serve it warm."

Whew, I thought.

"That's such a good point," said Tony. "That's exactly the kind of criticism we need to hear. Specific and something we can change."

I smiled shyly, turned red, and went back to the page in my notebook where I had been writing the day's observations. I knew that what I had said was correct, but I was embarrassed by having said it. I hoped that the cooks would not be upset by my comments or mad at me.

Instead I saw a different reaction on their faces: I had told Tony, their boss, that his food was not perfect, and I had lived to tell the tale.

"Let's hear what people have left to do," said Tony.

"Dress the bluefish, slice the sockeye," said James.

"I slice the fish," said Tony.

James didn't say anything. He had his usual blank look, as if he'd heard the words but was not sure what they meant.

"How many times are you gonna make the same mistake?" asked Tony.

Silence.

"You need to start doing things my way," Tony said in a raised voice. "How long have you been with us?" He shook his head. "Don't touch the fucking fish!"

Tony continued down the line.

"Jill?"

"Capers, dried watermelon, toasted hazelnuts."

"Super prepared," said Tony. "Nice job."

"Thanks!" said Jill.

"And I love the jacket," he added. Her jacket was covered with big red blotches.

"Yeah," Jill laughed, "it's me against ketchup!"

"Nate?"

"As soon as I get the sour cream . . ."

Tony laughed and cut him off. "Bobby?"

"Olives, lemons, peppers," Bobby said.

"Dakota?"

Dakota always carried with him a notepad that fit in his back pocket. He took it out, flipped through its pages, and read, "Cut whelks."

"That's it?" asked Tony.

"Yeah," said Dakota. His grin made it difficult for people to be angry at him. "Why? Is there something else you want me to do?"

"No, you're good, D," said Danny. He laughed and then whacked him on the right shoulder. "You're good, you're good, you're good."

"Cool," said Dakota.

"Matt?" said Tony.

"Well," said Matt, leaning forward on his elbows, which he had planted on his knees, and then sitting back and spreading out his arms and hands. He had the posture of someone telling a campfire story. "We've got this really gorgeous fish that just came in. Wait till you see it. It's fucking beautiful. Big, fat piece of the most beautiful tuna I've ever fucking seen. You think you have time before service to show me how you're gonna cut it up?"

Tony looked up. "For sure," said Tony. "Won't take long. Okay." He made as if to stand up, but Danny put up his right hand.

"Hey, Chef," he said, "just want to keep you up to date: I'm cutting up bones for the marrow and brining a baby pig."

"Awesome," said Tony.

As usual, the meeting ended with the cooks getting up slowly but then running across the street and into the kitchen as Tony or Danny exhorted them. This afternoon it was Tony:

"Are you jacked? Are you stoked? Are you pumped?"

Before he took off, Matt came over to me and said, with his wonderful grin that explained it all, "I like the hours here. I love what I do. And you know why? Because I don't have to deal with the normal shit like everybody else. I don't like the normal shit."

SEVEN

Some Words About the Food

AFTER NINE MONTHS AT CRAIGIE, I HAD EARNED TONY'S TRUST. I HAD also learned a great deal about how he made decisions. Tony knew that his guests or customers not only could afford to pay top dollar for the luxury of eating out, but they wanted to. He was different from most chefs in that way, having been a member of the upper middle class from childhood: Feeding the very well off was the same for him as cooking for family and friends. He was a member of the club. His affiliation added to his confidence and gave him a psychological advantage.

This emboldened him. The risks Tony took in his cooking were nowhere near as great had he been working class and alienated from his customer base. Having grown up in the same circles as his guests or customers, he was better equipped psychologically to anticipate their reactions to his food. He could take more "risks" knowing that what appeared to be risks to critics and outsiders were safe bets with people whose psychologies he knew intimately.

He was not afraid of reactions to his restaurant. If guests did not like his food and service, they needed to open their minds. This approach may sound arrogant, but it wasn't. It was a natural extension of Tony's choice upbringing, which provided him with the social information and self-respect needed to execute his highly personal cuisine, establish pricing, and provide fine dining that was informal. When he opened at his first location in West Cambridge, Tony had gone door to door in the Brattle Street neighborhood asking people what they wanted.

"'What kind of restaurant do you want here? What are you looking for in dining?' They wanted the food they'd had in Paris or Marseilles," Tony said. "The food they'd enjoyed in Provence: Bistro food! Gutsy food! Not just a good roast chicken, but chicken stuffed with sausages! Pork belly! Offal! Bones!"

"You knew before you opened your doors that you'd have people waiting," I said.

"People in West Cambridge have more sophisticated palates than in Boston. They travel," he said. "Three nights a week we still have the principal of a certain private school there who comes in to eat six- or eight-course tasting menus with his wife!"

"He must love your food."

No wonder the cost of private education kept rising; at $900 a week for three dinners out, and about thirty-six academic weeks a year, the head of school was dropping $32,400 per year to eat at Craigie, which was almost, to the dollar, the cost of sending one child to his school.

"People in West Cambridge are not afraid of trying new things!" Tony said. "Lamb's tongue. Beef tongue. Lots of mustard sauce! Sounds delicious, right? But other chefs were afraid to put it on their menus because they thought guests wouldn't be willing to take chances."

Tony sold out every order.

"Look, many other chefs don't appreciate the fact that our guests travel. Our guests know food. They've eaten strange and delicious food in the best bistros of France. Why dumb down the food? All I'm doing is serving the food people love to eat!"

The psychological and social advantages that Tony had over most cooks and chefs because of his upbringing meant that he did not have to wait to gain confidence strictly from personal achievement. Whatever obstacles he had—anger, organization, planning, focus—were related to being a confident, suburban, well-schooled, smart individual who was adored by his mother. Growing up white, male, and affluent meant that he got away with more than most people.

What did Tony do with these valuable cards he had been dealt? He did not need to worry about impressing anyone with his food. He was born lucky, and his food tasted like it had been cooked by one lucky guy.

In contrast to Tony, a working-class chef at a fancy restaurant cooks meals that cost far more than he or she can afford for a clientele that historically has regarded him or her as the help. To succeed in the business, these chefs must get over both the insecurity and resentment implicit in that social-psychological imbalance. The rise of celebrity chefs, the inflated sense of ego, came about, in part, as a defense against the pain that most cooks who slave away in upscale restaurant kitchens experience at work and at home.

Most line cooks never become chefs. Line cooking is a young person's job because of the physical demands, stress, and low wages. Famous chefs like Emeril Lagasse, Mario Batali, and Bobby Flay are the lottery winners, and while they give hope to the dreams of line cooks, they are also part of a delusion that misleads many into attending culinary school imagining that when they graduate, they will be chefs. But who will invest money with a young cook, who is deeply in debt, to open his or her own restaurant?

"I went to the CIA," Danny told me, "and even though the

Culinary Institute of America—I call it 'Skills USA'—gave me a four-thousand-dollars-a-year scholarship, the fees still came to twenty-two thousand dollars per year, exclusive of room and board. I graduated without a job owing the bank seventy-six thousand dollars! I was so broke when I graduated that I worked for the food services at Boston University for two solid years! Here it is, nine years later; I'm a sous chef at Craigie? I'm still in massive debt!"

Tony had none of the problems that plague most young cooks. He had no college debt. He and investors shared the same vocabulary. He had gone to the same types of schools as his guests. He knew that most cooks would never become chefs, and that made him special.

"I'm a rock star," he had told me.

Having been brought up without the social and financial insecurities of most cooks, he was able to cook what he liked to eat without worrying about how it fit into a recognizable cuisine.

As tempting as it might have been, though, he and his team could not say "It's Mawsian," or, "food without limits," as this would lead to misunderstandings, some deeper than others, and empty tables.

How did Tony describe the food to guests and when he trained cooks on what they would be cooking?

Without a clear definition of what he does, what he is looking for, and how to achieve precisely the flavors in the food, he ran the risk of cooking ad hoc. The danger was that in failing to articulate what he was after, he could not teach his crew to cook his food consistently. That was often true, night after night, day after day, as I watched the cooks hand Tony tiny spoons or thimbles of food for him to taste. They often lacked the confidence to say they had achieved the desired results, but wasn't their hesitancy a natural response to Tony's inability to explain his cuisine to them? The constant tasting, the uncertainty of his cooks, and his routine frustration and anger with them seemed due to Tony's failure to focus on defining his cuisine, but I wondered if it wasn't something else entirely.

Tony had created a system in the restaurant in which all critical decisions in the kitchen had to go through him. Since the food was him, it was nearly impossible for a cook to re-create what Tony was after without his direct involvement. What he was after was unwritten. What he wanted in a broth on Tuesday night might not be the same in that broth on Wednesday night. How is a "boudin noir–hoisin sauce" *supposed* to taste? Did "ramp kimchee" benefit from more vinegar? More sugar? More salt? How do we know these things?

The only person who could answer all the questions was Tony Maws, which led to constant misunderstandings.

Tony knew that having an indefinable, ever-changing cuisine meant that conflicts were more likely to occur in comparison to a restaurant that served classic versions of Tuscan or Burgundian food. There the guidelines were obvious. Follow the centuries-old rules, guided by a good executive chef or chef de cuisine, and the cook was set. Night after night, there was little improvisation.

Tony was being creative, but what was the psychological explanation for what amounted to a rebellion against the rules and traditions of many generations of chefs before him?

Under Tony's system, he was allowed to be angry at cooks who invariably misunderstood *him*. If he had chosen to have a paternalistic cuisine—specific to a region with clear standards for each dish as is true for all the best cuisines, the food of our fathers—he would be angry at cooks who misunderstood his *food*.

Anger in more traditional restaurants is directed at cooks who are slackers or incompetent, and not at cooks who, as was true at Craigie, constantly have to keep up with the chef's whims. No wonder Tony's tasting menus were called just that: "Chef's Whims."

I had never seen restaurant cooks more unsure of themselves than the crew I met at Craigie—constantly asking Tony if what they were cooking tasted right, or needed something else, or was done. It was not laziness or poor skills, but rather that they honestly did not know what he was trying to do because he could not explain it to them consistently.

I finally asked Tony, "How would you describe your food?"

"That's a difficult question," he said. "Creative French?"

"Oh, c'mon," I said. "It's not French."

"All right, let me think about it," he said.

He thought about it.

A fascinating thing about certain chefs is that being analytical interferes with cooking. Danny, for example, had told me, "There are two things I hate doing. The first is writing and the second is reading."

However, not being analytical complicates the single *most* important requirement of being a chef: *Teaching* cooks to cook the food.

"How about: snout to tail, sustainable food prepared using French techniques and Asian as well as local ingredients from as many organic farms as possible," Tony said.

"That pretty much covers everything," I said.

"Yeah, I see that," he said. He laughed. "Let's ask my mother."

I was charmed: Here was a top chef asking his mother what kind of food he cooks. Imagine if each of us could have the kind of relationship with our mother where we could call her up to ask: "Hey, Ma, what is it I do, again?"

"Tony's food is refined rusticity, French in technique, but it includes Asian ingredients and local products, too," said Marjorie. "He's all about sustainability."

That did not sound very appetizing. I also did not understand what she meant by Asia: Vietnam? China? India? Japan? Korea?

Thailand? As for *sustainability*, the word, like *organic*, does not hold the same meaning for each person using it. When you consider that the world's largest sustainable grocer is Walmart, you realize the word could signify almost anything.

Oh, well, I thought, how about, "really delicious," and suggested to Marjorie that we meet for coffee to talk about her son. We set a date.

Then it hit me:

Tony could not explain his food because he did not know what it was either! That was why he asked his mother. And since his food is so personal, his menu was the culinary equivalent of a teenager saying, *I don't know who I am!*

If Tony did not know what to call his food, and if his mother did not either, could his staff tell me?

I asked front-of-the-house servers and hostesses as well as cooks and sous chefs what they were serving and cooking.

I began at the bar.

John Mayer, Texas born, looking so clean it appeared that he just stepped out of the shower, and with the magnetic smile of a broker, had ambitions to work as a youth minister, but until that happened he was serving drinks. He enjoyed the contrast between helping kids choose Christ's path and making cocktails.

"It's not as much of a paradox as you might think," John said. "I was brought up Episcopalian. We like to drink. Jesus turned water into wine, didn't he?"

This tension between two very different ways of life added to the general fun at Craigie. John was not the only one working at Craigie who did not know what he wanted to do in five years' time. His solution to the conflict was an imaginative and youthful way to embrace contradictions. Soon enough he would have to choose: Working in a restaurant was a way to delay having to make the decisions associated with becoming an adult.

"Let's go crazy," sang Prince as John, Sally, and Ted worked at top speed to prepare the bar for service that night. Hands in constant motion, focus on the external: arranging glasses; stacking menus; slicing oranges, limes, and lemons.

"How would I describe the food at Craigie?" John asked rhetorically as he poured simple syrup from a jar into a bowl of sage and juniper. The aroma was intoxicating.

"It is French inspired," he said, "eclectic, rustic with emphasis on organic, local ingredients whenever possible with incredible meat and fish."

"That does sound good," I said.

"It's Tony's food," John said, "but heavily influenced by many traditions—Japanese, Middle Eastern, and American."

Prince sang, "Let's go crazy, let's get nuts, let's look for the purple banana, till they put us in the truck, let's go!"

"The food here," John continued, "can be very refined or it can be roll-up-your-sleeves cuisine."

As John spoke, his love for the food could be detected in the increased speed of his speech and the brightening of color in his face. Food was more than a way to sustain himself; it was spiritual.

"The last time I ate here," John said, "I had the pig's tails. Ate with my hands!"

"With your hands?" I asked.

"You bet! That's how they're supposed to be eaten," John said. He began to drawl. "And I shared the pig's head with a friend. You know what he called the food?"

"What?" I asked.

"Bad-ass food!" John said.

Sally came over. I had tried to engage her many times before, but she had always been shy and reluctant to express her ideas. She did not think that what she had to say was important, which may seem strange for someone who has to face a row of talkative customers, but having a well-defined role as a bartender, with a limited and repetitive script, was liberating. She could feign communication.

"His food is fine rusticity," Sally said, and then returned quickly to her chores.

"Uniquely Tony Maws," said Ted.

I pictured the three bartenders pitching these explanations to customers or guests seated on stools at the bar, newcomers flipping over the paper menus, printed daily, who were trying to figure out what was going on. The menu contained familiar choices—tuna, clams, bass, burgers, and chicken—but it had just as many strange terms. Terms that even for someone who writes about food serve as barriers to understanding: *squid ink anchoïade, nuoc cham, purslane, sauce vert.* In what sense are these words a reflection of a philosophy of cooking? Why are they all on the same menu? What chef is an expert at preparing this range of complex ingredients used in various cuisines? What do they mean?

It is fine if you are seated, hungry, and willing to try new things, but what happens to people who have never been to Craigie on Main?

The initial point of contact is the person who answers the phone: a general manager, host, or hostess. How do they describe the food to first-time callers who have heard or read about the restaurant?

"I tell them it's very adventurous, fun, and fresh food with a French background to it!" said Julia. She looked as young as a kid in high school: long tresses, the smile of a cheerleader, the wholesome looks of a girl next door. Julia was new, having replaced Kim, who decided to take a two-month road trip west with her girlfriend before returning to Boston to look for a new job. "I tell them it's influenced by Asian and Mediterranean cuisines, too? My dad? He eats out a lot? He loves the food here!"

The lack of specificity in all the answers provided by staff was puzzling. Did their amorphous descriptions of Craigie's food show that they misunderstood what Tony had taught them about his kitchen? By saying that the food was all things, or most things, they were not saying anything. Unless . . .

Unless the staff meant that Tony was some kind of culinary genius who could use a startling array of ingredients to evoke deeper tastes than ever before! That he was not confined to a formal tradition. There were right ways and wrong ways of doing things at Craigie on Main, but not according to Escoffier. It was the world according to Tony!

Julia kept smiling. She was genial and confident. Like the other hostesses, she was a diva. Always on. The effort looked exhausting.

"People call in to ask about the tasting menus," said Julia, "I tell them that we want to cater to what people like. You don't like raw fish? Fine, tell us what you do like. You love mushrooms? We can do that! It's fun. Anyway? I think that the fun of pleasing people with great food is more important than the style of cuisine."

"Look, all chefs are baddies," she said, and laughed. "And that's great!"

I turned to the cooks to find out more.

Danny, as usual, was a whirligig. His jacket unbuttoned, the U of his wife-beater exposed, he was scrubbing down the huge stovetop, stirring a pot of chicken stock, and screaming at Bobby, "It's not rocket science, get the fuck ready!"

Danny looked up from his chores and then back down again.

"We cook good food here," Danny said calmly, leaning into the stove, putting his whole body into each scrub. "We have no boundaries—we're not afraid to use ingredients from anywhere."

"Taste this," said Tony, appearing at my side, handing me a spoon with a blue-white dollop on it.

"What is it?" I asked.

"Jeez," he said, "just fucking taste it!"

"Wow," I said. Creamy, salty, sweet. Great consistency, too. "What is that?"

"Blue cheese dressing," Tony said proudly. "Kind of a culinary joke for a chef, a friend, who's coming in tonight for his birthday with eleven friends. The world's most expensive blue cheese dressing: It's made with St. Aubin cheese at twenty-four dollars a pound."

"Uniquely Tony Maws," said Danny, echoing Ted. Some kind of mantra, I guessed.

"Wow," I said again.

"Have some more," said Tony.

I did.

"Look," said Tony, "we don't have a tradition. All of us come from different places."

"And your food reflects that cultural diversity?" I asked.

"It helps me to be prolific," he said. "I'm interested in consistency, but I don't want to get bored either. It's like, 'What, I have to make the corn soup again?' When cooks come to work for me at Craigie, it's never easy, but it's never dull. Like our tasting menus which change all the time. Keeps us sharp."

It was now 5:30; the front door had been unlocked and dinner service could begin.

"Let 'em in," said Marjorie, "let 'em in!"

Nearly a dozen people stepped inside, out of the rain, looking like kids at a middle school dance: in awe, a little shy, excited about the night ahead, and hopeful. Stamping, shaking off the rain, folding umbrellas, wiping eyeglasses clear of condensation, accepting cloth napkins to dry their hair.

"Look," whispered one guy to his date, "there he is. That's Tony Maws! The chef."

The guest and his companion beamed, straightened up, made a

slight wave at waist level to Tony, and averted their eyes from him as Julia led them to their table.

I stayed in the kitchen at the pass, watching the cooks start work on the first orders coming in.

Matt was shouting an order to Timmy, whose long, cursive tat, *Fire in the Night Forever*, stood out on his right forearm:

"Hey, put that pan on the heat! Five orders of bacon all day!"

Then Matt said to Kyle and Carl: "Pigtails in thirty seconds!"

"Pigtails," said Kyle and Carl.

"We are walking that now," said Matt.

"We're playing the clam against the tail," said Dakota.

"Let's play the squash in one minute," said Matt.

"Squash," said Dakota, "one minute."

"Two sixes, all in, funky stuff," said Matt.

All the cooks said back: "Two sixes, funky stuff!"

"Let's get ready on four thirty-one four," said Tony.

"Let's get ready on four thirty-one four," said Matt.

"James, I'm giving you a dorade in thirty seconds," said Tony.

"Thank you," said James.

James did not seem to respond to what was going on around him but instead, showing no emotion, went about the work robotically.

I elbowed my way behind the two line cooks at the meat station until I reached Matt, who was supervising the grill.

"What kind of food do we cook here? Is that what you're asking me?" Matt said. He had a pair of tongs in his left hand that he used to turn the sizzling burgers. The fat in the butter and the delicious aroma of the beef captivated me. "It's really locally, seasonally in-spired. There are not many rules. It's French inspired."

He flipped the burgers. The beef had been cooked sous vide, at low temperature, for over an hour, and then put on the grill to get a good crust. The burgers would be finished under the blue, coiled flames of a blazing hot salamander so that the Vermont cheddar melted into the meat.

"We also get to work with cool equipment and use beautiful products," Matt said. "The best fish, the best beef, the best chicken!"

As the tickets flew in, the frenzy increased until it achieved a rhythm. The cooks were in a place different from the rest of us: not exactly a trance, but close to it. They worked as an ensemble, and it reminded me enormously of watching jazz musicians play. What kind of music or food was being created mattered less than the wondrous performance itself. All of them, as Tony had noted, came from different places, but here, in his kitchen, they were in the same place, moving as if they were connected to one another, anticipating reactions, helping out, establishing reliable, nonverbal ways of communication. It was flat-out beautiful, very different from the chaos out on the streets, or the spite and disagreements that characterize family life at times.

The relationship of the cooks to the food was hindered by Tony's inability to explain what he was after in his cooking, but being a key member of a functional group of people helped to compensate for that.

These were nights they would, I believed, always remember, as their first youthful experiences of a selfless profession. Give it a name, define it, establish rules: All of it would for certain make their lives easier, but until that happened, they had, at least, the comfort of going through a powerful experience together.

"Two octo all day, one pork," Danny shouted to Bobby. "Bobby! Two octo all day, one pork. Two octo all day, one pork! Bobby!"

"Two octo all day, one pork," said Bobby.

Under his breath, to me, Danny said, "I swear to God, what a moron."

Dakota, whose tattooed body, from the fork on his neck to the clown below his elbow, contrasted with his genuine innocence, piped up. "My knowledge of food, of what we do here, from what I've seen," Dakota said, jumbling up the words in his nimble excitement, "it's old-school techniques with modern amenities." He paused and grinned. "I don't know what that word means: *amenities*. I don't know French cuisine yet. I don't know American cuisine yet."

Then he returned to his station to cook food that, as yet, had no name.

EIGHT

The Son, the Chef

F I HAD TO DO IT ALL OVER, I WOULD WRITE THIS BOOK ABOUT MARJORIE
Maws. I say that only half-jokingly, as Marjorie is certainly as
interesting as her son, the chef. Unlike most people her age—she is
seventy-two—Marjorie personally achieved financial independence.
Her economic freedom contributed to her emotional confidence. I
think her achievement gave strength to her son and made it possible
for him to imagine his own future with assurance. Chefs also cook
with someone in mind, and it is my opinion that Tony cooked and
came up with new dishes to please his mother.

As in, unconsciously or not: What would Ma think? Hey, Ma,
you like this? Ma, is this any good?

Marjorie ate in his restaurant all the time, too, so she was able
to judge the food and service. She was not a cook, nor had she run
a restaurant before Craigie, and she'd never expressed interest in
going into business with her son. Tony, recognizing talent when he
saw it, persuaded his mother to be by his side, literally, when he first
opened, and to this day she still helped him run things. "He called

me out of retirement," Marjorie said. "'It's time,' he said. Time to open his restaurant . . . I had an entirely different retirement plan! But when he decided to open his own place, he called me to help him run things. I bought a book on how to run a restaurant, got other family members involved, and we were off. It's awesome! I'm so proud of him!"

A chef's mother working in the kitchen or on the floor or at staff meetings is extremely unusual. This was not a simple bistro or trattoria; it was a luxury restaurant. Picture Daniel Humm's mother seating customers or Paul Liebrandt's mom at the stove.

As a parent I felt intuitively connected to her: Of the fifty-five or so people working at Craigie, only Tony, Chuck, Santos, and Marjorie had kids. (By the end of my time at the restaurant, four more parents were added to the staff.)

Marjorie and I met often during the eighteen months I spent at Craigie. The best conversation we had was at Hi-Rise, my favorite bakery in town, for what was supposed to have been forty-five minutes but turned into two hours.

The opportunity to talk to a chef's mother! It was a psychologist's dream come true. How often had I heard the well-rehearsed and impressive remarks of famous chefs and wondered: What does your mother think of you?

"Tony's different from his brother, Alex," Marjorie said after we had sat down. "For one thing, Alex is an ardent vegetarian."

I knew from our conversations that Tony regarded vegetarians with . . . was it pity? Polite respect? An eye roll?

"Oh, Alex is a wonderful cook, too," Marjorie said. "Very skilled. He makes great breads and delicious ice cream."

"Is Alex also in the profession?" I asked.

"Not at all," she said. She took a sip of her tea. "Alex lives in London and is head of education at a foundation called The Holocaust Educational Trust."

I couldn't help thinking: *That* would make a terrible name for a restaurant.

"But Tony, was he always interested in being a chef?"

"No," said Marjorie, "not really. Not as a child, anyway. I never thought he would end up working in a restaurant."

Marjorie explained that both she and her husband, Stewart, had worked long hours. She said that she and Stew typically got home late and that dinners often consisted of chicken with soy sauce, iceberg lettuce, Pearl kosher hot dogs, take-out Chinese, and pizza.

I knew from Tony that his years of work with chefs Chris Schlesinger (East Coast Grill), Mark Miller (Chez Panisse, Coyote Cafe), and Ken Oringer (Clio, Toro, Coppa) had provided him with the knowledge and experience needed to cook professionally, but without a palate fostered in childhood, what is a chef creating in his or her kitchen? One reason the French, Japanese, Chinese, and Italian cuisines are so spectacular in certain restaurants is that the chefs have the flavors in their bones. They have a sense of what has been done up to that point, a huge vocabulary of specific dishes and ingredients, and an inclination to perfect or refine the food.

However, several chefs—exemplified by Ferran Adrià, Wylie Dufresne, Heston Blumenthal, and David Chang—are inventive because they either reject the past or have little past to rely on. They can cherry-pick what they like from any culture or cuisine, and if the result is unfamiliar to them and their guests, even better! At Momofuku Ko, David Chang's top restaurant, I had bone marrow in Gruyère broth. Where did *that* come from? But it was delicious and memorable. These new chefs saw themselves as futurists and food pioneers.

Was Tony a believer in this new way of doing things? Or did he have a tradition? Marjorie explained how Tony could have developed his palate as a result of Baba Hannah's foods, but she felt that he was also influenced by the food they had around them when they lived in the South End before moving to Newton.

The South End was not an especially diverse or food-oriented neighborhood, having once been filled with single-room occupancies, marginalized African Americans with low incomes, and Spanish speakers. Then gay men and affluent, young careerists moved in. But Chinatown was practically next door. Marjorie recalled a time when Tony came home from kindergarten, and he was so proud of himself for winning the award for best chopstick skills! He'd beaten all the Chinese kids!

But at home? Tony did not cook for the family. He was not obsessed with food from an early age, nor did he have much exposure as a child to great examples of cooking.

This was puzzling. If Tony had not grown up eating amazing food, if he was not surrounded by a family in the dining industry, where did his palate come from? Surely there were early behaviors that he showed his mom that gradually formed a pattern leading him to become a chef.

Marjorie explained that Tony was clear about how he wanted *her* to cook. From age eight or nine, he would ask her to cook food according to the directions on the package. He stood by her side, in the kitchen, and read the package—it could be macaroni and cheese, it didn't matter—and made sure that she was doing exactly what it said. Black and white, to the letter.

"'Mom, follow the directions on the package!' He was saying that when he was eight years old."

"So you were his first line cook," I said.

She wasn't, of course. She ran her own management consulting firm. People skills, but it had nothing to do with food.

She assumed that Tony had restaurant jobs as a teenager because he enjoyed the experience and was good at waiting tables. That he was good at selling the food and made a lot of money doing it. When he got older, he didn't know exactly what he wanted to do. She saw his discomfort with a couple of office jobs and then a year to be a ski bum.

That was when it occurred to her that he might want to be in a restaurant and cook.

"What was your reaction?" I asked.

"I thought if I championed it, he wouldn't do it," she said.

Marjorie saw right away that Tony could do it. During the summer, living at her house in Menemsha, he was twenty-three, waiting tables. He'd help out in the restaurant kitchen, too, doing little things, whatever the cooks needed. The chef took him aside and said, "Why aren't you cooking? You're good. Why are you content just waiting tables?"

"What did Tony say?"

"He said, 'I don't know why!' So he started cooking, which was a sacrifice."

"Why?"

"Because of the great money he always made waiting tables," Marjorie said. "He was such a great server!"

This was a long time ago, in 1993, when there was far less glamour associated with cooking and becoming a chef.

Marjorie's view was that cooking was a blue-collar profession back then. Cooks did not expect to progress. They didn't think about the next step. There was no Food Channel, there were no food shows, and there weren't many celebrity chefs.

"Then the Culinary Institute added a course: Media Relations," Marjorie said. "Media relations! Most of the kids there were never going to be chefs, but with this course the CIA got them thinking: 'Hey, I can be a famous chef, too!' I think that was a disservice. It misled them into thinking that if they went to the CIA they'd be famous chefs one day. Instead they went into debt."

"Maybe that's a problem with hiring cooks," I said. "Maybe they have the idea that line cooking is beneath them and that after a few months they can quit and open their own place or move up the ranks."

"Finding and keeping good people is a problem, yes," she said.

A huge part of Tony's success is due to his mom's direct involvement then and now. She continues to check the budget, supervise staff, take on design projects, handle difficult customers, run the website, and respond to written complaints.

"What was that like? I mean, his first restaurant?"

"We divided up the responsibilities. We had a fifteen-thousand-dollar budget."

"That's it?"

"That's it," she said. "I have good marketing skills. I have good organizational skills. I was soon working full time as business manager and marketing director. Some retirement! But I loved it! We brought in everyone we knew to help. We had three months to open up. We called ourselves Team Tony and later Bistrot Buddies. My brother is a lawyer—he helped with legal stuff. Alex and one of Tony's best friends from high school, Peter Leis, designed the website. We had friends to shop for antiques to decorate the restaurant, wallpaper the bathrooms, and sew and make curtains. Tony's dad, Stewart, and his best friend, Mike, did the wiring, plumbing, and construction."

"So it's always been a family affair," I said.

"Absolutely. We used to be much more like a family, too, when we first opened. Tony's cousin was involved. My niece helped with PR. Literally everyone who could manage it in our family was working for Tony in one capacity or another."

"And with families, anger has a certain legitimacy."

"I think we've made enormous progress in that regard," Marjorie said, "but, yes, anger management with Tony has always been an issue. The thing is: It's almost always legitimate. It's how he expresses his anger that can be a problem."

She shared her son's impatience with the cooks who were disorganized or did not work hard enough, but she understood that leadership required patience to nurture and train them. Marjorie felt that cooking for a busy room on a weekend night created enormous pressure, that it got to Tony, and that it led to his becoming enraged or even yelling. She wanted him to find new ways to deal with that pressure, ways that were more productive.

"Tony has a history of inappropriate responses. I know that Tony Maws is one in a hundred. I understand that. But I keep telling him: 'You can't expect people to work at your level! You can't treat the people below you as failing.'"

"To which he responds?"

"Oh, he thinks I'm fed up with him," she said, and laughed.

I laughed, too. We were both doing a lot of laughing. It was like talking about the boss behind his back. Guilty laughter based on fear and affection.

"Maybe if he responded to his frustration the way he responds to his son, Charlie, that would work," I said.

"That's exactly what I tell him. 'Talk to them as if you're talking to Charlie.' I don't mean that his staff are children."

"Of course not."

"I mean show them the same patience and love you demonstrate to your son," she said.

We were nearing the end of our long talk. Marjorie was driving to Hyannis later that morning to catch the ferry to the Vineyard. She would spend four or five days there each week, throughout the summer, coming back midweek to work at Craigie.

"It's so much fun at Craigie," she said. "It's cool. A high: When you stand at the pass and watch Tony cook? I feel mesmerized and proud."

"That's wonderful," I said, thinking of other people her age who lacked the rapport, trust, and intimacy with a child whose enterprise she was involved in so routinely and meaningfully. She must have done many things right as a parent. The question of palate aside, her ability to be frank with Tony, knowing he trusted her, surely had enabled him to cook with profound confidence. His mother loved him deeply.

"When I'm in the restaurant, the world is in color. My friends sometimes ask me: 'Hey, Marjorie, didn't you plan to retire? When are you going to retire?' But outside the restaurant, the world is in black and white."

"There's a great Italian saying Mario Batali quoted in his Babbo cookbook, and you made me think of it. 'No one gets old at the table.'"

"Exactly," she said. "The challenge we face is finding staff who want to share that kind of intimacy. Assuming talent and motivation, you have to buy into our mission."

"Which is?"

"Honesty. Being proud of being associated with that. If the fish is cut up wrong, don't serve it. No exceptions."

NINE

Rock Stars

I WAS RINGSIDE WITH TONY. "I DEAL WITH THE LIMITED SKILLS OF SOME of my cooks by using technology," he said. "Making things idiot-proof. I'm not eliminating the cooking, I'm just making it easier for them. Like the low-heat convection oven I use to keep the burgers warm. Like sous vide."

One reason for the rise of sous vide methods in restaurants—food that is poached in plastic packaging very slowly over low temperatures in a tightly controlled, reliable, and scientific way—is that it takes a great deal of guesswork out of cooking. With sous vide cooking, sous chefs can prep most if not all the protein dishes, except for items meant to be served raw, and instruct line cooks to finish what they started. Prep and line cooks work with sous vide, too. You do not need a great palate or high-level abilities to put things in Cryovac, place them into a machine that vacuum-seals them, and store the products in a walk-in for later use.

Most of the protein served at Craigie—pork, chicken, beef, lamb—starts out sous vide. No different from The French Laundry,

Restaurant Daniel, Momofuku Ko, Robuchon, and other top restaurants.

Sous vide cooking originated in France as an economical way to cut costs, as less protein is lost when poaching in plastic. Chef Joël Robuchon was among the first great chefs to see its potential. He introduced it to first-class passengers on the high-speed TGV trains. Wolfgang Puck understood that sous vide was the single most important technological advance in the business. With sous vide, Puck can have his food prepped in one location and have it shipped worldwide to his global empire of restaurants.

Chefs will tell you that sous vide creates more intense flavors because the methodology seals things in. This is true. It is also much easier to teach cooks sous vide methodology than to teach them knife skills. Tony permitted his cooks to work with sous vide, but only he could cut the fish.

What Tony lacked in tradition, he made up for by being passionate about how science can be used to solve problems in restaurant kitchens.

He loves gadgets.

One problem Tony had was that the sources of his palate, how he developed a superior sense of taste, were unclear. His lack of clarity complicated the task of trying to explain to line cooks what he was looking for in a dish.

I had seen this happen many times.

One night Zack handed him a dollop of diced cucumber in buttermilk, and Tony said that the sauce was too thick.

"But," said Zack, protesting, "that's how you wanted it last night!"

"That was last night!" yelled Tony. He had his hands on his hips and then pointed to the spoon and then to the stairs, gesturing for Zack to go down and do it all over again. "That's not how I want it tonight!"

The fluidity of Tony's thinking was creative, but how was a cook supposed to keep up with it?

Not having a tradition with established rules meant that Tony had, as his mother said, a legitimate outlet for expressing anger whenever his unclear, changing method of doing things was not followed.

With sous vide, Tony's cooks had a method that was relatively simple to put into practice and created the same results each time. The cooking involved technology rather than speed, hand-eye co-ordination, delicacy, or stirring. Sous vide methods are also used to create viscosity in shampoos and toothpaste.

I had determined that Tony had grown up in a very supportive household, was good with chopsticks from an early age, lived briefly in a neighborhood near Chinatown, bossed his mom around in her kitchen, began cooking professionally at age twenty-three, cooked in France for six months, and benefited from having a grandmother who loved food and cooked some dishes that involved long braises and slow roasts and an unabashed embrace of chicken fat, but it did not add up.

"I'm not even attempting to go to the science side of palates, the neurology," Tony said when I asked him how he had gone about developing his. "I feel as if I was in the right place at the right time. I fell into something. It was a combination of things. I was getting ready to leave the East Coast Grill. Chris [Schlesinger] said, 'Tony, it's time.' Chris said he had taught me everything he had to teach me. He thought I had more potential, that I could grow. So he said, 'Where do you want to go? I'll call whoever you like and try to get you a job there.'"

Immediately, France came to my mind. How its gastronomy had influenced Thomas Keller, Andrew Carmellini, and Daniel Humm, among countless other chefs who had not grown up with a French *grandmere* but who had recognized or felt that working in a French kitchen offered the finest techniques, rules, and methods. I thought, too, of Mario Batali, and Dave Pasternack, who went to Italy to discover the power of rusticity, regionalism, and ingredient driven cuisine. And David Chang, who had gone to Japan to learn about one of the world's finest cuisines.

"I wanted to work for Mark Miller," Tony said. "In New Mexico, at Coyote Cafe. He was a Boston guy originally and got what I call his doctorate at Chez Panisse back when Judy Rogers and Jeremiah Tower were in that kitchen."

France and Italy were important to his way of thinking about food, but Tony was essentially a New World guy, an Augie March of the kitchen.

"Mark had an unbelievable palate," Tony said. "He wasn't a great cook, but he could taste all the components of a sauce or a dish. All the spices!"

"That's an interesting way to define a palate," I said. "I think of it as an ability to discern when something tastes good."

"That, too," said Tony. "That's important, too. But for a chef it's also essential to know how to *create* the taste. You'd give Mark a mole to taste and he could tell you every spice that went into it."

That made sense. What I still did not understand is how Tony personally knew when he had achieved the taste he was after.

"It's simple repetition," Tony said. "I have some dish in mind or some variation of that dish and I cook it again and again and again and again, sometimes for months, until I think it's ready to put on the menu. Even the tasting menus, most of what's on them, are comprised of dishes I've thought about or tried for a long time. Okay, a lot of it's improvisation with an ingredient I know or want to try, but then . . ." He laughed. ". . . then you have to trust me!"

I still could not see how he developed his deeper sense of taste.

"You dive deeper, and deeper, and deeper," he said. "Palates develop over time. Look, think of it the way you think of music. What's your favorite rock album of all time?"

"*Let It Bleed*," I said.

"Excellent choice," he said and fist bumped. "One of my favorites, too, although I prefer *Beggars Banquet* because it's not as well known. So think about it: How many times have you listened to that album?"

"Oh, man," I said, "I don't know, maybe a bazillion. I still listen to it every day, no kidding."

"Okay," Tony said, "so I bet that you hear things in the songs other people don't hear, right?"

"It's interesting you should say that, because I was just listening to 'Midnight Rambler' the other day and I swear I heard chord changes in Keith Richards's playing I'd never heard before."

"Exactly!" Tony said. "Exactly! Cooking is like that, too. You cook something a bazillion times and you discover things in the dish you didn't know were there. You decide then to bring those things out. You might think a dish tastes the same each time, but there are subtle differences. I may decide one night to bring out different flavors in the same dish I've cooked for months or years in my kitchen."

"Ah," I said, thinking of how this drove his cooks crazy, this pursuit, this lack of a fixed address.

"It's a fucking pain in the ass," Tony said, "because I see things in a dish I want to bring out and meanwhile I've got to get the dish to the table."

"Yeah, well, even Keith Richards put down his guitar after a while and knew that he had nothing more to add to a song."

My thoughts were interrupted by Bobby and Danny, who were at Tony's elbow with things for him to taste.

First, Danny.

"Wow," said Tony, "this is great!" It was a piece of guanciale that had been cooked sous vide.

"Thanks!" said Danny.

"Perfect texture," said Tony. "Nice balance."

Bobby inched forward. "Show him what you got, Bobby," said Danny.

It seemed that Bobby had had enough of being teased by everyone in the restaurant, from waitstaff to Santos.

"Look," he said to Danny, in an expressionless voice, "my name isn't Bobby. It's Thomas."

Danny laughed.

"As long as you're working at Craigie, it's Bobby," said Danny.

Bobby shrugged.

"Whaddya got for me, Bobby?" asked Tony.

"Chorizo sauce for the octo," he said, handing him a spoon.

Tony tasted it.

"Needs salt," Tony said.

"I think the salt will come when I add the anchovies," said Bobby.

Tony looked at him with disbelief and rage.

"Bobby," Tony said, "it needs more salt."

"Yeah, I heard," he said, still completely unemotional. "I still figured that would come with the anchovies. The anchovies are very salty." Was he clueless that in Tony's eyes this amounted to a provocation?

"More salt, Bobby, more salt, more salt!" said Tony.

Danny jumped in. "If Chef wants to hear your opinion, Bobby, he'll ask for it. Now get the fuck back to your station and do what you're told."

Bobby's back to him, Tony said, "My way or your way, Bobby? My way or your way?"

To me, Tony said, "See what I have to deal with?"

"Bobby's sitting pretty," said Mary, who was slicing hydroponic watercress at garde manger.

A couple of other cooks laughed, but most of them were too caught up in the work they still had left to do in the ten minutes before the doors opened.

Tony stood up.

"Got to change for service," he said. Out of college clothes. "Be right back."

While I waited, I watched Mary and Jill work in garde manger: swift, fastidious, with total concentration.

Tony returned in freshly pressed chef's whites. He went from cook to cook, high-fiving each person, a couple of fist bumps here and there. A lot of steady eye contact: He gazed into their eyes.

"You ready, Dakota?" Tony said.

"Ready to rock, Chef!" said Dakota.

"Yeah, man!" said Timmy.

"Let's do it, Chef," said Danny.

I expected Tony to take his position at the pass, but he asked Danny to man it while he worked at the counter to its right. He took out a bowl, poured in a little olive oil, chili water, and a pure green liquid the color of English peas. He began whipping things up.

"You planning on turning that into a purée?" asked Danny, over his shoulder, as he sharpened knives.

"I don't know," said Tony.

"I'm just asking," said Danny.

"I don't know, I don't know, I don't know," said Tony.

Tony stirred harder.

"Uh-oh," said Danny, laughing. "Whoa! Hands off!"

"I don't know," said Tony. "*Back off!*"

"In three," said Drew.

Before the doors opened, Tony finished whatever he had been doing and asked Matt to hand him a small metal tray in which a beautiful, thick loin of tuna had been placed under a paper towel. Tony took out the fish, placed it on the counter, and began slicing perfect squares.

"For the tasting menu?" I asked.

"Right," Tony said.

"Doors open," said Drew.

People started streaming in.

"There he is!" said a guest or customer loudly. As if he had been shipwrecked and spotted land. "There he is!"

"Where?" asked his female companion.

"There!" He did all but point. "Slicing the fish!"

The two of them turned to the couple they were dining with and, starstruck, hesitated before Meredith, who wanted to lead them to their table.

What a gulf Tony's notoriety must create between him and his cooks, I thought, and between him and the ordinary world, the world of black and white his mother had spoken of only a few days before. No wonder he thought of himself as a rock star. No doubt he saw most of his cooks as roadies rather than as members of the band.

He had said that of the cooks working for him now, there were two people who might be rock stars. What had Tony seen? What made them different?

Jess was downstairs, in a tight corner, surrounded by counter-tops. On the surface of the counters were trays holding parceled-up meat, dead animals, bones, and blood. It was a dreary place to work: low ceilings, too, and gray walls, and her work space no more than a narrow counter on which she had placed a mixer, bowls, a tiny scale, a blender, a food processor, and stainless-steel utensils.

Jess's life was a little bit easier than working upstairs, though; being in pastry, she did not have to conform to the time crunch faced by the line cooks. The new rule at Craigie, Meredith and

Drew had announced last week, was that the first course must get to the table within ten minutes of the waiter putting in the ticket.

"Hi, Jess," I said, making my way past Santos, Gabby, and Alex.

Santos was butchering. Gabby and Alex carried trays of food between cleaning up. Constant cleaning! Bobby and James were downstairs, too, doing what, it wasn't clear, but it seemed to involve cooking. To my right was Aaron, tall and laconic and as thin and agile as a guy who ran track, who led the operation downstairs under Tony's guidance. Aaron kept count of supplies, supervised the prep cooks, helped bake the sesame-seeded burger buns, and made sure nothing was wasted. It was all arms and legs downstairs, not a frenzy, but still constant motion.

"Hi!" Jess shouted, over her shoulder, concentrating on the sorbet in the bowl before her.

"So, Jess," I said, "I'm here to find out why Tony thinks you might be a rock star."

Jess laughed.

"Is that what he said?" Jess asked.

I stood at her side.

"Hold on," I said, "let me look at my notes . . . 'Jess is one of the best pastry chefs I've ever had. She contributes to our menus—she's the only person in eight and a half years to be able to do that.'"

"I'll have to thank him," she said.

Jess brightened up the place. It was not just her positive outlook that did it, nor her pleasant mien. Her intelligence did it. She opened up lines of communication between herself and the cooks and in doing so established order.

Done with the sorbet, now Jess was kneading dough.

"I moved to Boston because of a boy," she said, pressing into the dough fiercely. "He didn't work out, but the city did!"

She had worked as a medical assistant for two years after getting her degree, and she spent her spare time going to farmer's markets and cooking. Like many in their twenties without a clear vocation or family business, she had worked hard to decide what she wanted to do with her life.

"One day I quit my job and applied to the Cambridge Culinary Institute, a one-year program, and after graduating looked for work," Jess said.

With a mother and a grandmother who are both artists and a father who taught math and science, Jess found that baking made sense. "It combines two elements in my family: the artistic and the analytical."

Jess rolled out the dough and then, using a wooden-handled slicer, cut it into thick, even sections. It was Jess's seventh month at the restaurant. Before starting there she had been a waitress and later, briefly, a pastry cook at a French bistro in Boston's South End.

At Craigie, Jess is one of four women in the kitchen. "I'm a woman in a man's world. It's a challenge getting respect from everyone, especially from guys who come from other countries where they aren't used to having women at work tell them what to do. They do what I tell them to do. They have to. We have a job to do." She parceled out the pieces of dough and began to brush them with melted butter.

"I just think we always have to prove ourselves," she said. "The thing is: Being a girl, I'm like that naturally. Knowing that I have to prove myself, so: I prove myself. Being a girl in a restaurant kitchen, if you say you can't do something, you're judged. But, as I said, I'm not like that. I never ask a guy to do something for me simply because he's a guy. Gets me in trouble sometimes . . . On my second day here, I was carrying a huge batch of poached quince downstairs—I wanted to seem tough enough—and I sprained my wrist."

Unlike the women who worked in the front of the house—behind the bar, waiting tables, and at the door—Jess, Jill, Rachel, and Mary wore little makeup, talked like sailors, and relied solely on their cooking to establish connections between themselves and their co-workers. I loved their vigor and found it inspiring.

"So maybe being a leader among the men might help you to build the skills you need to take your career to the next level—to be a chef?" I asked. "Having faced adversity, you might get stronger. Ironically, being a woman in a man's kitchen, which is a challenge, forces you to be a leader."

"Yeah, maybe, and maybe not. I joke fairly often; I say it a lot to Mary: I feel very maternal. Especially with the young boys cooking here. Sometimes it's so mindless! I'll say to one of them, 'Just do what I'm asking you to do and make me a better mom.'"

Dakota ran past us carrying a small aluminum tray. It was the middle of service, but seeing a CD of DMX on the counter, he stopped in his tracks.

"Dude!" he said. "Dude! Whose is this?"

"Mine," I said.

"You listen to DMX?" Dakota asked, incredulous. "A shrink who listens to DMX?"

"It relaxes me," I said, ironically.

"Whoa, dude!" He put down the tray, and raised his left palm. "High five! Dude! That man is fucked up! Fucking crazy! You know DMX stole a 1988 Cadillac and ended up doing a three-month bid?"

"I thought it was for reckless driving," I said.

"Dude, he makes some cold music," said Dakota. He began to sing: "'Where my dogs at? Where my dogs at? We right here, bro!'"

"Dakota," said Jess.

"Okay, okay," Dakota said, "I get it! I get it!"

He picked up the tray he had been carrying and headed toward the walk-in.

"Dakota's gonna make me a great mom," she said.

Jess was placing the buttered dough on a long baking pan. She began to sprinkle brown sugar over the dough, scooping up the mixture with her thumb and three fingers. The immediacy of what she was doing was poetic, not something to puzzle over, but action with clear meaning. Not a classroom or playing field at college.

"I'm here six days a week, fifteen-hour days," Jess said. "I love the pace, the team-oriented approach to the work, and I love the opportunity to create."

"And when you're not here?" I asked.

"Hah!" she said, finishing off the pastry. "I watch movies in my bed or sleep."

Well, I thought, Jess is someone who gets it: The complete surrender required to work in the restaurant, the need to do what you're told to do by the chef, the importance of coming up with new ideas that will appeal to the chef, and the ability to tell cooks to follow your rules. Her energy and poise were unique. I could picture her in charge of her own restaurant one day.

"It's something I think about for the future," Jess said. "A bakery café–restaurant."

"Like Joanne Chang?" I asked.

Joanne Chang owned three wonderful bakery cafés, each called Flour. After graduating from Harvard with a degree in applied mathematics and economics, she had turned to bread, pastry, soups, and sandwiches. I could only imagine the reaction of her parents when she told them that her $200,000 education would be used to open bakeries.

"I love her food," said Jess. "Maybe one day." She handed me a spoon. "Taste this."

"Wow, delicious. What is it?"

"Anise, ginger, salt, celery. Not done yet."

As I watched her finish the dessert, I noticed Bobby standing still and staring into space. He sipped milky-colored iced coffee from a straw. His blue cap was at a tilt, but he did not notice.

"BOBBY!"

It was Danny.

"BOBBY! What the fuck, Bobby! Show me the Peking pancakes for the fucking pig! Fuck, Bobby! Upstairs! Now!"

"Later, Jess," I said.

Jess nodded.

I followed Bobby and Danny.

Upstairs, an hour into service. The cooks were moving so quickly that it seemed as if they were in a film that had been fast-forwarded.

The music playing was Coltrane's "My Favorite Things."

Danny called me over.

"I never see my wife anymore," Danny said. He was plating dinners as he spoke. "It used to be okay. Now it's not. She's a chef, too. When she was working in restaurants, we had similar hours so we could see each other in the morning, but what happened is now she's baking. She was looking for a spot for the past two and half years—finally opened one a few months ago: Treats on Washington. Only I literally, and I mean literally, never see her." He looked drained of emotion. "She works from six A.M. to six P.M. six days a week, and I'm here six days a week from noon to midnight."

THINKING ABOUT THE SACRIFICES THAT DANNY MADE TO WORK IN THE restaurant preoccupied me, but I needed to talk to Jill.

As I made my way toward her, saying, "Behind you! Behind you!" I heard thick slices of peeled potatoes hit the hot oil of the Fryolator. The sound was explosive.

"Crazy," I said.

"I love it," she said, her shoulders hunched, as she began to chop up pitted, dehydrated black olives. "Love being driven. Love being focused."

She handed me half an olive.

"Wow." *Wow* had become a big part of my vocabulary since coming to Craigie. "This is really delicious!"

She looked at me with a huge smile. "And?"

It is the cook's way of saying: What do you taste? Why does it taste good?

"You taste a nutty flavor, then salt, then almost a sweetness. It's umami. A long finish. The first thing you taste isn't the next thing or the last thing."

"Amazing, huh? It's a great example of why I love working at Craigie. The food gets better by technique, not enhancement."

"That's fascinating," I said. I was not sure I understood what she meant. "Say more."

"How am I doing with three sets of burger condiments, Jill?" shouted Tony.

"On it, Chef," Jill said.

"Am I in the way?" I asked.

"No, it's cool," she said, elbowing me out of the way, swiveling in place, and lining up three tiny white ceramic trays onto three longer white ceramic trays. "I can talk and do this at the same time."

"Okay," I said.

"I mean that Tony's cooking is all about skills," Jill said. "Modern techniques of bringing out the essence of how something should or can taste. He doesn't add something to a dish to alter its essence. I'm learning so much every day!"

Jill spooned house-made ketchup into three trays; then the sliced pickles; then tiny, pickled onions. She wiped surfaces clean and carried the trays gingerly to the pass. She had a forceful presence and, while not petite like her co-worker Mary, she moved with the grace of a dancer.

"I guess food was always important to our family. I come from a big family!" She began dicing Armenian cucumbers into cubes smaller than Jujubes. Each one was perfect and identical. Anticipating my question, moving with speed and dexterity, ignoring the commotion created by Danny and Matt who were yelling at Bobby and Kyle who had fallen behind, trying to get them into shape again, she said, "There are six of us, brothers and sisters."

She interrupted herself to call Danny over to look at the cucumbers.

Danny scampered over in a mad hurry, approved, and turned around to find poor, hapless James, looking downcast, with a bowl of ramp kimchee for him to taste. "This isn't how we do things at Craigie, James! C'mon, get your head out of your ass! Even slices, small pieces!"

James nodded like Eeyore and made a move as if to toss the ramps into the trash, when Danny started screaming at him, ordering him to never throw anything away without talking to him first. James returned to his station.

Jill continued, "I always wanted a professional career in restaurants, and growing up in Bay Ridge, in Brooklyn, I had great opportunities to work in the city. From about ninth grade on, it was lots of places. I even got a gig working for David Chang at Momofuku Ssam. *That* was a trip!"

Jill mopped her hands on a small white towel and started the next task: making candied lemon mignonette for the raw oysters. "Chang would sneak into the kitchen sometimes, a cap pulled down, pretending we didn't know he was the chef. I mean, we're talking about David Chang, for goodness' sakes! He was always clowning around. I loved working for him."

She said, stirring, "I wanted to go to culinary school. So I got into Johnson and Wales and found new places in other parts of the country were pretty interesting, too. I mean, check it out: Just before I came here, I did a four-and-a-half-month internship with Corey Lee at Benu in San Francisco."

Lee had run the kitchen at The French Laundry and was, by far, one of the country's leading chefs in his generation.

Mignonette done, she handed it off to Timmy, who was working on the oysters.

"Corey had me do everything," she said proudly. "I did all the prep stuff, stocks, staff meals, I cleaned everything. *I did whatever I was asked to do!*"

Jill could have stayed in New York or San Francisco, or gone to Chicago, L.A., or Las Vegas, all places that attracted talented cooks. But she decided on Boston after one of her brothers had moved to Charlestown, which was about an hour's drive from Johnson & Wales.

As Jill worked on making the beds for the eel platings, she said that California would be too far from home and New York too close. "I thought I'd look around here and see if maybe Boston was a decent place to cook. I tried out places owned by Boston's so-called great chefs. I had a shitty meal at Clio. I had a crappy meal at Menton. L'Espalier was okay. I even did a stage at L'Espalier. On my fourth day, the chef offered me a job cooking. But I didn't like the food enough to stay."

Behind us Danny yelled out: "PUT THE FUCKING BURGERS IN NOW, BOBBY!"

Eel setups done and handed to Tony at the pass, Jill was on to the next task, which was to plate small versions of terrines for a duo of tastings.

"I ate here once before I applied for a job," Jill said. "There's no avant-garde shit here."

I could see what Tony saw: commitment, knowledge, big heart, passion to learn, doing whatever needs to be done, a no-nonsense way of talking. That was Jill: Take her or leave her. She was not as interested in what people thought of her as what they thought of her cooking. I loved that about her. It spoke to her maturity.

Then she was on to the arugula for the ragoût, the pickled peanuts, the hearts of palm, and the preserved watermelon.

"What's this?" I asked, pointing to pale pink discs wrapped in sealed sheets of plastic.

"Compressed watermelon," Jill said.

"How do you do it?"

"It's a fifteen-minute process."

"Sous vide?"

"You bet," she said. "I Cryovac the melon with white balsamic, essential oils of lime and ginger, salt, and chili water. Here, have a taste."

It was, of course, delicious.

"Nice salt in that," she said.

I watched her make little cubes out of it.

"Beautiful," I said, admiring her finesse.

"I have this urge to kind of baby things. But cooks aren't leaders. It's not just a matter of skills that divides them from chefs, although obviously they're necessary. Chefs know exactly what tastes good and why, and can lead cooks to create what they're after. It comes down to leadership. Chefs lead, cooks follow."

Tony hired Jill after a one-week trial.

"You were right," I said to Tony, when I left Jill's side and returned to the pass.

"About what?" Tony asked.

He was drawing red lines through tickets that had been completed but stopped and looked up.

"Jess and Jill," I said. "Rock stars."

"I told you," Tony said.

Meredith strolled up.

"Four out on eleven," she said.

"Got it," said Tony.

Danny was yelling at Bobby again: "It's chess, not checkers, Bobby!"

Matt smiled and said, "That's what I always say!"

"It wouldn't surprise me if Jill opens her own place," I said to Tony. "Right next door. A good, home-style restaurant serving beautiful food."

"I hope so," Tony said, "because if she does, I'll be one of the first to invest!"

TEN

Chef's Night Out

I HAD MET HIS ROCK STARS AND I HAD MET HIS MOM, AND NOW IT WAS time to meet Tony in a place where he was not defined by his work. I wanted to see how he behaved and spoke outside the restaurant. To talk to him in the world of black and white where he was an ordinary person, a civilian like the rest of us, and no longer a chef.

I had been at Craigie ten months. It had become my focal point: the place I spent the most hours outside my home.

I don't get out much. Unless I am traveling, which is usually work related, I prefer to be at home with my wife and dogs, writing, reading, running, or cooking. Listening to hospitalized psychiatric patients or the painful narratives of outpatients in distress fulfills my strongest needs for intimacy outside family.

That had all changed with Craigie. The narrowing of contact with the world at large helped me appreciate and understand Tony with greater vigor than if I had been a person with a wide array of social relationships.

The world of his restaurant had become deeply appealing, a place

I wanted to be in as much as I wanted to analyze it. That phenomenon of seeking to belong was familiar to me; it is how I try to be of help to my patients: through affiliation. Namely, I had to at the very least imagine what it is like—how it feels, how it shapes thinking—to live in their world. Without empathy, trust is impossible, of course, and without trust we do not live outside ourselves.

I had a sense of who Tony was as a chef. Who was he as a person?

Danny was at the pass at ten P.M. the night I decided to get the chef out of the kitchen.

"Yo, *Doctah* Haas," Danny said. It was his usual greeting, which was invariably followed by a high five or a fist bump. "What is shakin'?"

I had been to dinner with my wife and afterward seen *Rise of the Planet of the Apes* on opening night. When Danny learned this, he stopped cold. I had never seen him with a more serious expression. He had been putting in final tickets for the night and crossing off what had been done. Tony was in the dining room, stopping by VIP tables and thanking guests for coming in to eat his food.

"How was it? Was it any good? I mean, that remake in the eighties? That sucked compared to the original. Sucked! I only saw the original as a rental; you probably saw it at the movies. Was what you saw, what I'm asking is, was what you saw as good as the original? As good as Charlton Heston?"

Dakota, working on some burgers, overheard us.

"Dude," Dakota said, "you saw the ape movie?" He flipped the burgers onto a metal tray to cool. "How was it?"

Soon the kitchen was abuzz with my news.

All the cooks wanted to know: "How was it? How was the new *Planet of the Apes*?"

"Did the apes look real?" asked Dakota.

It was not just the movie that interested the cooks. Friday night, and I had had the freedom to go out with my wife, to a restaurant, and see a movie. Any movie. These were galley slaves, in comparison, with one or two nights off a week and then too exhausted to go out and enjoy what nearly everyone outside the restaurant world usually took for granted: Dinner and a movie with someone you love.

I was about to answer Danny's original question when he was presented a plate that held ragoût of brisket and pastrami, chanterelles, and a farm-fresh egg. Danny shifted the egg yolk with his fingers and handed the dish off to a runner.

"This walks," Danny said. "This walks. My ragoût walks."

Then he turned to me, as if there had been no interruption, "Well, was it as good as Heston or not?"

"Not as good," I said. Having seen the original as a young adolescent may have colored my sentiment about the first movie. Memory has a funny way of distorting perception. "But lots of fun. Better than the remake."

"I love ape movies," Danny said, before turning and saying to Bobby, who, standing behind him, was moving a thick slice of pork belly on the grill as if he had all night, "Cook, Bobby, cook! Don't just fucking stand there!"

Just then Tony returned to the pass. "Hey, bro, give me another hour to finish up and I'll be ready to roll."

Tony looked over the tickets, patrolled the stations, and got a couple of cooks back into gear. He helped Timmy finish cooking an item for the tasting menu that night: guanciale-wrapped sweetbreads pan seared and served in a beer jus.

I tasted the jus and was slammed by its deep flavors: crazy delicious, nuts.

Danny turned to Bobby and said: "Hey, Mr. Erroneous, downstairs! Get more stock!"

▪ ▪ ▪

AN HOUR LATER, TONY, AS CALM AS COULD BE, DESPITE THE FRENETIC pace of the kitchen, asked, "Where are we going?"

"I don't know," I said. "Not my neighborhood."

"Not his neighborhood," Tony said to Danny with a sneer.

"Not his neighborhood?" said Danny with a fake sneer.

They both laughed. It was a big deal: going out with the chef. Tony did not pal around with the cooks. Like many chefs, he felt that he would lose authority by doing so.

"Green Street Grill?" I suggested.

It was within walking distance from the restaurant; I had read a web review that described it as kind of a bar first and a restaurant on second thought, lively, and with a decent scene attractive to people in their twenties and up to their fifties.

Tony pursed his lips, looking thoughtful, and nodded his head. "Excellent choice," Tony said.

"That's a good choice," agreed Danny.

Word had gotten out for days that I was going to interview Tony away from his kitchen.

"Let me change and we'll get out of here." Tony went downstairs and returned about five minutes later in his usual outfit. He dressed like a kid and made me think of Gramps in a Grateful Dead T-shirt. He had been cool at school and was cool now, too, unlike many men his age. He had never stopped being cool, never wore a suit to work; cooking kept him young.

During our short walk over, the street came alive. Pressed together on sidewalks were groups of white, Indian, and Chinese college kids dressed up to go clubbing, and the locals, most of them black, perhaps from the housing projects a block away, eyeing it all with pleasure or dull resignation for now. The fire station was brightly lit; the entrance to the Salvation Army shelter next to it was crowded with homeless men. We made small talk about baseball as we passed by an ice cream shop, a cheap Chinese restaurant, an Indian restaurant, a McDonald's, a Cambodian restaurant, an Irish pub, and a hole-in-the-wall serving Tibetan food.

"You hungry?" asked Tony, when we were seated at the Green Street Grill and handed laminated menus.

The place was jammed and we had been given one of the last tables, way in the back, by the swinging kitchen doors and the women's restroom.

"No, I'm good," I said.

The waitress came over, very cheery, and we ordered a couple of drafts.

"I'll have an order of the chicken wings and a small salad," Tony said.

Then he handed back the menu.

"Chicken wings and a salad?" I asked.

"Hey, I'm hungry," Tony said. "Don't knock it!"

"I didn't say anything negative."

"Yeah," he said, "but I saw that look."

"Probably tastes pretty good."

"You got that right."

"So what's going on?" I asked. "What's new?"

"What's new? What's new is I'm down a cook and Meredith just gave one month's notice today, which sucks."

"Is that unusual? One month's notice?"

The beers arrived. Cheers, glasses clinked, sips.

"My mother is apeshit about it," Tony said. "After two fucking years, she quits. With one month's notice. She's a fucking GM, for fuck's sake. How about three months' notice?"

I knew better than to interrupt.

"What happened is that Meredith wanted a raise. We offered

her a raise. We offered her a big raise! We're coming out of a recession and we offered her a big, big raise, but she said no, she wants more. More! Fuck that. I am so pissed."

"Then if it's not the money, if the money's good, then it must be something else."

The food arrived. Crispy wings stacked on a big white plate with a little cup of hot sauce in the middle. Salad of iceberg lettuce and tomatoes drenched in oily dressing. Tony dived in. The way he ate—as if it were his first decent meal in days—made the food look appetizing.

He held a wing in the air and nodded his chin.

I shook my head no.

"You don't know what you're missing here," he said.

"Maybe the something else is Ted," I said. "Having a boyfriend in the restaurant may complicate things."

"You think?" Tony said, ironically.

He had worked his way through half of the wings. Clothespin-shaped bones lay on his plate. Dutifully, he raised forkfuls of salad.

"Ever since Meredith got a new boyfriend," Tony said, "she's stopped taking feedback."

He was down to his last two wings. He waved one at me. "You sure?"

"I'm sure," I said.

"She stopped looking up to me," he said, pushing the empty plate away. "When I tell her to do something, she gives me this look of indifference. It wasn't always like that. I'm not getting her respect."

"Maybe she's worth a better offer that you could make her."

"We made her a great offer," Tony said. "I'm sure she's run this all by her ex-boyfriend. He's a restaurant GM, too. He knows numbers. But the difference between what he makes and Meredith makes is that she's, what, twenty-four or twenty-five, and he's in his late thirties—he knows what he's doing, I know him. He tells her she's worth the money. But I don't think so. I mean, I'm the one who figured out how to sell the more expensive wine, not her! I'm the one who raised menu prices, not her! I'm doing *her* job."

I nodded my head and kept writing.

"Part of the problem for Meredith is that she sees the prices going up and thinks: 'Oh, the restaurant's making more money, so *I* should make more money!' But we're not making more money: Food prices this year have shot up! The price of quality fish has skyrocketed. I won't compromise on food. The money isn't going into my pockets—it's going to meet food costs."

I looked up from my notes.

"Look, it's not just Meredith—it's the business," he said. "It's the business, the business, the business. It's hard to keep good people."

It *was* the business. I knew that by now. Tony had spoken of "the business" before, making it clear that no matter what he did, no matter what proactive steps he took, no matter whom he appeased, and no matter what he did to change working conditions, the restaurant business remained attractive to many people who could not fit in anywhere else.

Only Santos had been with Tony from the start. Several people lasted a couple of years or more. Others had stayed weeks or months.

"Danny's cutting back to four days a week in September," Tony said.

The waitress returned to clear the plate and our empty glasses, and we ordered two more beers.

"Yeah, it's time," said Tony sadly. "He's been with me four and a half years. He misses his wife. It was fine when Danny's wife had a schedule like his, but now they never see each other."

"How about you and Karolyn?" I asked.

"It's a little better," he said. "Back when we first opened, she worked for me in the front of the house. That had its ups and downs, but at least I got to see her. These days I see her on Sundays, sometimes in the afternoons when she brings Charlie by, and before she goes to work in the morning."

"That's not a lot of time."

"In September Karolyn's quitting her job," Tony said. "That's gonna cause financial stress, but it's time, she says."

"What then?"

"I don't know. We'll see."

The beers arrived.

I had also seen on Craigslist that Tony needed a hostess.

"So you're down a GM, a cook, a hostess, and your sous chef is going to work four nights instead of six."

"Look," Tony said, "longevity really is a problem. Money is one issue. I can be a pain in the ass is another. The work at Craigie is harder than it is at other restaurants. The hostesses are divas. I don't have multiple revenues—different restaurants, say, where I can move staff if they get bored or want more responsibility or more income. I'm not complaining, I'm just telling you what it is!"

He also had no one he could depend on other than Jess to help him make changes. But it didn't seem that Tony, as a mentor, encouraged his crew to come up with ideas.

Many chefs, as leaders, recognize that their work gets easier and that it is often more enjoyable in the kitchen when sous chefs can begin to create rather than just follow orders, and when line cooks ask more questions. Tony insisted that he did ask them to be more inquisitive and use their imagination, that he would be thrilled if that ever happened, but I did not see much evidence of that. I knew, too, that if the cooks felt that their ideas mattered, they would stick around.

"Last call!"

It had been years and years since I had been in a bar at closing time.

■ ■ ■

"SO, TONY, I'VE GOT TO ASK YOU: WHAT'S THE STORY WITH YOUR FATHER?"

"My father?" he said. He laughed. "We're gonna talk about my father?"

"Sure," I said. "Why not? Unless you don't want to."

"Sure," he said, grinning. "I'm happy to talk about my father. What do you want to know?"

"For one thing," I said, "you never mention him. So I figure there's got to be a story here. I see your mother all the time. I see Karolyn and Charlie. I've even met your in-laws! But your father? Not a word."

"No mystery," Tony said. He laughed again. "You know, he was in the restaurant tonight."

"He was?" I asked. I was struck by the fact that he had not mentioned this to me when I had been there.

"Yeah, you missed him," he said. "He was in with his best friend, Mike. He comes in about once a month. It's fine."

"Fine?"

"Yeah, it's fine," he said, "but it's always the same bullshit: He turns to the waiter and says to his friend, 'See all this? Without me, there wouldn't be a restaurant!'"

"There's a story about Philip Roth's father, Herman, how he went to a synagogue in Miami and that someone there asked him for a signed copy of one of his son's books. So the next week, he brings in a book by Philip Roth and it's signed, 'Best wishes, Herman Roth.'"

"It's complicated," Tony said. "After my parents split up, my father remarried. My father changed. He's different the last ten years. Stranger. More self-involved. He used to be funny. I don't know. Different."

None of this accounted for the anger in Tony's face and voice.

Then he paused.

"I'll tell you one thing that really pisses me off," he said. "He's got a son, Matthew. He spends more time with Matthew than he does with Charlie. I'll call him up: 'Dad! When was the last time you saw Charlie? It's been, what? Weeks?' Matthew has Little League, soccer practice, some school event. He's busy. He's too busy to see his own grandson!"

"How old is Matthew?" I asked.

"Fourteen," Tony said. He laughed. "Can you fucking believe I have a fourteen-year-old brother?"

We paid the check, the room cleared out, and the staff switched on the lights.

"Well, Tony," I said on the sidewalk, "I have a theory."

"Yeah?"

"My theory is that a lot of your anger toward the cooks stems from anger toward your father," I said. "I also think that your cuisine is an effort to establish your own identity—a sense of self that owes nothing to your father."

He laughed so hard he had to steady himself against the wall of the restaurant.

"Oh, shut up," he said, finally.

I laughed, too. Tony was right, and I knew it. There were limits to what I understood about him, his food, and Craigie on Main. To get beyond those limits, I had to take the next step.

ELEVEN

Taking Ownership

T ASTE THIS," TONY SAID.

On the plate was half a head. The color was caramel, nearly, and hazelnut. Eye closed, blond eyelash still. I could see a neat, little, even row of teeth.

"You tear it off with your fingers," he said, "and dip the skin and fat, fleshy meat attached to the jaw into the boudin noir–hoisin sauce."

For the life of me, I had not understood why he was roasting a pig's head to achieve the same effect that roasting a duck, Peking style, would have achieved just as easily. Nor why he had the need to do away with the traditional sugary-sour plum sauce and substitute for it a thick concoction of blood sausage.

Until I tasted it.

The fat from the pig's cheeks was fattier than what is found in a duck. The skin was crispier. The sauce sent ribbons of flavor in my direction rather than the one big taste found in traditional hoisin.

"Good, huh?" said Tony.

"It is," I said, "and once you get past the face on the plate . . ."

"No, man," Danny piped in, rushing over, wiping his hands on the towel he always kept tucked into his waistband. "Mister Pig is part of it. Got to be piggy!"

We were always tasting things, trying out food that might make it to the menu, enjoying the usual items, Tony making certain that dishes had been cooked correctly.

Everything tasted deeply flavorful. Paying top dollar for first-rate ingredients helped. One afternoon Tony showed me a tray of twelve pint-sized containers of raspberries.

"Forty-eight dollars," he said.

"That seems like a lot," I said.

"It *is* a lot," he said.

Tony had introduced all sorts of high-tech equipment into his kitchen and was not the only chef who understood that technology belonged alongside slow braising, making stock from scratch, and any number of traditional cooking techniques, but he was among the very few who used it in widespread and effective ways. Ironically, having access to expensive ingredients and technology also introduced an element of unintended detachment from the work. Some cooks came to believe that they were assembly-line workers using technology with nearly perfect ingredients rather than men and women whose ideas and efforts mattered in the cooking process.

A few days later, at the routine, preservice meeting for cooks, Tony brought this problem to everyone's attention. As usual, we were seated outside, under the locust and sumac trees, Tony with a new, short haircut, same slight beard. He got his hair cut very often, as he was on display. He rested his elbows on his knees and leaned forward. He had a way of making a calm look seem like an angry one because of his intensity.

"Yesterday," Tony said, "we talked about a challenge." He paused. "What was that challenge? Jill?"

"Better communication as a team," Jill said.

"Right," Tony said. "Collectively, as a team, there's a level of communication that's needed that doesn't exist now."

The cooks looked down; a few closed their eyes.

"It can be something as basic as making certain that by two forty-five each day the kitchen has been swept and mopped," Tony said. "Or, more broadly, having discipline. Not just about cooking the food, but about everything we do. Not being afraid. Working as part of a system."

The group's silence made me think of a driver who has been pulled over by the police.

Danny spoke: "I think people need to take more ownership of their own station."

Tony glanced up at him.

"Making sure at the start of the day," Danny continued, "that you have everything you need. Making sure your surfaces are spotless. Cleaning up quickly at the end of the night."

"These are not things we should need to be telling you at this point," said Tony.

Timmy, seated next to me, clutched his cooking notes tighter. On his right arm: a duck, a pig, a scaly fish. He opened his eyes but then closed them again and pouted.

"It's baffling to me how one side of the kitchen doesn't know what the other side of the kitchen is doing," said Tony. He seethed with impatience. "Again, basics. If you go into the walk-in and you need basil, you need to ask yourself: 'Is anyone else using this?' What if you use up basil that someone else needs? Or what if one of you goes into the walk-in, doesn't see basil, and asks Danny or Matt to order some, not realizing that someone upstairs has plenty?"

Tony paused again to suck in air.

"It's not just a waste of money," Tony said, "it's the fact that you all aren't working efficiently. This is very troubling to me."

His emotional range became constricted, his voice deepened, he spoke even slower, and then almost in a whisper so that you had to lean in to hear him, he said, "Patrick, what do you think?"

"I'm still learning where things go," Patrick said. He had been at the restaurant less than a month. "I need to ask people more questions when I don't know."

Tony went around the circle, asking each of the silent cooks what they thought of what he had said.

"Kyle, what are your thoughts?" Tony asked.

"I try to make sure that my station is good to go," Kyle said. "As perfect as I can make it. I try to work independently. I'm not saying that I don't communicate with the other cooks—I do. But at a certain point, I just have to focus on what I'm doing and make sure that, to the best of my ability, it's right."

Matt jumped in. With Danny cutting back in a couple of months, Matt's role in the restaurant might become more important—if he could be more assertive, if he could do the work. Matt's style was certainly more low-key than either that of Tony or Danny. As a big guy, he had a more imposing physical presence than either man, maybe that was it. Both Tony and Danny were easily lost in a crowd. Or it could just be that he had a different perspective.

"We need better organization," said Matt. "Even if you go into the walk-in and see things in a row—you need to ask, 'Is that everything? Are products upstairs?' We need to develop systems. Systems of where and how we put things away."

A huge tractor-trailer emblazoned with the red-and-white Coca-Cola logo roared by and drowned out all other sounds. About twenty seconds later, we could hear again.

"As I said," Tony said, "it's not just a waste of money—it's too much work, it's a wasted effort. I'm talking about ownership, keeping clean, and increased efficiency."

Michael, another new cook, small and uneasy, ginger-colored hair, so many tattoos on his arms as almost to be sleeves, spoke up. He had been hired on a trial basis just that week and said, "We need to know: This is where the herbs live. This is where the pickles live."

As Tony continued talking about being disappointed in the cooks, a slow transformation could be seen in their faces. Yes, they were being chewed out, but it was because Tony had expectations of them! *He saw their potential.* If Tony did not care, if he did not believe in them, he would not have said anything. It was difficult to be told that they had failed, but if they worked harder, they could do it.

To lighten the mood, which was vacillating between abject shame and pride, Dakota spoke up: "If there's stuff in the walk-in five or six days, it can go staff. We can use the elderly stuff for staff."

"Fair enough, D," said Danny. "Staff eats elderly."

He and Dakota started laughing.

"It's not just about waste," said Tony.

Dakota and Danny stopped laughing, but Tony was no longer angry.

"It's about growth," Tony said. "Growing as a team, growing as a restaurant."

Then, in what seemed to be a response to our conversation at the Green Street Grill only a few nights ago, Tony began to talk pleasantly of encouraging his cooks to express their ideas.

His mood shifted. His posture shifted. He even smiled invitingly.

"You can all have as much say as you want," Tony said.

This statement seemed tantamount to a revolutionary, liberating force. As much say as they wanted? *The cooks?* The same cooks who, night after night, had heard drummed into their heads: "My way or your way?" The same cooks whose taste buds were derided when they presented something for Tony to taste? "More salt!" "But, Chef . . ." "More salt, more salt, more salt!" Now suddenly, because to my ears it sounded sudden, he was telling them they could speak up?

"I am waiting for people to say that I am wrong on such-and-such project," Tony said. "That they have another idea. A different idea."

If the cooks were surprised, they did not show it. They barely moved. Up to that moment Tony had run a kitchen where his word was law, where contradicting him was seen as wrong, without merit, and if repeated a possible case of insubordination.

Maybe Tony's change of heart came about because he realized that his strategies of control and motivation were ineffective. He had created a work environment where people did not progress as an act of rebellion against his authority!

"Regardless of where you are on the food chain of cooking," Tony continued, "you will need to think about the food."

He paused, put his palms together, and looked up.

"And in doing that," Tony said, eyeing each cook until the look became a gaze, "you will be accomplishing more than just doing what you're told. At some point, should you one day become chefs, in charge of your own kitchens, you will have to design a menu."

The cooks nodded in agreement.

"Look," Tony said, "a menu doesn't have to be that inventive. I'm talking about your future here, not just Craigie. But even if your menu has tournedos Rossini . . ."

The cooks began to giggle: How old school and corny! Especially compared to Craigie! The food at Craigie was cool! They were cool!

". . . even if it's tournedos Rossini," Tony continued, "you'll have to know what's in the dish and how to order what you need to make it."

"How do you spell Rossini?" asked Dakota.

"I'm serious," Tony said. "I want people to think creatively—to take ownership of what they're doing, and to plan their lives for the day when it comes time to move on."

Now the cooks looked sad and scared. They dreamed of opening their own restaurants, but it was one thing to feel oppressed by the system that Tony had imposed on them and another to take responsibility for their work and plan their future.

Other than Matt and Danny, who were higher up the so-called food chain, and besides Jess and Jill, who were burgeoning rock stars, only Bobby—Bobby?!—seemed to be absorbing the message. He was nodding his head vigorously in response to everything Tony said. Maybe all along he had been taking the heat because he believed that one day he would become a chef.

"We have five or six conversations sometimes when we're chopping," continued Tony. "Think about it: five or six conversations about what it is we're doing!"

"Like," said Danny, "'We have a lot of beets, what the fuck are we gonna do with all these extra beets? I mean, what the fuck?' Then there's this conversation: 'We have a lot of beets. What else *should* we do with these beets?'"

"Google *beets*," said Tony. "Come up with an *amuse bouche*."

"The first conversation is not as good as the second," said Danny. "The first is: 'What the fuck? Rotten beets!' The second is: 'What can we do with the beets?'"

This amounted to a revelation for the cooks. They were inexperienced and insecure about what they could and could not do. So it was not just great ingredients, amazing technology, and Tony's intelligence and skill that accounted for the food? It was *them*. They had a stake in it! To hear this from the chef felt very good, and I could, at last, see satisfaction in their faces. They began to limber up—moving like athletes before the big game, stretching, moving their heads from side to side, flexing.

"Are we good?" asked Tony.

"We're good," said Matt.

But did Tony, with all his talk of wanting the chefs to contribute, mean it? Or was he co-opting the revolution?

"Chef," said Danny, "one other thing."

Danny had put up his hand. Tony nodded in his direction and raised his eyebrows: *Go on.*

"We have some veal left over," said Danny. "I was thinking: Why don't we grind it up and add it to the burger grind?"

"No," said Tony immediately. "All wrong! Not enough fat in veal. It won't add anything to the burger to put in expensive meat!"

So for all his talk about wanting his crew to participate, he had gone ahead and put down his sous chef in front of the cooks. He could have said, *I'll think about it.* Or, *why do you think that will work?* But instead he had belittled the idea with near urgency. For sure that would stifle any other proposals.

Danny took it in stride, nodding back, moving restlessly. As usual, he scratched his wrists.

"That it?" said Tony.

"Rabbits," said Matt.

"What about *wabbits*?" asked Tony.

"What do you want me to do about ordering rabbits?" asked Matt.

"Order *wabbits*," said Tony.

The meeting was breaking up. Dinner in an hour.

Tony stood up and said, "Work on thinking about the food. You are not robots."

Dakota stood up, too.

"Hey, Tony! Tony," he said.

The cooks had gathered their notes and were about to make a run for the kitchen.

"Yes, Dakota?" said Tony.

"Can you eat all rabbits? I mean, all of them? Even pet bunnies?"

TWELVE

Theory versus Practice

I T WAS A CONUNDRUM, THAT MUCH WAS CLEAR, AS TONY AND THE COOKS struggled to come to some resolution. In theory, Tony was shifting, or trying to shift, toward a more inclusive model in which the cooks felt able to think independently, propose ideas to him, and in doing so move up the food chain. In practice, neither side was budging much.

On top of this, a quiet, almost undetectable discontent was becoming evident in the front of the house. Since Meredith had given notice, a kind of fairy-tale atmosphere had developed. Not a happy fairy tale, but one in which the queen left the castle after making love with one of the knights, where all the other ladies-in-waiting and knights did not know what would happen to them.

In the midst of all these changes, it was summer and many regulars were gone, while in their place were tourists, businesspeople in town for conventions and meetings, and "foodies" who had heard about Tony's winning a James Beard award a couple of months back.

"It's a difficult crowd to cook for," Tony told me on the hot July night when James went over the edge, Bobby showed his stuff, and waitstaff pulled together. "They don't know what to expect, and it's hard to make them happy. We can do it—we've done it before—but it's harder than usual. When we don't know our guests, it becomes more of a challenge."

The first guests or customers had arrived and been seated. In a far corner facing the room, at a choice table, a much too casually dressed couple (Obama T-shirts and baggy old jeans) took their places, held menus out that Chuck had handed them, and started to look nervously around the room.

"Are they regulars?" I asked, nodding in their direction.

"Not at all," Tony said.

"But you gave them a great table."

Tony smiled, sharpening knives, and calling out, over his shoulder, "I need a lobster, bass, and sword."

"I'm in the hospitality business," he said. "There aren't any VIPs in for this seating, so they get one of the best tables in the house."

I watched from the short distance of the kitchen, beside Tony at the pass, as the couple looked over their menus. It didn't take long for them to put in orders: Fried clams, striped bass.

"They ordered the same things," I said.

"They probably think it's safer that way. Look, a lot of the features of my menu items aren't familiar to people coming here for the first time. I designed Craigie that way—that's how I like it. That's one reason I won't serve California wines. Because people might know them. I want them to step out of their comfort zone."

I understood the theory, but thought that the practice of keeping great California wines from small or exclusive producers like Peter Michael off the list uninspired. I also thought that if the chef wanted to hear my opinion, he would ask me.

I took a menu from the clip that held it on the wall, and Tony and I studied it. We were in the middle of service and as we went through the menu, he shouted out orders, expedited dishes, and watched over the cooks.

The couple at the corner table dug happily into their crispy clams.

"Tuna sashimi *with watermelon*," said Tony. He was proud of his ability to surprise people who then looked to him with added respect because he had changed their ways of thinking about what tastes good. "Oysters with *candied lemon*. Rigatoni made with *farro* flour and served with a *boudin noir* ragoût. Salad of Bibb lettuce with *crispy pig ears*. Swordfish wrapped in *pork belly*. Breast of chicken stuffed with *chicken sausage*. Now, tonight, and really more so since winning the Beard, we have to be on our game. We have to please people who don't know us yet. Everything we *do* here is about trust."

As we spoke, the cooks to our right and left, as well as directly behind us, struggled to keep up with the pace. Garde manger was falling behind, but Matt went over to help, and the cooks kept up their rhythm.

"Generation Y," said Tony. He shook his head angrily. "Always been told they're special. At home, in school. Mustn't damage little Johnny's or little Janie's self-esteem by saying that they're doing a lousy job! Wah, wah. They don't understand: You want praise, you have to earn it. That whole mentality of not wanting their feelings hurt? Complicates things!"

In practice, I could see that his cooks did not accept criticism well. In theory, they figured that one day they would be chefs. But without criticism, how did they expect to learn the craft?

"Most of these cooks here will never be chefs," said Tony. "I don't know what the exact numbers are, but less than fifty percent of culinary school grads are cooking after ten years. And the percentage of cooks who become chefs? It's got to be less than five percent.

When I tell them what to do, I'm doing them a favor. I'm trying to teach them."

Danny ran up behind him clutching a pan in which three big, juicy, cheese-drenched burgers sizzled. I could imagine the flavors of the meat and cheese and onions without tasting them. In theory and practice, the dish was flat-out delicious.

Tony asked Danny to show him where they stood with orders. They looked over tickets.

"You stay on that side," Dakota shouted to Timmy.

"I am on my side," said Timmy.

"The fuck you are," said Dakota.

"Guys, guys," said Danny, "don't make me come over there."

Timmy and Dakota scowled, but got back to cooking.

After tickets had been counted, Danny zipped back to the stove and began basting the world's largest pork chop, which was a special for two. Bone-in, luscious, a dark crust formed from the sear in the pan.

"Man," said Matt, "that's fucking beautiful!"

Danny nodded as he spooned the fat and gravy over the browning chop. The spoon hit the side of the pan four times. Clang! Clang! Clang! Clang!

"Verbal for two," said Danny, "One pork for two."

Drew, at the pass, his face expressionless, readied a runner to take the pork to table fifty-one.

Things were going swimmingly. Cooks moving quickly and with precision, no one coming to stand at Tony's elbow and ask him if what they were working on tasted the way it was supposed to. A restaurant kitchen, even the worst, is a hotbed of commotion that when it is working is a lovely sight: At last, purpose! A sense of purpose that lasts hours! When the crew is moving in sync, at high speed, the only question is: Can I cook the food the right way?

Except that something was wrong with James. Dakota was the

first to notice. He alerted Danny with a tilt of his chin and a whisper, "Danny. Hey, Danny."

"Gotta go," James was saying. "Gotta go, gotta go."

James was staring into space. His hands were not chopping or slicing. His hands? His hands were at his side.

Danny came to James's side. "Whassup?" said Danny.

"James," said Dakota.

"Four pork, six pork, six pork all day!" shouted Tony.

"Dude," said Danny. "James, you all right?"

"Gotta go," said James. He was stationary, but agitated. He looked as if at any moment he just might scream, but his face stayed blank. "Gotta go, gotta go."

"Hey, Tony," said Danny. "I need you over here."

Tony looked over his right shoulder. He had not seen what was happening, but he did now.

"Danny, please take the pass," he said.

Tony and Danny switched places.

"Hey, James, what's up, buddy?" said Tony soothingly.

"Gotta go," James said. Out of breath, his voice pausing between syllables. "I gotta go, gotta go."

"That's fine, James," Tony said. "That's okay. Can I help? What's going on?"

James undid his apron strings, lifted the apron over his head, held the apron in his clenched right hand, and, stepping behind Dakota and Timmy, vanished down the stairs to get his clothing and gear and then, no doubt, ran back up the stairs and out the back door. "What the fuck?" asked Dakota.

"No idea," Tony said.

James was never seen again, not in the restaurant, not on the streets, nowhere.

Meanwhile, the kitchen was picking up greater speed and Tony was needed at the pass.

"Danny, can you take over from where James left off?" Tony said. He was not calm, but he was trying to sound calm.

Danny took James's place, and Bobby went over to where Tony directed him, which was next to Danny.

The kitchen began to rock then, harder and faster than I'd ever seen before. No one said a word about what had just happened. What was there to say? A cook had lost his bearings. All it meant for now was: People had to work harder to compensate for the loss.

While all this was happening, Tony started in on Bobby.

Tony yelled: "You don't cook! You don't cook! You don't cook!"

I squeezed back to where Bobby was working.

"Do you know what he means when he says that?" I asked him.

"He means," said Bobby, "that I'm overthinking things. That I just need to cook faster."

"C'mon, Bobby," Tony yelled again. "Two pork belly! In the window! Get them in the window!"

The bellies cooked, Bobby raced to get them to Tony at the pass.

He was not in the clear yet. Danny berated him: "Bobby! Pretend you fucking care! Some of us care!"

After this, all through service, Bobby kept up with the orders. He did not talk back, question what he was told to do, or look hurt or upset. He had to show the chef that he could get the job done.

Later, after service was over and surfaces were being scrubbed down, I asked Tony if Bobby was okay. He had been screamed at all night.

Tony laughed.

"Ask him," he said. "Hey, Bobby!"

Bobby came running over.

"How was your night?" asked Tony.

"Best yet," he said with a smile. "Best so far."

"See?" said Tony. "Bobby thinks he had a pretty good night."

A couple of days later, I brought up the topic of Tony's father again, but in doing so omitted his name. "So, Tony, when do I get to meet him?"

Tony looked up from pink invoices. Dakota was standing on the other side of the counter holding a deep stainless-steel bowl of daikon broth and waiting for Tony to taste it.

"Hey, how's it going?" Tony said, putting his hand out to me. "Meet who?"

"Meet your father," I said.

"This is too thick," Tony said to Dakota.

"Add water?" asked Dakota.

"Chicken stock," said Tony.

"Got it, Chef," said Dakota.

Dakota danced off to find stock.

"You want to meet my father?" Tony laughed. "Why do you want to meet my father?"

"I met your mother," I said. "I think your father is part of the story at Craigie. I mean, you hardly ever mention him. Issues, right?"

"I can arrange it," he said. "Why don't I arrange for you to have dinner with him here?"

"That'd be great," I said.

Tony laughed again.

"Issues! What kind of issues?"

"Anger issues," I said.

"Oh come on! I'm not an angry person!" He laughed even harder than he had the night we left the bar, and then fell onto the counter and slapped it with his palms.

"Anger issues!" he said. "What a fucking shrink!"

"You don't get angry at your cooks?" I asked.

"Of course I do," Tony said between laughs. "Anger issues! The cooks deserve it when they don't do their jobs! You sound like my mother!"

Danny walked over to us.

"Fucking shrink," said Danny. "I suppose I have anger issues, too. Want to meet *my* father?"

I could see their point. Anger came so naturally to them, the emotion was as fundamental to their work as having good knife skills, that an outsider telling them that they had issues seemed ridiculous.

"Anyway," I asked, "how are you going to arrange this dinner?"

Tony typed on his iPhone.

"Up to you now," Tony said. "Stewart, meet Scott; Scott, meet Stewart."

I stayed at the restaurant for a few more hours, interviewing and observing the cooks and front-of-the-house staff, and by the time I left, Tony's father had e-mailed me: "My busy super tennis dad schedule keeps me pretty busy, but Wednesday at seven could work for me. Stew."

ON WEDNESDAY NIGHT, THE RESTAURANT WAS JAMMED. IT WAS EARLY September. The kids were back at college and regulars had returned from holidays. The place had familiar rhythm.

As usual, I went over to stand by Tony at the pass. He was sharpening knives, crossing off tickets, and shouting orders.

"I guess I'm the first to arrive," I said.

"Oh, he'll be here," said Tony. "Just you wait and see."

Moments later, a tall, lean man wearing eyeglasses, grinning broadly, strode in. He had a black cap on: *U.S. Tennis Open 2011.*

"Hey, Tony!" Stew said. "Good to see you!"

They shook hands.

"Dad," said Tony. His voice was more reserved than it had been with me. "Hey, how are you? Good to see you!"

Tony introduced us.

"So were you at the U.S. Open?" I asked.

"That I was," Stew said. "I've been many times! Great seats! Love it! Started going forty years ago! Stan Smith! Bob Lutz! John McEnroe!"

"My parents used to go back then, too," I said.

"Your parents are probably closer to my age than your age," Stew said.

I did not understand the logic of Stew's comment. Tony saw my puzzled look, rolled his eyes, and smiled.

"So, Dad," Tony said, "where'd you eat in New York?"

"Where'd I eat?" Stew said. "Oh, here and there. Nothing out of the ordinary."

"Yeah, but where?" Tony asked.

"I told you," Stew said. "Nothing special. Some Chinese place. Whatever. Wherever."

I could see that Tony was disappointed that his father did not share his passion for food, but he also looked relieved. Food was Tony's world, not his father's. Still, it was a shame that he did not appear to appreciate how much it meant to his son.

"After dinner on Sunday, a friend of mine took us to meet a friend of his, a famous writer, I forget her name," Stew said. He looked at me. "I hope I'm not offending you. I'm not saying you're not a good writer."

Again, I did not understand his logic.

Meredith came over to us.

"Are you ready to be shown to your table?" Meredith asked.

We were led into the bar area to the corner table that the cooks and servers called "The Hot Tub" because of its shape and size.

The whole way over, Stew talked rapidly and with great animation. He had the vigor of a man half his age. I did not have to ask him anything. He did all the talking. He oozed with charm and reminded me of Larry King in looks and voice. He towered over Tony.

"Back when Marjorie and I were married," Stew said, "we lived on Rosalie Road in Newton Center. Among our neighbors were Jonathan Kozol and Bernie Katz."

"Oh, I know Bernie," I said. "He was one of my mentors. A great psychiatrist!"

"That's right," said Stew. "I figured you might know the name. Anyway . . ."

The waiter arrived with menus and took our drink orders.

"Anyway," Stew continued. The man was a great raconteur, from an age when people entertained one another with jokes and stories, when individual lives had more dimension. "Anyway, Bernie and I bought a racehorse . . ."

"Would you like to order off the menu?" asked the waiter when he returned with our drinks. "Tony suggested that he cook for you, but it's up to you."

"I'm happy to have him cook for us," said Stew, "as long as he doesn't send out too much food."

"Sounds good," I said.

"Excellent choice," said the waiter, scooping up the menus and returning to the kitchen.

"Where was I?" asked Stew.

"Racehorses," I said.

"Right," he said.

From racehorses it was off to Stew's early life on Madison Avenue. I still had not asked him anything.

"You know that show, *Mad Men*?" he said. "That was me! That was my life! I was cute, tall, and good looking!—I'm taller than

Tony and his brother—and I dated supermodels and stewardesses! It was pretty wild, let me tell you!"

Our first course arrived. Three precise *amuse bouches*: cured fluke with carrot frond broth; cauliflower and cilantro with smoked corn purée; and house-smoked bluefish rillettes with huckleberries.

"Wow!" I said after taking bites. "This is so powerful and delicious! Each one of these is very distinctive."

Stew wolfed the food down without comment, but he ate everything.

"I was among the first Jews to be hired by a big marketing firm," he said. "Dunbar. They came over on the fucking Mayflower."

"Now, Marjorie," I asked, "does she have a background in marketing, too?"

He ignored my question.

"Marjorie went to the University of Michigan," Stew said. "Going there was a tradition in her family. That's why Tony ended up there: He didn't work that hard in school. He was a C+ student, not that smart."

"Oh, c'mon," I said.

"He didn't apply himself," he said.

The waiter returned with our second course: raw slices of bright red tuna with ponzu, a little bit of shiso and red onion, and tiny cubes of dehydrated watermelon. Delicious, of course, with great textures.

"Here's my relationship to cooking," Stew continued. "I was between companies and doing freelance marketing consulting. I met Madeleine Kamen. Heard of her?"

"Sure," I said. "Famous cookbook author."

"Exactly," he said. "Madeleine hired me to market her. I made her famous."

"This was before chefs were celebrities," I said.

"Just the beginning of that trend, right," he said. "Then, after the divorce, I joined a men's group. Chris Schlesinger was in it. When Tony finished college and didn't know what he wanted to do with his life . . ."

"You introduced him to Chris Schlesinger?" I asked.

"That was me!" Stew said. "Chris hired Tony to work as a line cook at East Coast Grill!"

The third course was brought to our table: miso-and-sesame-grilled *hiramasa*. It was a stunning, thick fillet of fish with dense flavor. Stew dug in happily.

As he ate, he rhapsodized about Marjorie. I had a hard time picturing the two of them as a couple, but I know that it is impossible to understand any marriage, failed or successful. His eyes lit up, his voice deepened, and he spoke more slowly when he talked about his ex-wife. I wondered if he still loved her. I wondered if he still carried around that hurt. For all his bluster, Stew's vulnerability made him very appealing.

Our fourth course arrived.

"Spice-crusted striped bass collar with pea shoot greens and Sicilian olive oil," said our waiter.

He put the plates before us: very beautiful, very flavorful.

"I'm a New York Jew," Stew continued between bites. "P.S. seventy, the Bronx! I love stories! I'm an out-of-the-box thinker!"

"Smart like Marjorie," I said.

"Oh, she's one of the smartest people I ever met," he said. "She is phenomenal! A great study!"

He spoke at length of his ex-wife's intellect and talent, and then about himself.

"I'm just a marketing guy," Stew said. "I could be Larry David. I'm not as brilliant as Woody Allen."

Our fifth course was a spectacular ragoût of blood sausages, an egg, hen of the woods mushrooms, and corn kernels. The presentation alone was satisfying, and when I began to eat it, slowly savoring each bite, the effect was soothing.

"Amazing," I said to Stew. "This is so unbelievably tasty!"

"It's good," he said. "I like Tony's cooking." He paused. "Where was I? Oh, Tony. I was talking about Tony."

Stew had not been talking about Tony. He had been talking about Marjorie, whom Tony resembled much more so than looking like him, and then himself.

"Tony wasn't very big," Stew said, "but he always had very good hands. You know when he was a kid? They drafted him in Little League to be a catcher because of his hands!"

"Did you ever figure that he would one day be a chef? You mention his hands. Anything else?"

"We knew that Tony had some kind of artistic ability we didn't understand," said Stew. "Maybe it runs in the family. My grandfather—my mother's father—he was a cabinetmaker. He made his own tools. He made magnificent statues, too. He carved them."

"Wasn't your father a tailor?" I asked. "I saw a photo of him when he was a young man in Lithuania."

"That wasn't my father," Stew said. "That was my uncle. He lost his family in whatever."

Whatever? I thought. He meant the Holocaust, but being incessantly upbeat, Stew could not even say that word.

Our sixth course arrived. Good thing the portions were small; the richness of the dishes was nearly overwhelming. Plates of veal and sweetbreads and parsnips. Salty sauce, sweet parsnips, dense sweetbreads. It all came together.

"Tony never focused on anything until he started cooking," Stew continued. "He did it without anyone pushing him."

"He found his calling," I said.

Tony had to find something with high stakes that only he could do. With two very successful, driven parents, he needed to prove to himself, *and to them*, that although academics was not an area where he would excel, nor sports, nor marketing, he could achieve greatness worthy of their respect and pride.

"He did," said Stew. "Good thing, too! I come from a complicated family. I wanted Tony to be a success. It didn't matter what he did. When he goofed around at U Michigan his first two years I told him, I said, 'If you didn't want to go to college, why didn't you say something?'"

"Complicated family?"

"I have a brother who went to federal prison," Stew said. "They found marijuana in his house. He was locked up for several years. He was growing it and selling it. Guess how they caught him?"

"No idea."

"The crazy guy had tapped illegally into a power line to get the electricity needed for all the growing lamps in his basement."

"Wow."

"I wanted to see Tony make something of himself," Stew said. "I helped him any way I could. I did all the electrical work at the first restaurant. The thing is: I can see gears in my head! I love mechanical engineering."

TONY BROUGHT THE DESSERT OVER—STRACCIATELLA CHEESE WITH melon sorbet—and sat down next to his father.

"Gentlemen," he said with a bemused look, "how was everything?"

"Delicious," I said.

"Wonderful," said Stew.

Stew's pride in his son was unalloyed at that moment.

Tony propped his chin on his elbow and listened to his father talk about him.

"I took this kid to Little League every game and every practice," said Stew.

"That he did," said Tony. "You were a great dad."

"He was a good ball player," said Stew.

"Yeah, Dad, but tell him about what happened when I struck out or missed a catch," said Tony.

Stew looked genuinely surprised.

"What happened?" he asked Tony.

"He would yell at me," said Tony. "Say I was a lousy player! Tell me I needed to practice more or I'd never be any good!"

"Oh, c'mon," said Stew, laughing. "I did not!"

"You did!" said Tony. He laughed, too.

"Yeah, well, maybe that did you good, Tony," I said. "Without your dad's high expectations of you, maybe you wouldn't have pushed yourself to become a chef. Maybe that's also where your yelling comes from."

Tony shook his head.

"How about *your* father?" Tony asked me. "What was he like when you struck out?"

"The opposite of your father," I said. "My father would blame the umpire and say he was blind, or he would put down the game and say that it was stupid and unfair."

Tony's father looked at me. Our dinner had lasted three hours.

"You could write a book about me," Stew said.

II.

THE SAVIOR'S BUTCHER AND OTHER TAILS

All of us have kids and spouses and pets and hobbies, but that's not where we *live*.

They operated on the principle that you weren't ready for a task until you admitted it was beyond you.

FROM *YOU THINK THAT'S BAD*, BY JIM SHEPARD

THIRTEEN

Shadows

SEVERAL DAYS AFTER DINNER WITH STEWART, I WAS BACK IN THE RES-
taurant on a Tuesday afternoon. Staff meal had just been served
at the pass: rice from South Carolina that Matt had explained was
an heirloom heritage variety recently said to have been rediscov-
ered; stewed, smoked pork shanks; and long-braised collard greens.
It was leftovers from a benefit dinner held the night before when
Tony had cooked with Sean Brock, another James Beard award-
winning chef, from Charleston.

Danny handed me a plate and told me to dig in. He needed to
insist: I felt part of Craigie, after a year, and not part of Craigie. I
was not an outsider, but where did I fit in?

"Crazy good, dude," said Dakota between bites.

Fist bump to me, back to his plate.

I had come to Craigie to try to understand what motivated Tony.
As an outsider, I had observed that the intensity of his anger was not
just about working in the restaurant, but related to not being an
academic star but being expected to excel in school; striking out at
bat and being told it was his fault; having a father who competed

with him; and growing up in a wealthy community of high achievers but having very little clue, until his early twenties, of what he needed to do to accomplish comparable success.

I now understood that Tony was trying to define himself by cooking food that could not be categorized. Which made sense: He was not easily named, either. His food reflected that amorphousness.

When the family meal ended, cooks came forward to clear away the pass and bring the pots and plates and flatware to soak and be scrubbed clean. The kitchen returned to its state before service: shoulders bent in, everyone focused on the station in front of them. Nothing abstract: no future, no past.

Then Tony ran from the bar area into the kitchen shouting: "Let's go! Let's go! Everyone stop what they're doing!"

He ran to the top of the stairs.

"Everyone upstairs! Now! Move it!"

"What's going on?" I asked.

"Bunny's birthday," said Tony.

Every staff birthday was celebrated at Craigie with a song and cake.

"Hey, Bobby," said Tony. "Your turn."

"My turn?" Bobby said.

"We always choose a different cook to lead each singing of 'Happy Birthday,'" Tony said, giggling. "Today's Bobby's turn!"

"No, I can't," Bobby said, backing away, walking in reverse toward the stairs leading down to prep. He was laughing, but he didn't think it was funny. Like many cooks, Bobby was shy and awkward with people and more confident around food. "No, no, I can't!"

"Chef didn't ask you, Bobby," said Danny. "Now get back here and fucking sing!"

Bobby sang.

When the cake was cut, I watched from a distance and heard the laughter and saw the happiness that comes from feeling lucky and working hard and being part of something larger than oneself.

"Hey," said Tony, running up to where I stood apart.

He handed me cake.

"I wanted to make sure you got a piece," he said.

"Thanks," I said.

"Welcome to the family," Tony said.

When he said that, I felt a rush of sentiment. I think of myself as an outsider and take pride in observing rather than joining, so when a knot rose in my throat, it was surprising. Just like almost everything that happened at Craigie: The improvisation forced me, and everyone else, to explore and accept personal dimensions that had been hidden by habit. Tony made people change their habits, their likes and dislikes, their tastes in food, and ultimately how they viewed themselves. That is powerful cooking!

Shortly after the birthday celebration, I said to Tony, "I want to shadow your staff. In the hospital, residents and medical students and interns work with the doctors by following them as they take care of patients. So here at Craigie I want to work with a number of your cooks for the next four months. I'll do everything they tell me to do."

"That's fine," said Tony at once. "I just want you to take owner-ship of your work—Work hard!"

"I'll do it!"

He put up his hand: High five!

"Who do you want to start with?" Tony asked.

"Santos," I said. "He's low in rank, but he's here all the time. He's indispensable."

Tony laughed. "Excellent choice," Tony said. He laughed some more.

"What's so funny?"

"Santos is going to beat you down!" Tony said. "He's tough! You are gonna be his bitch!"

Tony explained that a typical day for Santos started at nine A.M. and ended at eight P.M., six days a week, but I said that I did not need to be with him for eleven hours each day for twelve out of fourteen days to understand and appreciate the psychodynamics associated with his work. Instead, I proposed a few days for several hours for two weeks.

Tony agreed.

Afterward, I would work with Bobby, Jill, and Dakota. While doing so, I would carry around my notebook and write down everything of interest.

Tony went to the top of the stairs and motioned for me to follow him.

"Santos!" Tony shouted.

"Yes, boss?" came a voice from below.

"I got someone for you," Tony said.

Tony's eyebrows shot up. He looked at me as I heard Santos's footsteps thud up the stairs. Santos moved heavily for a small man.

"Santos is going to fuck you up," Tony said.

"Yes, boss?" asked Santos.

"Scott is going to work with you," Tony said to him. "You'll be his boss, tell him what to do. He will do anything and everything you tell him to do. Okay?"

"Okay, boss," said Santos.

"Good luck," said Tony, and then he returned to the kitchen while I followed Santos back downstairs.

Wordlessly, Santos walked to one of the two walk-ins and withdrew a large stainless-steel tray that held two large fish. Then we went to the prep area where on one side butchering took place and on the other side desserts were being prepared by Mary and Rachel.

Santos, his back to Mary, his head bent over the fish, which he had now placed on a cutting board, said something to her in Spanish. He put on surgical gloves and toweled the fish dry. I caught, "Work, boss, this guy."

"What's he saying?" I asked Mary, who was convulsed with laughter.

"He wants to know why you're following him around," Mary said.

Santos had not understood what Tony had told him to do. I wondered just how often that might have occurred. I asked Mary to tell Santos in Spanish what Tony had said to him in English.

"Oh, said Santos, beginning to cut off the head of one of the fish. "So for the couple of weeks I'm this guy's boss!"

"That's right," said Mary. "*El Jefe* wants you to be *his Jefe!*"

Santos nodded his head and continued cutting the fish. Now he slit open its belly and separated the body from the spine.

"What's the name of the fish?" I asked.

I held the cutting board steady for him.

"I don't know," said Santos. "See this ice?"

He showed me a tray of ice beneath the first tray that had held the fish.

"Yes," I said.

"It keeps the fish cold," Santos said.

He took a pair of scissors and began snipping the thinnest pieces of fish away from the bone.

"Sexy, huh?" said Santos.

Then he opened a drawer from the chest below the cutting board. The drawer was a mess. It held a hammer, knives, and crumpled-up towels. Santos took out a pair of tweezers.

"Touch this," Santos said. He indicated the part of the fish that had been below the head.

"Okay," I said.

"Lots of little bones," said Santos.

He began to pull out each bone with the tweezers, working fast and meticulously. The entire process took about twelve minutes.

"So nice," said Santos. "This fish? One of my favorites."

Having cleaned the fish and broken it down, Santos set to work on the second fish. I took the tray that had held it and put it in one of the sinks. It was all I felt capable of doing. The work was humbling.

When I returned to Santos, Tony was beside him. He had his hands on his hips, and he was scowling.

"Santos," said Tony, "you are not cutting the fish close enough."

Tony held up the fish's head, which had been tossed in a white bucket used for garbage, and showed Santos how he had left on about an inch of product.

"This is why Pasternak cuts most of his own fish," Tony said. He was referring to Dave Pasternack, the chef at Esca, which is arguably the best Italian fish and seafood restaurant in the country. "This is an experiment at Craigie. Normally I cut my own fish."

"I know," I said.

Santos did not say anything. His expression did not change, either.

"Listen, Santos," said Tony, "you have to push up with your knife. You're pushing down."

Tony illustrated.

"No waste *carne*," Tony said. "That's fucking *dinero*. If it's in the *basura*, it's a fucking problem."

Santos nodded his head. He did not appear to be in the least upset.

Tony saw the open drawer.

"And clean up your space, Santos! It's a fucking mess," he said.

Tony walked away. I felt embarrassed for Santos, but he still showed no reaction. He went on cutting the fish. When he was done, he threw away the spine and the head.

"And now the *dinero* into the fucking *basura*," Santos said with a big laugh. "Now you take the trays upstairs to wash."

I stacked four empty trays and carried them up. Santos showed me how to tilt them and place them in an industrial Hobart washer. I lowered the levers on both sides of the square machine, and seconds later with a loud whoosh and a cloud of steam, everything was clean. I waited until the trays were cool enough to handle, and then I carried them back downstairs, where Santos showed me how to put them into racks.

Then we returned to the walk-in.

"That's a different fish," I said, when Santos took a large metal tray out from a shelf in the walk-in.

"Striped bass," Santos said.

We headed back to the prep area. As cooks ran past us, turning this way or that, they shouted, "Corner! Corner sharp! Corner! Corner sharp!"

At his workstation, Santos took the fish off the tray and placed it on the surface of the cutting board. I held the tail while Santos placed a thick meat cleaver at the point of the gills and then slammed a hammer onto it so that the head came off. The black gills fanned out as he hit the fish. Dark, clotted blood, nearly black, plenty of it, began to pool around the head. The sound of the hammer coincided with the cleaver and the flesh and the wood until it was musical.

"I need towels," said Santos.

I got him towels.

When I returned, Tony was at his side.

"*Mas o menos or mas todos perfectos?*" Tony said to Santos. He was shouting at him.

Santos continued to waste product.

"Santos," Tony continued, "part of the problem is your knives. You need to sharpen your knives! You're using dull knives."

Then Tony went away again. Santos got a deep plastic tray filled with water and put a few earth-colored sharpening stones in it. He sharpened his knives on the clean surface of the stones. It took him as much time to sharpen the knives as it did to cut the fish.

We went back to the walk-in and brought back a huge piece of swordfish. We unwrapped the green paper around it.

I touched the skin, which felt like a racing swimsuit. The flesh itself was the skin color of a Caucasian. When Santos cut the skin from the fish, I threw it away. It was hard for Santos to boss me around. Despite what Tony had said about him, he seemed to be a person who had never exercised authority over anyone.

"Here," said Santos, handing me a small tub of white powder. "Taste this."

"What's it for?" I asked.

"For the fish," he said.

"What is it?"

"*Activa.*"

"What's it for?"

Santos shrugged. I decided to stop asking him so many questions. He cut the swordfish into big chunks.

He got out sheets of greasy brown paper from the walk-in. We took off the top sheet, and beneath in were two layers of very thin, house-cured guanciale. I threw away the greasy paper.

Santos placed one chunk of swordfish on top of the guanciale and sprinkled the activa on top of it using a tiny silver-colored sieve.

Then Santos told me to place each new chunk of swordfish on top of four or five slices of guanciale and roll the fish forward. Once that was done, I had to roll plastic wrap around the guanciale-wrapped swordfish. The plastic wrap kept breaking or sticking together.

"It's easy," Santos said.

"For you," I said.

Mary laughed.

Santos showed me how to lean my whole body into the wrap so that it broke at my elbow. Forty-five minutes later we had eight rolls of swordfish, which equaled sixteen portions for dinner that night. I felt as if I had passed an important exam. The feeling of accomplishment was powerful, and I supposed Santos felt it, too.

"Now I must cut the striper," he said.

I carried the portioned swordfish back to the walk-in. Santos took out the striper he had broken down a short while ago. We returned to the workstation.

"Where's my scale?" asked Santos.

I found the scale and handed it to him.

"Each piece has to be one hundred fifty grams," Santos said.

He took his newly sharpened long knife and positioned it a few inches alongside the striper. He cut the first piece and weighed it.

"That's one hundred seventy-four grams," I said to Santos. "What will you do with the extra weight?"

"Family meal," said Santos. He cut the portion down to 153 grams.

My job was to take the extra pieces for family meal and put them into a small clear plastic container. When Santos had finished with the striper that had been on the long tray he carried in, I put the tray into the sink.

As I worked, I watched Santos weigh the fish portions. I wrote down each size: 176, 164, 160, 168, 160, 162. I did not understand why Santos did not take one correct portion and measure it against the fish to create equal portions. He could also have weighed the whole fish and calculated the number of 150-gram portions he could get from it. However, both methods involved planning and math, which were not approaches that Santos knew. Tony had not taught him how to do the job correctly but was angry at him for making mistakes that caused waste.

"Into the *basura*," said Santos, throwing away a few tiny pieces that were not to be used for family meal.

Two more fish were on another tray.

"Are you going to clean the char now?" I asked.

"It's not char," said Santos.

"What is it?"

"I don't know."

Tony came by to look at our progress, and I asked him.

"It's gray mullet that's been sustainably raised in Spain," Tony said. "A beautiful fish with deep flavor!"

It was intriguing to see what the chef knew and what the cooks knew. Knowing less about their work meant that the cooks were less engaged in what they were doing.

"Here," said Santos, handing me the clear container of leftover striper. "To the walk-in."

"Where in the walk-in?" I asked.

"Top shelf," said Santos, "on the left."

The handle made a loud puckering sound when I opened the door to the walk-in.

When I returned to Santos, there were more trays to put into the sink and more trays to carry upstairs. The repetition of my work, done in silence, with indie music playing low on a radio next to Jess, made for a numbing, calming experience. It was possible to forget complex thoughts and language and simply *be* the task.

"Where is the brine?" asked Santos.

I found the brine for him.

He tried to cut the mullet into seventy-gram portions but had the same difficulty as he had had with the striper.

"For tasting menus," Santos said.

Once the mullet was portioned, I carried it to the walk-in with

Santos. Behind us we heard screaming upstairs: "How many times? How many times?" The noise of a blender muffled the voice, and neither of us could say for certain who it was.

We had more mullet to clean. Santos took a small silver-colored device from his drawer. It looked like a mallet.

"Here," he said, handing the scaler to me, "try to scale the fish. Think you can do it?"

"Show me first," I said.

He held the fish by the tail and brushed away from himself vigorously.

"Easy," he said.

He handed me the scaler.

"Now you," he said.

I stood over the sink, tail in hand, and began scraping. Scales the size of a baby's fingernails flew into the air, caught the light, and soon covered surfaces near me. The flesh under the scales was firm, but malleable.

"What do you think?" I asked Santos after a few minutes. "I'm afraid to go any further because I don't want to damage the fish."

Santos examined the fish.

"It's good," he said, "it's good."

Then he scaled it some more.

We went back to portioning the swordfish.

"Take the sword up to Matt," said Santos when we were done.

I went upstairs to the kitchen and found Matt at garde manger, where he was supervising the cooks.

"Matt, for you," I said.

"Thank you," said Matt with an amused look. "Thank you very much."

When I went downstairs to finish the fish with Santos, we had more striped bass, huge and bloody, to work on.

Santos grinned at me.

"Sexy, no?" he said. "This is more sexy, no?"

He grabbed the gills and gave it a whack with the hammer and cleaver. I knew my turn would come soon.

BY THE SECOND WEEK WITH SANTOS, HE WAS MORE COMFORTABLE TEACH-ing me, and his confidence in my efforts felt good.

"Matsutake," he said. In front of us was a big box of the largest and most beautiful matsutake mushrooms I had seen outside Japan. "Perfect. Sexy."

Tony, in apron, came over to us.

"I have a forager in New Hampshire who finds these for me," Tony said.

Santos took a small black-handled knife and trimmed the frills of the mushroom tops. When that was done, he placed the dozen or so cleaned mushrooms in a small container and returned the rest to the walk-in. Next up were the chanterelles.

"Beautiful chanterelles," I said.

I had shopped for chanterelles for my wife and myself earlier that day at Whole Foods and returned home empty-handed as the mushrooms for sale were dark, torn, and spongy in texture. The chanterelles in front of Santos were perfect.

"Nice," said Santos. "Ready, always ready. *Sí?*"

"*Sí*," I said.

"*Sí* is yes in Spanish," he said.

"I know," I said.

"I know you know," he said.

He laughed. The other Salvadorans laughed, too.

Santos then handed me a knife identical to the one he was using and motioned with his hands to do what he was doing. I held each mushroom with the index and middle fingers of my left hand, rest-ing the stem against my thumb, and slid the knife down gently in a scraping motion. Once the stem was white, I placed the mushroom on a board and cut off its end.

"This is for stock," Santos said, picking up the scrapings and tip and placing them to the top left of the cutting board.

He took the trimmed mushroom and put it to the top right.

"This we must wash," he said.

As we worked, Santos told me how to get it right.

"Maybe lose money," he said, "don't cut so close."

I watched him work with speed and accuracy.

"Like this?" I asked.

"Good," said Santos.

We continued to trim the golden mushrooms.

"So you are writing a book about Santos?" he asked with a smile.

"You're in it," I said.

"Good," he said. "The book should be about Santos. You don't have to write about anyone else. Except maybe Mary and Jess. Sexy!"

The women laughed.

"See these mushrooms?" Santos said. He pointed to a pile of the chanterelles. "These are VIP family meal. Staff meal."

Convinced that I could do the job, Santos pointed to the entire box of chanterelles, about four or five pounds of them, and indicated that I was to trim all of them. He helped another cook move bags of ice. I was flattered to think that Santos had confidence in me and set to work rapidly until Tony showed up at my side.

"Don't throw away my mushrooms," Tony said.

I looked up, surprised.

"You're cutting off too much stem," Tony said. "Let me show you how it needs to be done."

He illustrated by taking my knife and scraping the stem. I had been cutting.

"Got it?" he asked.

"Got it, Chef," I said.

He turned to Santos.

"Danny needs the fucking ribeye, Santos!" Tony said. He started to yell. "I mean, what the fuck? He needed it hours ago! You told him you'd have it. Where the fuck is it?"

"I'll get it," Santos said.

Santos went to the walk-in and returned with a huge slab of ribeye that needed to be broken down and portioned.

"Perfecto," said Santos.

He sharpened knives and sliced open the bag holding the beef.

"Santos," said Tony, watching him cut, now speaking gently, "do you remember how last week you hung your head in shame? You didn't do a good job, right? So I want to see you get it right this time, okay?"

"Yes, okay," said Santos.

"I want this fat," said Tony. He took the knife from Santos and stepped in to cut the beef. "This is good fat."

Santos nodded.

"This fat?" said Tony. He cut some more. "This fat I don't want."

Santos nodded again.

"Tell me if you understand," said Tony sweetly. "Tell me if you *don't* understand. Do you understand?"

"I understand," said Santos.

"Good," said Tony, handing him back the knife and heading upstairs. He patted Santos on the shoulder. "Do a good job, please. I know you can do it."

Tony had spoken in a voice gentler than I had heard from him. He had a protective side; he was angry and disappointed, yes, but now I saw the good paternalism behind the emotions. He wanted Santos to experience the pleasure that comes from being successful.

At one point Tony may have regarded the people who worked in his restaurant as separate from his family, but his actions showed me that his employees *were* his family, and he considered them as such, whether he acknowledged it or not, which was what made the work so difficult, complicated, and meaningful.

"You see all this beef?" Santos said to me. "Beautiful."

Danny came racing down the stairs, shouting, "Where's my fucking beef, Santos? I need that beef!"

He ran past us toward the walk-in. He grabbed a box of greens.

"Danny," said Santos, "where's your father?"

"Probably banging my stepmother about now," said Danny, and then he raced back upstairs.

"Nice," said Santos, ironically. "Very nice."

He continued to slice the beef.

"Sharpen my knives," Santos said to me. *"Muy importante."*

As he cut, I trimmed.

"Not like that," Santos said to me.

He stopped cutting the beef and took my knife to show me how he wanted the mushrooms to be trimmed.

"Too much stem," Santos said. "Don't waste it. It's money."

He made a gliding motion into the mushroom.

"You understand?" Santos asked me.

"Yes," I said.

"Good," he said, handing me back the knife.

The way he spoke to me, his manner as well, were an homage to the way Tony had just taught him.

I returned to the task and Santos went back to cutting the beef.

We cut our products for well over an hour.

To my right, Santos began to portion the meat and place each piece in a plastic bag with about half an ounce of butter.

When I was done with my mushrooms, I helped Santos bring the bagged beef to the Cryovac, where each portion was vacuum-sealed.

"Into the *máquina*," said Santos.

We lined up the bags, six at a time, against small metal hooks on the two sides of the inside of the machine, lowered a lid, and then Santos pressed a button. About five minutes later, the bags had the air sucked out of them and then Santos and I took them back to where we had been working. Gabriel, one of the prep cooks, built like a minotaur, took a black magic marker and labeled each one *19*, for the date. Then he put them back in the tray, which Santos handed to me.

"Put these in the deli," said Santos.

"The deli?" I asked.

"The walk-in," he said.

Gabriel then took my bowl of cleaned chanterelles to a sink to wash them and cut them up. I felt the proprietor's sense of loss. Those mushrooms were mine! The customers or guests who enjoyed them that night would be enjoying my work. I am certain that everyone who worked in the restaurant felt connected to their food in that way, and to one another.

The pace was picking up: 4:10 in the afternoon, only eighty minutes before service. Food was leaving the prep area for the kitchen upstairs, and food was arriving to us for final preparation before it was cooked. Gabriel lowered huge bags of purple, tangled octopus onto ice in the sink to my left.

"I'll be right back," Santos said to me.

He returned with swordfish and rolls of guanciale that had been pressed flat.

"Same as the first day," I said.

Santos unrolled the guanciale and I placed the swordfish on top of several slices, but I was doing it wrong.

"You forget," Santos said. "You forget what I showed you."

He showed me again.

"Okay?" Santos asked. "Show me," he said.

After I showed him that I had understood, he nodded his head and pursed his lips in approval. "I think," Santos said to me, "that in a couple of weeks you'll be a pro."

"No, Santos," I said, struck by his generosity, "more like a couple of months."

"No, a couple of weeks," he said.

Danny showed up between us.

"*Doctah* Haas," he said, his expression completely deadpan, "what'd they call you growing up?"

I was surprised by his question. No one had ever asked me that.

"I don't know, Danny," I said. "What did they call *you* growing up?"

"Groundhog," he said without hesitating. "Then when I got to be about ten, they called me Scamps 'cause my last name is Scampoli."

"Scamps," I said, laughing.

"Okay, so how about you?" he said. "What'd they call you?"

"Gee, I don't know," I said. "Scott. Scotty. Why?"

"Never mind," Danny said, and ran back upstairs.

The rest of the cooks followed Danny as it was the daily meeting before service. I stayed downstairs.

Within minutes, the four prep guys were having a lively conversation in Spanish. Santos left the conversation and began to butcher fish next to me. I continued rolling the swordfish and guanciale in plastic wrap.

"Every time Chef sees me," Santos said, "he says, 'too much meat thrown out.' I'm not complaining, but it would be nice to get out of this kitchen sometimes just for a few minutes."

"To clear your head," I said.

"Exactly," said Santos. He thought a moment. "What do you do when you fight with your wife?"

"I walk the dogs," I said. "I say, 'I'll be back in twenty minutes, honey.' When I come back, we've both calmed down."

Santos nodded his head sadly.

"Nice," he said. He leaned into the knife and exerted pressure on it so that it glided into the flesh of the mullet. "I can't do that here."

FOURTEEN

Attacked, Detoxed, Let Go

Several days following my first two weeks with Santos, I e-mailed Tony to remind him that I was coming in on Saturday. The plan was to work with Santos for eight hours starting at noon. Usually, I came in without notice, but on weekends, when the restaurant was busiest, I sometimes sent in reminders. Most often I got no response or a terse *Cool*, but this time Tony wrote back: *Sorry, but it's just too crazy, down two cooks, talk early next week?*

This was the first time in fourteen months of observing and working at Craigie that Tony had asked me not to come in. E-mail is notoriously robbed of emotion; I had no idea what he was feeling when he had written his refusal, and being curious I pressed on.

So I shouldn't come in as planned? I wrote.

Moments later, he replied: *Not today. Sorry.*

Hmmm, I wondered, what was up? Was he backing out of the project? I e-mailed him again: *Then Wednesday, okay? Deadlines loom.*

From Tony: *Sorry, Scott, but I'm not too concerned about deadlines right now.*

This was so completely uncharacteristic of him that I began to worry if he was all right. I had told Tony the week before about my concerns.

"I'm worried about you," I had said while standing in his cavelike office. He looked surprised but flattered that someone in the restaurant had interest in his emotional life. His job, after all, was to take care of staff and guests. No one at work cared if he was down or anxious, but I did.

"No, no," Tony said. "Why? Do I look worried?"

"You do," I had said. "Danny is cutting back next week. Meredith is gone. I can see you're disappointed in the cooks."

"Normal," he said, "all normal."

"Okay," I said, "but I get paid to worry about people, and you look worried."

"I'm not!" he said, laughing and protesting with raised, flat hands, as if surrendering, "I'm not!"

He said he was not worried, but his behavior suggested otherwise. It had been clear from the modulation of his voice, his increased distractibility, and his impatience. However, I knew that I could not convince him.

It was not that he was trying to keep emotion from me. After so many months of getting to know each other, he trusted me enough to tell me all sorts of personal things. No, he really believed that he was not worried, which I respected. Denial is the engine of resilience, and to be a chef you must be willing to bounce back.

After going for a run, still thinking about how down, worried, and preoccupied he had been even before the latest e-mails in which he had told me to stay away, I texted Tony: *Please let me know if there is anything I can do to help you.*

He texted back moments later: *Santos got jumped last night. Not sure what's up. Think he's in the hospital. Know how to butcher quail?*

I gasped.

OMG, I M so srry, I texted back. *Where is he? Which hospital? We have no idea,* Tony texted. *Sucks.*

Returning home, I tried to calm down by walking the dogs, and that worked for the duration, but I could not get the news out of my mind. I felt helpless. Was it my place to visit Santos? Would I be overstepping my bounds? Tony's message was: Not now. I could not challenge him or question how he wanted to handle the disaster, but it upset me. I had met Santos more than a year ago. How could I help?

I had to wait. It was not going to be easy, but Tony had made it clear that *he* needed time to sort things out. After all, the attack on Santos had come on top of whatever it was that had worried him the week before.

When I came into the restaurant five days later, the next Wednesday, Tony put out his hand to say hello, and I asked about Santos.

"Sounds like he actually got into a fight with one of his apart-ment mates and they got thrown in jail," said Tony.

"Unbelievable," I said. Worried about Santos? No, now I was mad at him! How could he jeopardize his job by getting into a fight that landed him in jail? It must have been some fight! He wasn't a kid.

"I want to kill him," said Tony. "I'm pretty pissed. It was the *last* thing I needed."

"I think I will kill him for you," I said to Tony in what I hoped was a therapeutic tone.

"I would kill him, but we're weeded," Tony said. "I'll revisit this when we're stable."

I mulled this over while Tony texted, responded to e-mails, and talked on the phone. I thought about Santos. When he left work, he was all wound up. How did he alleviate stress?

I did not think that the stress from his work was the cause of the altercation; I understood how Santos had to take responsibility for fighting. However, leaving a stressful work environment and returning home without some outlet for pent-up emotion must have contributed to the poor judgment and impulsivity implicit in acting out.

All the cooks left the kitchen late at night after spending hours on their feet, getting yelled at, cooking at great speeds, shouting, and occasionally getting burned. The floor staff? On their feet as well, and night after night keeping their truest emotions under wraps while they took care of hungry people wanting to feel very important.

Staff were not in relationships outside the restaurant to which they could devote much time. Most of the most passionate experiences of their lives took place at work. The focus was about pleasing guests, cooking the food, and doing what the chef required. Love or personal fulfillment had little to do with it, which, ironically, was a relief; until, that is, they became aware of the emptiness, and then they felt stress. The stress, too, having been repressed while at work, was often magnified.

Still, working at Craigie was a way to subvert the challenges of emotional commitment that are at their strongest developmentally in one's twenties. Spending more time in the restaurant with the family *there* meant being able to remain forever young: unconquerable, unquenchable, and without limits. Get the food hot to the table, and you're good to go.

This also meant that stress stayed at its peak. Disappointments and acting-out behaviors were common among cooks and servers at Craigie and other restaurants. The subtlety, satisfaction, and patience that come from long hours with loved ones were missing. Life outside the restaurant was incomplete.

"So," I said, finally. The *very* last thing Tony needed to hear now was that working in his restaurant stressed staff out. I knew I needed to change the subject. "I guess I should think about shadowing another member of your staff. How about Bobby?"

Tony looked up.

"Bobby?" he said. "This is Bobby's last week. He gave me a month's notice."

"He did?" I asked. "What happened?"

"You saw what happened," said Tony. "He couldn't keep up. He couldn't do the work. He gave notice before I let him go. He didn't get it. He was here for months and he never got it."

"I thought he was getting better."

"Maybe," said Tony, "but it wasn't good enough and it wasn't consistent."

He went back to answering e-mails.

"How about Dakota?" I asked.

This was the story that Tony had not told me, and what had caused him so much pain.

"We knew something was wrong," Tony said. "Dakota was coming in looking washed out, as if he was hungover. But he wasn't. He wasn't hungover." He paused and pursed his lips. "He was strung out. So last week, on a Sunday, he calls me on my cell phone and asks me to drive him to a detox. My HR guy found him a bed. He calls me to ask him for a ride."

"That's beautiful that he trusted you," I said.

"It is," he said. "I guess. But, look, I'm a chef. I'm running a business! I'm glad to help him out. I felt good about being there for him. But it's hard to be the guy's boss and do that. I drove him to the Dimock detox in Roxbury," Tony said.

Dakota was in rehab to get treatment for a heroin addiction. After driving him to the facility, Tony pulled up to the door and told Dakota that he had to walk in there by himself.

A few days later, Tony heard from Dakota. Once he was discharged, he was not sure what to do next: He could go back home to his parents in the Midwest or stay in Boston and either look for a new job or see if he could return to Craigie.

Tony's lawyer recommended that he terminate Dakota, but he felt that this would be abandoning him. No matter what ended up happening, there was a more immediate concern: Dakota wanted Tony to help him clean out his apartment; he was afraid to go back there alone because "stuff" was there.

"What a mess," I said.

"Welcome to the biz," said Tony.

I thought then of what it really takes to be a chef, and what advice I would give someone who aspires to be one. Running a restaurant starts with knowing how to cook, but the essence of the job, the skill that separates the best chefs from everyone else, is managing people: purveyors, cooks, floor staff, city health inspectors, immigration officers, electricians, plumbers, investors, the media, and guests. Once you can cook, it's like the shrink said at the end of *Portnoy's Complaint*: *"Now vee may perhaps to begin. Yes?"*

To try to lessen the tension Tony was expressing, I showed him a quote I had enjoyed from a review of Adam Phillips's new book, *On Balance*, that had appeared in a recent issue of *The New York Review of Books*:

> In Freud's original helplessness, we are infants crying for food, and therefore for our lives. When nourishment arrives, in the form of the encompassing warmth of the mother, a state of complete and unrepeatable satisfaction is experienced—a state of grace in religious terms—that we are doomed to try to recapture in later years.

"Interesting," I said. "Probably helps to explain why people are eager to eat out, and why chefs have become celebrities."

Tony nodded sadly.

"I think about these things, too," he said. "When I'm not driving cooks to detoxes or trying to find out which hospital my butcher is in."

FIFTEEN

Destroy All Robots

O N MONDAYS, WHEN THE RESTAURANT WAS CLOSED, TONY WENT TO the farmer's market in Central Square and often phoned me while shopping. He was in a better mood this particular Monday than he had been the week before: laughing, talking animatedly; it always made him happy to be around food.

He had a simpler relationship to food than to people. It upset him when he could not please others or when he failed to meet their expectations. He could not change people or improve them the way he could food. Too bad that the biggest part about being a chef is not cooking, but managing people who have more ingredients than cassoulet.

"How about Jill?" I asked.

We were still discussing whom I would shadow next. Dakota had extended his stay in detox, Bobby was gone, and Santos was MIA.

"I figured Jill would be good," I said, "because she's in garde manger, and she can teach me how to do some basic things."

"Excellent choice," Tony said. "The problem is that Jill isn't in garde manger any more. I need her on the line. It's gonna be a crash course. Big promotion. Normally, it would be four months of training to go from garde manger to the line, but it's gonna have to be four weeks . . . But we'll see. I have faith in her."

I could hear him buying brussels sprouts, apples, Bibb lettuce, and spaghetti squash.

"So who's left in garde manger?" I asked.

I wanted to work in garde manger because it was a step up from prep, but without the intensity of the line. Garde manger meant assembling cold appetizers, making brines, organizing the components needed for cooking on the line, and making sets of condiments. It was not easy, but it did not require the speed and focus of the line.

"Nate," said Tony. "I'll assign you to Nate. He's an interesting guy. Quirky. Yeah, that'll work."

A couple of days later I returned to the restaurant and found Tony at the chef's counter. It was late afternoon, and the cooks were humming along, trying to finish up projects needed for the night.

"How are things?" I asked.

"Better," Tony said. "Still crazy, but better. Danny is gone except for Sundays, so Matt's my only sous chef."

"I misunderstood, then. I thought Danny was cutting back to four nights a week from six."

"That was what he did for two months," Tony said. "Now? Now it's just Sundays. Danny is helping run his wife's bakery in Brighton, but most of the time he's 'Danny the Nanny'!" He explained that Danny's sister-in-law, a single parent, had a baby she needed help taking care of while she worked as a physician in New Hampshire.

"Meanwhile Dakota came back this morning and Santos showed up yesterday."

"Lots of commotion," I said. I thought back to Lydia, who was now running a very low-key, neighborhood restaurant, and Danny, helping his wife take care of her sister's baby, after Craigie. Very atypical for sous chefs. It seemed that both Lydia and Danny wanted a break after years of intensity with Tony.

"Totally," said Tony. "Let me ask you something: Will people still want to eat at my restaurant after reading your book?"

"Of course," I said, "your food is delicious and your staff is very pleasant. Why would you ask?"

"Because it's like the Bronx Zoo in my kitchen!" he said.

"No," I said gently, "it's not. It just feels that way because you're in charge."

"Hmm," said Tony, and he went back to reviewing the menu, crossing out dishes he would not be serving that night, adding others. Then he glanced at his watch, looked up, and yelled: "Okay, everyone! Finish up what you're doing! Outside! Now!"

It was freezing, almost November, but we all took seats beneath the trees next to the restaurant. Shivering.

The weekly contest among cooks got under way. Tony invited each of the cooks to create an *amuse bouche*. The winner got his or her item served to guests. It was a competition, not a collaboration. Today four dishes were presented to Tony: rye crisp and roasted duck breast, some kind of horseradish custard with braised celery strips, a cheese and apricot concoction, and a chocolate and hazelnut dessert. It was very complex, with talk of slow cooking at 118 degrees, many unusual ingredients, and talk of methodology that would not have been out of place in a college chemistry class.

Tony offered support to each cook, clearly impressed both by their efforts and by the end product, with the clear favorite, for now, a dessert made by Jess, about which he said, "I like it! But bump the hazelnut up next time!"

After telling the cooks that the results of the contest would be announced at the end of the week, Tony became serious. So much had·changed since I had first come in. The restaurant was in crisis. His trusted sous chef of nearly five years was gone but for Sundays, his butcher was just out of jail, and one of his best line cooks was newly sober and perhaps unreliable.

"The past couple of months have been some of the roughest months in my years as a boss," Tony said. "It has been an absolute, tremendous challenge, and unfortunately I have also been noticing an attitude in my kitchen. If you want to improve what you do, if you want to enjoy working at Craigie, there can no longer be any excuses. There's always going to be a reason why something has gone wrong, but excuses don't fix things."

Tony spoke compassionately and with disappointment, without a trace of anger, which made it harder for the cooks to absorb and accept what he was saying. He had a habit of being extremely frank.

"Craigie has never been about expensive plates or expensive tablecloths," Tony continued. "We can't hide behind that stuff. We're about the food—we've always been about the food. So when we're not working as a team, it shows. What I see instead of teamwork are a lot of islands. I don't see people having each other's backs." He paused. "I don't see people doing their homework, taking notes, and communicating. We are not consistently walking the walk. You need to be accountable: This piece of fish ends up on the plate the way it is supposed to."

Sadness informed the tone of Tony's voice.

"We can't rely on people not with us any more," Tony said. "But change creates opportunity, and we need to embrace that. Problems? Of course. Talk to me. Anyone who has asked me, 'Can I talk to you?' I have always talked. If you think I am inaccessible, that is not true."

If the cooks had come to Craigie thinking that they were there to cook food, they were correct about that being the starting point. What they may not have known, especially the kids fresh out of culinary school or for whom this was their first job cooking professionally, was that this was a new home. Hearing Tony talk was like eavesdropping on a dad upset with his son for striking out: He knew the kid could do better.

Tony took out a new book that had arrived in his mail the day before: *Momofuku Milk Bar*, by Christina Tosi.

"I read this almost all the way through from the moment I got it," he said, "and I like Christina. I met her when we were both working at wd-50—I was doing a stage there. She and I share the same outlook on the need for a level of consistency and a level of organization in everything we do."

He opened the book and began reading to his cooks.

The chapter was about "Hard bodies who go above and beyond, who never complain," compared to "Soft bodies—we like them as people, but don't want to work next to them." He closed the book and looked at every cook. "I would love to see Craigie filled with hard bodies."

This was not a speech any of the cooks could deliver. It was not harsh, and it was not forgiving. The tone required maturity and vision. The cook who could learn to speak that way had a chance of becoming a chef.

"We need to adjust," said Tony. "We will keep on doing what we are doing. I will make sure that happens." He paused, not for effect, but because he was overwhelmed momentarily by the emotional power of what he was about to say. "Craigie on Main *will* continue."

These were dark, cold days, I could see that, and the faces of the cooks showed what they were thinking and feeling. A lack of certitude, disappointment in themselves, fear, and not knowing what would come next if they could not meet the chef's expectations.

When the meeting broke up, the cooks sloughed back to the kitchen. Tony took Nate aside and told him that for the next couple of weeks I would be working with him.

"Cool," said Nate. "This could be cool."

Nate had shaved his head again and, as usual, showed little emotional response to what had just been said to him. Language was important to Nate, but it was not that important. I followed Nate in. His sleeves were rolled up: skull-and-crossbones tat revealed. We went to a small back room, next to the wine cellar, where Nate copied down the pickle brine recipe from a laptop. The pickles were for the burgers.

"All the recipes we need are in a file here," Nate explained.

We sat next to an electric meat slicer and beside a box holding squash and pumpkins. The subway rumbled beside us; I heard rapid footsteps above. A food dehydrator hummed behind me.

"Basically, we're gonna *mise* this out," said Nate. "Assemble it. The burger pickles are a pretty rare project—we make them about once every month and a half."

I helped him grab supplies: stainless-steel bowls, a scale, knives. Then we walked over to the prep area.

Santos was working on octopus. He was subdued. Both sides of his face showed scars. It looked as if he had been cut by knives. He nodded hello.

"If you'd been here earlier," Nate said, "I could have had you working on the cucumbers. Next time. I'll want you to mandoline the shit out of them."

As we worked, Nate talked about himself. He had all the qualities of a shy person, more interested in things than in communicating about things, but he talked a little about growing up with a father who was a career officer in the U.S. Navy.

"We moved around a lot," said Nate.

Not forming attachments to a community may have had an impact on Nate when he left home to attend Ohio State.

"I was failing out at college," Nate said. "I lasted one year and one semester. I didn't go to class." He laughed at himself.

"I watched cooking shows," Nate said. "I sat around and thought: I gotta figure out what to do or my parents are gonna kill me."

Eventually, returning home to Virginia, Nate got a job washing dishes, then doing prep, and, finally, becoming a sous chef.

"That's impressive," I said.

"It was basically a sandwich shop," he said.

Nate put himself down at almost every opportunity.

He spoke blandly of visiting his brother, who offered him a place to stay. Nothing to do, feeling aimless, Nate saw an ad for a cook at Craigie and applied. "I wrote a cocky e-mail," he said. "My subject line was, *Willing to start at the bottom and rise meteorically.*"

He said it in a way that was self-deprecating, as if to say, who was he fooling? He worked at Craigie about six days a week, from noon to one A.M., but he was still doing prep and garde manger, still lacking skills needed to work the line.

"You can get the spices we need for the pickle brine," he said.

He handed me a list and directed me to shelves of jars and containers holding forty-eight different spices. Then he went off to another prep area to work on something else.

My list:

35 grams fennel seed
31 grams coriander
42 grams black pepper
42 grams yellow mustard seed
10 grams juniper
10 grams allspice
18 grams bay leaves

I took down each container and weighed the spices on a small scale. Their colors, aromas, and the silent precision of the task were mesmerizing.

Gabriel was peeling shallots next to me. Both of us started to cry.

When I had finished weighing the spices, I returned with them to Nate. He was engaged in a heated conversation in Spanish with Santos.

"It's illegal in Boston," said Nate.

"What are you talking about?" I asked Nate.

"You don't want to know," he said.

"I'm just curious," I said.

"He's talking about cutting my penis off," said Nate.

Santos smiled a fake evil smile.

"I will do it for him," Santos said.

"You asked," said Nate.

"I did," I said.

Next to Nate was a large tray of fresh, dark, gnarled horseradish roots. We began to peel them together and weigh the results. Then we chopped them up into small pieces.

"Working prep can be harder than the line," Nate said. "It's hard to stay motivated and focused. There's no one telling you what to do."

I took a small, wet towel and cleaned off the board where I had been cutting the horseradish. I swept the peels into the trash.

"When I make fresh horseradish at home," I said to Nate, "I peel the roots and cut the pieces and pop them into a food processor. Why are we cutting them up this way at Craigie?"

"It brings out more flavor," Nate said. "Also, because honestly that's how Chef wants us to do it."

I was struck by his lack of curiosity. It was not sufficient to say that it was how the chef wanted it done. Here was another difference between the cooks who advance and the cooks who don't. Skills aside, cooks who ask questions are more likely to become chefs. The questions lead to a dialogue. By knowing more about what they are doing, the cooks engage more in the process.

"Sweet, sweet, sweet," said Nate.

We were on to the next task: julienning purple onions. Slicing them in half, carefully removing the peel, snipping off the ends, and slicing thin pieces rapidly.

"We'll make about three gallons of brine in a huge steam bath," said Nate. "When it cools, we'll add the pickles. Got to work on the pork skin, too. We'll *mise* it out for Chef, then he'll cook it because he doesn't trust us to cook it. That's the way a lot of chefs work."

"What will he use the pork skin for?" I asked.

"I'm not sure," said Nate. "A braise? A ragu? I don't know."

He asked me to go upstairs and get him a few containers. It was the middle of service and the atmosphere was potent and frenetic.

"How long?" Matt was saying. "How long? Someone please say something."

Matt's style was different from Danny's, more deliberate, tighter, and derived from his huge physical presence. He did not have to shout to be heard.

"Two minutes," said Jill.

Jill moved quickly between the grill and garde manger.

"Thank you," said Matt.

"Fish is down," said Jill. "Let's go, guys."

I returned downstairs with the containers. Nate was pouring the contents of a "foie gras kit" into a bowl.

For the remainder of the evening, I helped Nate out on small, manageable tasks within the limits of my ability. Nate had a home at Craigie, that was clear: more intense than ordinary family life and better defined. It was, I could see, preferable to the chaos he faced outside the restaurant. Here he got things done.

It made up for earlier failures.

Then it hit me: Danny had asked me what my nickname had been as a child because we were all starting over in the restaurant. We were kids again with a second chance.

Before leaving, I asked Nate to give me his e-mail address so that I could confirm with him when I would be in next to work with him.

"Destroyallrobots at gmail dot com," Nate said.

"Wow," I said.

"I wish I could be more entertaining," he said, "but I'm a super awkward person to begin with."

When I came in the next morning, I walked over to catch up with Tony at the chef's counter.

"Dakota's sleeping on my couch. He called me up and said that he had to get out of his place," Tony said. "He had no place to go."

"Karolyn doesn't mind?" I asked.

"She's okay with it," Tony said. "This morning Charlie gave Dakota one of her brownies. Loved it. Now he'll never leave!"

"How long is he staying?"

"I don't know."

"And you say this isn't your family," I said, gesturing to the cooks who were showing up for prep.

Tony laughed, and I went downstairs to find Nate. He was writing down a list of what was in the walk-in. We stood next to two white tubs of huge split bones being brined.

Nate finished writing and we went back upstairs.

"Chef," said Nate, "one last thing. Are there any projects I should know about for tonight? I know I should get pork neck bones roasted and I'll double-check, but I'm pretty sure there's also a whole pig. Anything else?"

"Why don't you make a list of everything you're doing and e-mail it to me?" said Tony.

"Got it," said Nate.

We went back downstairs. Being with Nate involved a great deal of going from one place to the next.

"My father said that he'd be happy with me flipping burgers,"

Nate said, "as long as I could support myself." He laughed. "But I don't know if he meant it literally."

Before he sent the e-mail to Tony, Nate and I opened a UPS Next Day Air box from Blue Moon Acres in Buckingham, Pennsylvania, that held two and a half pounds of small containers of microgreens, including wasabina and tatsui. He stacked the containers, brought them into a walk-in, and then broke down the box.

Then we went back to the laptop so Nate could write the e-mail.

He titled it *Brines and Cures*. Then he just sat there for a while and looked at the screen.

"What's the problem?" I asked.

"It's only the second e-mail Chef has had me send him on inventory," Nate said, "so I don't know exactly what I'm doing."

"Ah. You have to make note of the brines, though, right? Dates when they were started?"

"Right," he said. "It's crazy, but from what I'm seeing, it looks like the way we've done the brines, all of them will be done on the same day!"

"That's not good."

"No," he said. "They should be spread out."

He finished the e-mail, sent it, and said, "Okay, I have a big prep list, we'd better get going."

The list had been written by Matt. Nate copied it into his small black notebook.

"Wait a second," Nate said to me. "Can you read this word? How good are you at reading lousy handwriting?"

"Good," I said. "I work in a hospital." I looked at the word. "I think it says *fennel*. As in fennel broth. Does that make sense?"

"It does," said Nate. "Thanks."

I had assumed that we would next try to find a clean place to work, but Nate went back upstairs. This time it was to get three knives and a rod for sharpening them. He handed me a knife and a cutting board and we set to work, side by side, in garde manger, in the open kitchen.

"I think I'll have you working on the ketchup. Take these," he said, handing me four onions, "and dice them."

I diced one, and Nate showed me what I had done wrong and how to make it right.

"You're chopping, that's wrong," he said. "Dice them."

When that was done, Nate handed me two inch-long pieces of ginger root and a spoon.

"Use the spoon to peel these," Nate said, "and when you've done that, dice them, too, and add them to the onions."

This did not take long.

"Good," said Nate, "now since you seemed to enjoy working on the spices the other day, I'll have you go downstairs and grab the spices for the ketchup."

We returned to the cellar.

He handed me a list, divided into three parts, with fourteen ingredients on it.

"Get two Cambros," Nate said, "and double batch them."

"Cambros?" I asked.

"That's the brand of the containers," he said, and returned upstairs.

The ketchup, made in-house, contained mace, clove, yellow mustard seed, agave syrup, turbinado, and many other fresh and powdered ingredients. To suggest using the bottled stuff would have been anathema to Tony's philosophy of cooking. This was only the ketchup; I could easily imagine the complicated steps, precision, and focus needed to do everything in this kitchen. I thought of a favorite quote from one of my favorite books, *Akenfield*: Bell ringers coordinate church bells to ring in an elaborate sequence over dozens of miles, from village to village: "We attempt the difficult, but there is no virtue in what is easy."

Standing there, measuring liquids, powders, and seeds, felt complete. The ceiling was low, the space was a narrow corridor dimly lit, but I was part of the crew making ketchup!

Nate came back downstairs as I was finishing up.

"How often do you make ketchup?" I asked.

"About once a week," he said. He began to stir. "It's very cool, isn't it? All the ingredients we put into it."

"What do you do with the onions, ginger, spices, and liquid?"

"We sweat it, grind it, turn it into sauce, and reduce it until it's sticky. Then we add four big number ten cans of tomatoes, reduce everything by a quarter, and then buzz and pass it."

"Buzz and pass?"

"Blend and chinois."

"This is all a ton of work. I mean, this is only the ketchup!"

Nate nodded in agreement. We began to set out the next set of tasks when Santos came over.

"What's up, buddy?" Santos said to me.

He had altered his voice to sound as if he had been born and raised in Boston.

"Hey, Santos," I said.

"What's with this guy?" asked Santos.

Santos motioned to Nate.

"Santos," said Nate, "any time you need something, you ask me, but otherwise you give me a hard time."

Santos laughed.

"Why are you a son of a bitch?" he said to Nate. "Is that right? Help me with my English, Nate."

"See what I mean?" Nate said to me.

I heard the slight clatter of wheels, and Dakota appeared a few feet away on a skateboard.

"*Doctah* Haas," he said, mimicking Danny. Fist bump. "How *are* you doing?"

He looked pale and as if he had just tumbled out of bed, hair all over the place, unshaven.

"Good," I said. "You?"

"Good," he said.

Nate smiled in wonder at Dakota's apparent social ease.

"What time are you in tomorrow?" I asked Nate.

"Day off," Nate said. "Every Wednesday."

"What will you do?" I asked.

"You know," Nate said, and he quit stirring, "you have to take care of yourself. Your body? It's like a spaceship: It requires care, it's the only one you'll ever have. So: I'm probably gonna join a gym."

"Good idea," I said.

"I need more balance in my life," Nate said, and went back to stirring.

SIXTEEN

A Chef in the Making

I T TOOK A FEW WEEKS BEFORE TONY'S TALK TO THE COOKS ABOUT TAKING more responsibility had any effect. Things began to turn around slowly, related to what he had said, but also due to emerging talent. Tony's two new hires, Patrick and Orly, were demonstrating top skills. Jill had taken a position of authority on the line. Tony got himself an assistant from New York City who doubled as a new GM: Carl.

Business, too, was picking up. Fall going toward Christmas and then the New Year were the busiest times for Craigie, next to college graduations in May and June.

I attached myself to Jill and told her that I wanted to shadow her. I was ready for the line.

"You're gonna learn a lot with me."

On my first day with her on the line, Jill had me observe her preparing the sweat for the mussels. She sliced celery stalks very rapidly.

"This involves carrots, fennel, celery, onions, and white wine," she said.

When she was done with the sweat, she said, "Produce orders are coming in. Want to learn how to do them?"

"Sure," I said.

We ran downstairs and joined all the other cooks who were opening boxes, filling plastic trays with product, and breaking down the cardboard. It was frantic, but there was a great deal of laughter and joy. Abundance!

"You put paper towels on the bottom of the trays," Jill explained, "then put the product on top, and then put another paper towel over it."

We dumped a big bag of green leaves into a tray.

"Spinach?" I asked.

"Fava leaves. Want to have one?"

I had never tasted anything quite like it. It does not make sense, but the texture enhanced the flavor.

We worked on other boxes—beets, thyme, rosemary, Belgian endive, carrots, pea shoot greens—and as the cooks passed by Jill, each one asked her, "How are you feeling?"

"Better," Jill said. "Better, thanks."

"Can I ask?"

"I had mono. I *have* mono. But I'm not contagious any longer. Last week was tough because I was completely exhausted from the work and then after work I had to drive to Providence, Rhode Island, three nights a week—that's where I live with my girlfriend. I hoped to find something closer, but that's not gonna happen for a while. Or maybe never."

Matt came running by, and he saw the beets.

"Golden beets!" Matt exclaimed. "Ask and you shall receive!"

After all the product was divided up, Jill and I wrote labels and the date on masking tape, affixing these to each container.

"Can I bring them to the walk-in?" I asked.

"Definitely," Jill said. "Take these three containers in. The herbs go on the middle rack on the left."

I went into the walk-in and then noticed that I had rosemary, thyme, *and* endives. I put the herbs where I had been told, but where did the endive go? I did not want to go back to Jill and ask her. I looked around and found more endive and put my tray there.

When I returned to her and told her what I had done, and why it had felt like a problem at the time, she said, "Oh, you got it!"

Everything we did in the kitchen was part of a larger process and, when things worked, the smallest activity had meaning.

"We get at least one delivery a day," Jill said, "and sometimes four a day!"

By the end of our first day together, she was promising to start me on grilled cheese sandwiches.

"We use pork belly. The sandwiches are amazing."

Then she put out her right arm, made a fist, and beckoned me to do the same so we could bump.

WHEN I RETURNED TO THE RESTAURANT TO CONTINUE WORKING WITH JILL, I checked in with Tony, who was at the chef's counter. He looked glum.

"Where've you been?" he said with a big smile.

Maybe he wasn't glum.

"Busy writing," I said.

"It's been, what? Five days? A week? Lots gone on since you've been in," he said. "I want to be sure you get it all."

Tony's outlook was puzzling to me because it was so unlike most of the other successful chefs I knew who spent time planning or opening new restaurants, on the road doing promotions, or shilling for products. Tony found resonance and identity in *one* restaurant, at the pass or behind the stove, and it was an environment over which he had control. The world, with its variables, is much more perplexing. Things went wrong at Craigie, every day and every night, but what *really* went wrong?

A batch of stock got ruined, cooks did not work as a team, a customer sent back the food, the cooks fell behind in prep. These were all important problems, but compared to the stresses outside the restaurant? These were problems that could be *solved*. Hence, the appeal. Unlike the unpredictability of the world outside, there was control inside Craigie. Beets needed to be peeled properly, knives sharpened, chicken cooked at a low temperature, and so on. It was nothing like being stopped for driving under the influence, failing a physics exam, leaving a marriage, arguing with your landlord, or missing a flight.

Still, it was always super highs and extremely deep lows. When Tony told me that there were protests against a new plan for tips he and Carl had established, he called it a near coup. But it was not a coup; no one got hurt, no regime was overthrown. He told me that Dakota was back in rehab and in crisis. It wasn't a crisis; he was getting treatment. He had even been in touch with both Dakota and his mother. He said he had hired a new cook, Marian, describing her as a potential rock star, citing time she had spent at Cafe Boulud and 11 Madison as amazing. But was she? She had been at Craigie only a week. How did he know if she was any good? Hyperbolic rather than static, drama rather than calm.

It was the day before Thanksgiving and, for the third year in a row, Tony and the cooks were preparing a meal for the firefighters at the station down the street. He was also having a Thanksgiving dinner in the restaurant for twenty-four friends and family.

"Hey, what's up, buddy?" Jill said to me.

"Give me something to do," I said.

She handed me a small knife and gestured to a pile of potatoes. We both began peeling.

"These peels would make great chips," Jill said, "but no time for that, unfortunately."

She explained that after the potatoes were boiled and mashed, she was going to add creamed leeks to them.

"Awesome," Jill said. "In a little while, the cream will caramelize and it will get sweeter."

While the potatoes boiled and the leeks cooked, Jill and I went downstairs to work on the sandwiches. She found a large loaf of bread.

"If I can get started on this now," Jill said, "I won't have to deal with it during service."

Before we started making sandwiches, however, we had to go back upstairs to clean the plates, pots, pans, and utensils we had used for the leeks and potatoes. The rule at Craigie was that everyone had to do their own dishes until five P.M. I loaded a rack and shoved it into the Hobart.

"And that's how that goes," Jill said.

Between the time we worked on the mashed potatoes and were to start making sandwiches, it was time for staff meal, which was served routinely around 2:30 to 2:45 in the afternoon. Today's selection was salad, fried potatoes, and "Buffalo" swordfish. The food was nothing like what the cooks made for guests, but it was no different from a parking lot at a BMW factory filled with the cars of the workers who assembled the luxury vehicles but could not afford to buy one.

"Okay, buddy," said Jill, after we finished eating. "We're gonna go make sandwiches!"

I loved her attitude. She was like a comrade: the ease of her movements, the way she seemed at home in her body. She was refreshing, no diva, and when we spoke, I felt comfortable. She did not judge me or herself.

We went back downstairs, to a dark corner, where Jill and I set up a prep area. We unrolled plastic wrap, arranged cutting boards, and took out a tray of house-cured bacon. Then Jill sliced the bread in half.

"Fuck," she said.

"What?" I asked.

"It's fucking rye. Fuck!"

"What do you want instead?"

"Pullman," she said. "Fuck." She held a knife in her hand, and put her head down. "Fuck. Hold on. Fuck. Fuck, fuck, fuck."

Jill found Matt. Matt explained that all he had was rye in the house. We returned to our prep area. We had to put everything back where we had found it.

"So now I have to do what I was hoping to avoid," said Jill. "I'll have to work on the sandwiches after five, and during service. That really sucks."

Then Jill led me to the Robot Coupe. It had just two buttons: green and red. I loaded its container with mushrooms for a duxelle: hen of the woods, shiitake, chanterelles, and beech. One flip of the switch and I had pulverized them.

Next to me, Jess, in her own world, was making pastries, while listening to a Q-Tip rap on her iPod: "Breathe and Stop."

Mushrooms done, I returned upstairs, where the room was filled with the sounds of "Tumbling Dice" from *Exile on Main Street*.

As Jill and I melted huge chunks of butter on the stove—more butter than I had ever seen used in cooking before; it must have been at least two pounds for twelve potatoes—Tony spoke about his new hire.

"Marian is great," Tony said. "I'm very excited about her. Watch her work."

Marian stood about ten feet away, moving with more speed and precision than I had seen in most other cooks at Craigie.

"Go talk to her," said Tony.

Breaking away from Jill, I walked toward Marian, who was ruddy faced, with bright orange hair, blushing from exertion as she leaned in to slice a loin. Her sleeves were rolled up. I saw pink and white scars from burns on both of her arms. Marian talked about how she had been working at her family's restaurant in Wisconsin up until she answered an online ad for a cook at Craigie.

"Scott," Jill called me over. "Scott, salt!"

I ran to get her salt. She added a ton of salt to the potatoes and leeks.

"Pepper!" Jill said.

I ran to get her pepper.

Then we stirred and tasted.

"Fucking incredible," Jill said. "Okay, let's see what Chef thinks."

She brought Tony a small, hot bowl of the mashed potatoes. He tasted them, closed his eyes, nodded, and said, "Thank you, Jill. These are delicious."

She beamed.

Tony walked off to check on the progress being made by the other cooks.

"The wives of the firefighters are gonna want to murder us," Jill said. "These are gonna be the best fucking mashed potatoes their husbands have ever tasted!"

We headed back downstairs to organize her prep area.

"What are your Thanksgiving plans?" I asked.

"After service tonight, I'm driving to Brooklyn," she said. "I'll probably get there around three in the morning. Then it'll be a meal at my parents' place, with all my siblings, and nieces and nephews, and then I'll have to drive back here. Should be back by midnight. I have to be in the restaurant on Friday morning at nine."

I wondered about someone who sacrificed so much of the love that many take for granted. She would miss the fullness of the family holiday to prepare food for customers in a restaurant.

Perhaps, however, that was the point: a good excuse for avoiding family. Saying that she would love to spend more time with them, but unable to do so, out of her hands, she had to work.

What seemed at first to be a downside to cooking long hours in a restaurant may have been an advantage.

We started cleaning up, and then Jill stopped, her hands on the table.

"Omigod," Jill said, "I fucking love Thanksgiving!"

ON BLACK FRIDAY, JILL AND I WERE BOTH IN THE RESTAURANT EARLY.

She looked exhausted, shoulders slumped, moving slowly, drained of color. We stood beside a huge, deep pot of bubbling stock that smelled of bones, fat, and liver. Thin white bones protruded from the scum on the surface.

"I'm really busy today," Jill said, "and there's not much I can have you do, but if you go downstairs, I can set you up with the cheese. It needs to be shredded for sandwiches. Think you can handle that?"

"Sure," I said.

"Great," she said. "Go to the dairy walk-in. On the bottom right you'll find plastic trays of cheddar cheese and Comte. It's for the world's fanciest grilled cheese sandwich. That Comte is something like thirty dollars a pound. Cool, huh? So I want you to cut them into blocks about this size."

She held up a small plastic container as big as a one-pound box of butter.

"Got it," I said.

"Okay," she said, "now go do it!"

Downstairs, I went into the walk-in to search for the cheese, which was not as easy as I thought it would be. Few things were labeled, and trays were stacked on top of each other and stuff was misplaced. I did not want to disturb the cooks, so I sniffed around, unwrapped cheeses, and found what I was looking for by smell rather than sight.

The next step was getting knives. Each cook had his or her own set. I have Japanese knives at home but had forgotten to bring them in.

I saw Santos.

"What up, buddy?" he said.

"Santos," I said, pointing to some knives, "are these yours? Can I take one?"

"For what?" Santos asked.

"Cutting up cheese," I said.

"Okay," he said.

I took the cheese and the knives to a small platform near Tony's office and began working. It did not take long for me to stab myself in my left palm, but the wound was superficial and painless, so I dried the blood with a paper towel and kept cutting.

When the cheese had been cut into blocks, I got the Robot Coupe. It had not been cleaned properly. I scraped away bits of whatever had been left there. Flipping the switch, I fed the cheese into the machine and watched shreds of it fly out and into a big plastic tray I had set up at its spout.

"Buzz that cheese!" said Santos when he walked by.

Finally, I covered the tray with a lid and labeled the date on it with a black marker. Santos had a marker.

At last, job done, I presented my work to Jill for approval.

"Thank you, Scott," she said. "Very helpful."

When it was time to leave that night, a curious, satisfying thought came to me: What if this really *was* my family?

RETURNING TO THE RESTAURANT A FEW DAYS LATER, I FOUND JILL TEARING up sage leaves downstairs. I joined in. Afterward, she had me go upstairs and check on two enormous sweet potatoes by sticking a long needle into their flesh.

"Not done yet," I said.

"No worries," she said.

She said she was not worried, but she looked down. I asked Tony what was going on.

"Jill had a tough night last night," Tony said. "It happens. I told her it happens to everyone. She felt like it was the worst thing that could have happened to her, but I told her, 'Hey, this is just the beginning of your career! This is what makes you better.'"

I walked downstairs to her.

"Oh, shit," Jill said.

"What?" I asked.

"I always feel like I'm fucking behind," she said. "I could come in at nine twenty in the morning and still find a way to fuck it up."

I did not see it that way and I told her so. It was obvious that Jill was highly skilled. However, she was so caught up in what she saw as failure from the night before that she did not believe me.

The answer to the dilemma, she decided, was simply to work harder.

"What the fuck," she said as she rummaged in the walk-in for shellfish.

Eventually she found mussels, shrimp, whelks, and razor clams.

"Scott," she said, handing me a few empty trays, "can you bring this up for me?"

"Where?" I asked.

"Dish pit," she said.

I did what I was told and then came back to her.

Marian walked behind us sweeping with a small, yellow broom.

The kitchen was calmer since Tony had spoken with the cooks about hard and soft bodies. Less screaming, less name-calling. For one thing, there were now four women working the line when before there had been two. For another thing, the crew had more reliable, higher-level skills.

"Very weird to be in it," Jill, said.

"In what?" I asked.

"It," Jill said. She gestured around her. "This."

She had posted a list in front of her of the day's tasks: *Herbs, whelks, mussels, razors, sammies, sweet pot, Brussels.*

There was no end to it. It was true what Jill had said: No matter what she did, no matter how many projects she completed, there was always something left to do.

Orly walked over from garde manger to offer her philosophy on the predicament of being a cook. Tall, pigtailed, having spent the past seven years cooking at a resort in Jackson Hole, Orly was at once playful but focused and tough, like a volleyball player. She had worked in kitchens since finishing high school and was now twenty-five but with the maturity of a person much older.

"Practice doesn't make perfect," Orly said. "Perfect practice makes perfect."

Jill nodded but remained distracted. She gestured to the board she was using to clean the shellfish.

"They keep giving me the same shanty-ass board," she said.

Jill removed each razor clam from its dark, long shell.

I carried the dirty equipment to the Hobart and threw out the shells.

"Okay, everyone," Tony shouted, "photo shoot!"

"Photo shoot?" asked Jill.

She did not look up from the clam shell she was prying apart.

Tony had told me that *Serious Eats* was stopping by to make a video of him cooking the burger.

Jill shook her head and smiled angrily.

"What?" I asked.

"Nothing," Jill said. Then she added, "Everyone's so fucking serious." Then she stopped what she was doing and said resolutely, "Look, this . . . *this* is the craziest kitchen I've ever worked in. *The craziest kitchen.* Bar none. We'll talk."

I RETURNED SEVERAL DAYS LATER, BUT IT WAS JILL'S DAY OFF. AND WHEN I went downstairs looking for Nate, I learned he had quit.

"Hey, Tony, where is he?"

"Gone," Tony said, without looking up.

Tony was hunched over his laptop and had opened the page to a travel site. We had talked about my family holidays, going back decades with my parents, at a place called Crystal Waters, in Negril, Jamaica, and after I had put Tony in touch with the property's owner, he had booked a cottage. My relationship with him and his staff at the restaurant was taking intimate turns.

"Yeah," said Tony, looking up and raising his eyebrows. "He flipped out."

"During service?" I asked.

"No, thank goodness," said Tony. "What happened was this: I mean, you've worked with Nate, you know he wasn't doing a great job. He wasn't getting it. We had the regular review with him, me and one of the managers, and we told him that. No surprise, right? But he got very upset and started crying."

"That's very sad," I said.

"It is," said Tony. "No doubt about that."

Jess came by to ask Tony to taste a dessert made with pecans and caramel. I had some, too, and it brightened up my day. What Jess conjured with sweets was mood elevating. Perhaps she should supply inpatient units, which would decrease the need for antidepressants and mood stabilizers. Fine, people would put on weight, but what if hospitals built gyms and told patients that they would be required to exercise to have Jess's desserts? Clearly, having these thoughts while eating the sweets was distorting my thinking. Jess was a great pastry chef.

"Nate's parents drove up for Thanksgiving," Tony explained, "and he had a meal with them in a restaurant. The next day he calls me to say he's going back home with them. He wants 'balance in his life,' and he 'wants to figure things out.' No notice," Tony said. "He just quit. So now I'm down a cook. Again. Welcome to the business!"

"What's Nate going to do?" I asked.

"No idea," said Tony. "For now he's living at home. Look, he's young, he's only twenty-two, and maybe working in a restaurant isn't for him."

Patrick came by from garde manger with a spoon of pâté.

"Too salty," said Tony grimly. "I'll need to work on this with you."

WHEN I CAME IN THE NEXT DAY, JILL WAS AT THE STOVE PREPARING STAFF meal with Tse, who was a new cook in garde manger. She was using whatever meat and vegetables she could find to make stew in a big pot. Then she would boil white rice and put together a salad.

"You're just making it up as you go along," I said.

"You got that right," she said.

Marian was scrubbing down surfaces and singing: "Ninety-nine problems and a bitch ain't one of them."

Jill chopped scallions and threw them into the stew pot. I took a few scraps of meat that had fallen out and put them back in.

"When can we talk?" I asked Jill. I lowered my voice to a whisper. "You said that this was the craziest kitchen you've ever worked in. I want to find out what you mean."

"I don't know," she whispered back.

She chopped up some spices, threw them into the pot, and stirred.

"Lemme ask you something," Jill said. "Have you seen the Paul Liebrandt documentary?"

Chef Paul Liebrandt, the chef at Corton, in Tribeca, was regarded by critics and chefs as wildly innovative, creating a cuisine never before seen. I had eaten at Corton some months back and enjoyed the food immensely.

Finished with the stew, having added some bits of sweetbread to it, Jill started to shell steamed mussels. She removed each mussel, shoved it to a side of her cutting board, and put the shells in a corner of the board.

Suddenly Tony was at her side.

"Don't put the shells on the board!" he shouted. "Find a container!"

She nodded. I found her a container.

"It's my fault, Tony," I said. "I was distracting her by asking her questions."

"Fucking Scott," Tony said, and walked away.

I could not tell if he was angry, and thought to apologize further, but then I realized that not being able to read his mood was more interesting than the mood itself.

"You gotta see that movie," said Jill, as she shucked more mussels. "I mean, here's this chef working insane hours in his restaurant, totally consumed by what he's doing, and his personal life is a shambles."

"Do you think that's necessary?" I asked Jill. "To be a great chef, you can't have a life?"

"Yes," Jill said.

Then she let out a deep sigh.

"What time is it?" she asked.

There were no clocks in the kitchen; none of the cooks wore watches or carried cell phones when working. Only Tony knew what time it was.

"Two twenty-one," I said, looking at my iPhone.

Staff meal: two thirty.

Jill and I carried pots and pans to the Hobart.

"I'm the youngest kid in my family," she said, as we loaded the dishwasher, "and my father paid for me to go to Johnson and Wales. I got a scholarship the first two years that cut the tuition in half. That helped, but think how much it cost him to pay for the six of us. But let me ask you something: Would you work one hundred hours a week for eight dollars an hour?"

"Is that what it comes out to here?" I asked.

"Pretty much," Jill said. "Plus, four days a week I have to drive an hour and forty-five minutes each way from Providence to get here. I stay at my brother's in Charlestown every Saturday night."

I live about a mile from Craigie. My house had four empty bedrooms on the top floor. I told Jill she could have a room for free for one night a week after the Christmas holidays. She said she would think about it. So far I had discussed with Tony the benefits of a detox for Dakota, planned his family vacation, and offered housing for Jill.

"And of those one hundred hours," Jill continued, "I get stomped on about sixty of them . . . Sometimes I wish I could just turn around when I'm driving. Seriously. I see an exit ramp and I swear I think I'll just get off and go back home."

"So why do it?" I asked.

"I wish I didn't have such an awesome family," she said. "They paid for me to go to college! So I don't have to work here. Which in a weird way makes it harder. I wish I had no choice, that I *had* to do it. Having a choice makes it harder."

Jill felt emotionally obligated to her father, who had paid for her to be a cook. She did not want to let him down. But what about the work was attractive to *her*?

When I asked her about what she enjoyed about cooking, she said it was fun, but the expression on her face was the opposite of someone having fun. She said that being at Craigie made her feel special, that she would not work for just anyone, and that Tony had taught her a lot.

"I don't want to do catering," Jill said, "and I've been a private chef. I worked for a family in Providence my first three years of college. I babysat for them, too!"

Carlos, another new cook, interrupted our conversation. He had a steady gaze, a short haircut, and a wide, open face. He just appeared at our side, wordlessly, with a big smile.

Then he handed me a spoon that he dipped into a small bowl of orange liquid, which he explained was tangerine-habanero sauce. He stood and waited while I tasted. The sauce was sweet and hot, so deeply flavorful that I could not resist taking a couple more spoonfuls.

Carlos nodded happily.

"Staff meal!" shouted Matt.

Jill grabbed a bowl, filled it with rice, and topped that with the stew. The other cooks had gathered in the bar area and were eating together. It was freezing, the first week in December, but Jill, dressed only in cook's whites, ate alone and outside.

I watched her leave.

When Jill returned about ten minutes later, I helped her carry a couple of containers downstairs to the walk-in. They contained golden raisins in muscat and pine nuts, which would become a sauce for the fish. Then we set about making the sandwiches that were served with the pumpkin soup. Jill put plastic wrap on a work-table and placed eight slices of huge Pullman bread onto the plastic. After spreading lots of butter on each slice, she pressed on massive amounts of grated Comte and cheddar cheese. We cut each slice in half. Jill stacked the bread in a plastic container. She placed a paper towel between the two layers. Then she disappeared.

I went back upstairs just as Karolyn came in with Charlie.

"Jamaica," Karolyn said to me.

"Should be lovely," I said.

"I'd go to Cleveland," Karolyn said. "I just want to be with my husband and have him relax." She definitely knew what she was getting into when she fell in love with a man who was passionate about what he does. She knew that she'd never live more than one mile from the restaurant and that they would spend long hours away from each other. She once said to me during a visit, "I know it sounds cheesy, but Tony has more integrity than anyone I know."

BEFORE I RETURNED TO THE RESTAURANT A FEW DAYS LATER, I DOWN-loaded the documentary that Jill had insisted I see: *A Matter of Taste: Serving Up Paul Liebrandt*. Early in the movie, a quote from Thomas Keller about Liebrandt's cooking caught my attention, as it applied to Tony's cooking as well.

"You don't know if his interpretation of a dish is a good one or a bad one," Keller said, "because you've never had it."

If something tasted good, the dish was a success, but the extremely personal style of Liebrandt, and Tony, made the chef more important than a culinary tradition.

In the movie, Chef Liebrandt spoke of having a lonely childhood in England, noted that his parents divorced when he was very young, described being sent away to boarding school where meals were disastrous, and said that there was no food culture in his family. The accumulation of these experiences, so utterly different from the narratives of the great French and Italian chefs, who had told me of being raised on farms or by parents with knowledge and passion about gastronomy, helped me understand why Tony and Liebrandt had created their own cuisines. Neither man had an obligation to, or feeling based on experience of, the past. They were inventing inside a gastronomical vacuum.

"This is my place, the kitchen, being here," Chef Liebrandt says in the film.

It was a place where he found meaning, as outside the restaurant, challenges for Liebrandt had fewer resolutions. In the kitchen, how he acted led to predictable results. No wonder chefs got enraged when things went wrong: So many of the feelings typically developed in relationships were displaced onto their cooking because only here could they control the outcome of the emotional tie.

"In this business it's hard to form relationships," Liebrandt says in the movie. "I have no family in this country. I don't have any friends because I work so much."

The movie shows Liebrandt's devotion, his fascination with the work, and his blind rage when his staff lets him down. In one scary sequence, he chastises two young cooks who look like boys: "If you ever bring me a dish like that again, I'll put your heads through that fucking wall."

Later, one of the cooks, looking sheepish, says: "My work life is going really well, but the rest of my life? Not so well."

The poignancy of the cook's predicament is not lost on the viewer: The cook is trapped between trying to withstand the hostility of the chef and pursuing a life filled with even greater uncertainties. That the hostility is at least reliable is the hallmark of a dysfunctional family.

For all the discomfort Tony's crew expressed at being bossed around by him, they embraced his order. Without him, they had to make personal choices, take responsibility, and commit to independent decisions. By placing themselves in a structure where they were told what to do and when to do it, they took on less risk. In a strange way, this was liberating: If you don't know who you are or what you can do, there are few better places to find out than in a restaurant kitchen or in the military. You wear a uniform, you follow orders, and how you feel does not matter to the person in charge. Being in the weeds while in the restaurant was nothing compared to being in the weeds in real life.

Returning to Craigie, I ran over to Jill. She still had not found a time to tell me why she felt that Craigie was the craziest place she had ever worked. "Why did you love the Liebrandt movie?" I asked her.

Jill put off telling me her reasons until we were together at staff meal. "Okay," said Jill, "the reasons I loved it? Number one: The food looked so fucking cool. Number two: Liebrandt looked like a fucking psycho. He had these crazy eyes. You can just tell there's something different about the guy. The best part of the movie was the last still frame, after he gets the two Michelin stars. He's in a tux, he's smiling, he's got that smirk, right? I mean, what the fuck was that? It was, like, what's he thinking? Did he even know?"

With that, she got up, grabbed her plate, and ran back into the kitchen.

"I'm so in the weeds," she said.

III.

FAMILIES

SEVENTEEN

Family Holidays

IT WAS A SATURDAY IN DECEMBER, AND THE PACE WAS FASTER THAN ever.

"Hey, come here," Tony said to me. He was ringside. "Check this out," he said.

He showed me the results of the 2011–12 Zagat survey in the Boston Business Journal. Craigie was number three. The only restaurants ahead of it were Abe and Louie's (number two), which is a steak house that is part of a large restaurant group, and Legal Sea Foods (number one), which has several locations.

"We're ahead of Barbara, Ken, Michael, Jody, and Frank," Tony said. He was grinning, and immediately I thought of the Gore Vidal quote: "It is not enough to succeed. Others must fail." Tony was naming chefs Lynch, Oringer, Schlow, Adams, and McClelland.

"Congratulations!" I said. "That's great news!"

He was in a great mood not just because of the survey results. His cooks were working with greater cohesion lately.

There was less screaming in the kitchen.

New inspirational signs had been taped above the workstations by the crew:

Where's the place, big baby?

REDEMPTION!!

KEEP KLEAR!

It came down to changes created by Matt as the new sous chef, and Marian, who was emerging as a likely sous, too. Tony had greater confidence in them.

However, not everything was peaches and cream.

Conflicts in the front of the house at Craigie had escalated in the past few weeks since Tony had instituted his new system in which bartenders shared tips with servers.

That afternoon I wandered into a tense meeting.

"There is not enough delegation of tasks between server and back server," said Carl. He looked like a young attorney: small, fine hands, a voice that suggested familiarity with power, and the propriety of a golfer. He looked a little like Dick Cavett in his heyday. Carl was chairing the meeting of more than a dozen servers, back waitstaff, and bartenders. Tony sat in, listening. "To me it should be instinctive."

A few people nodded their heads.

"Richard, no offense," said Carl, "but you had fuck-all to do, and you should have paid more attention to everyone in your section. It's my fault, though; I should have been on it. The thing is? I'm glad you sold the dessert wine, but your other five tables suffered."

Sean, a server sitting to my right, garbed in a wool cap, with a grizzled beard, wearing Persol eyeglasses, was getting angrier. He glared at Carl.

The atmosphere was getting ugly, and more barbs were exchanged. People belittled one another and spoke with sarcasm.

"There's a missing element in the culture at Craigie on Main," Tony said. He had not spoken until then. "Either I'm not hiring correctly or people have attitude problems. Clearly we need to do a better job of giving you the tools to do the job." He paused. As the only person in the restaurant who worked front of the house and in the kitchen, Tony had more knowledge than anyone else in the room.

"People have to work better as teams," Tony said. "We've been through this; I was unwavering. If you cannot act accordingly, I'll have to make very tough decisions about people." No one said anything, and movement was minimal. Tony had become furious. It was obvious that the staff was acting out their disgruntlement over the new wage program by not cooperating with one another.

"We have had the most discussions about this and related subjects in the past month," Tony said. "Will I allow this to continue? Will we have an antagonistic atmosphere here at Craigie on Main? Absolutely no way. I'd rather start from scratch. We need a system that relies on communication, growth, and education. That's not happening right now."

Tony's comments shifted the discussion. The more cooperative and positive-thinking individuals now felt comfortable enough to speak up because Tony supported their position.

Katie, one of the servers, went on at length about the need for commitment. Short brown hair, a ready smile, always on the go. The kind of person who looked like she would raise her hand to tell the teacher that he had forgotten to assign the homework. Tony grabbed my notepad and pen and wrote: *She's fucking the best!*

Bunny added to what Katie had said.

"You have to memorize flash cards," Bunny said. "You have to be accountable. You have to run the cheese plate you're terrified to do. You have to mess up the script and then be able to nail it."

Tony chimed in.

"We ran an ad this year," Tony said. He was beginning to calm down. "And it read, *Prima donnas need not apply*. That stands. I don't want to hear people say 'I can't' or 'It's not my table' any longer. That kind of attitude is not conducive to what this place is about. The water cooler shit has to stop. You might think people can't hear what you're saying, but they can. You can't be bitching, you can't trash-talk other people. It doesn't work that way. From now on, I'm calling for a zero-tolerance policy. I don't care if there are one hundred and forty covers on the books, I'll send someone home. I'm counting instead on continued positivity from people."

It was the kind of leadership that I felt could have been there from the start. Although Tony did not acknowledge his part in the trash talking, it was clear that if he kept his anger in check, behaved compassionately, and was genuinely paternal, his staff would grow with him.

Just as he finished addressing his crew, Tony's phone rang. It was his mechanic. Jill's car had broken down earlier that day. She had phoned Tony and he had arranged to have it towed to the garage where he had his car repaired.

A WEEK BEFORE CHRISTMAS, I ASKED TONY IF I COULD FEED THE STAFF. I could not accomplish what they performed at tables and over stoves, but each cook was responsible for a staff meal regularly, and this was my effort to fit in and be one of them, as well as a way to thank everyone for allowing me to be part of their lives.

"Awesome," said Tony.

I dithered between buying prepared food and cooking at home. If I bought the meal, I could avoid any personal criticism, but that seemed cowardly. However, if I cooked for the cooks and the chef, I had to face the possibility that they would hate my food. So naturally I decided to do both.

I ordered three trays of pizza from Galleria Umberto, which is a neighborhood place in the North End, with truly the best square

Sicilian slices I have ever tasted, served up by Ralph and Paul Deuterio from eleven A.M. until they run out, six days a week. Lines are out the door.

I also bought an enormous bone-in pork butt. I had cooked this cut of meat many times before, usually turning it into North Carolina pulled pork sandwiches, inspired by my fantasy of having had an African American grandmother in whose steamy kitchen I had learned the craft. I decided against that method this time. Tony had worked the line at East Coast Grill, where the kitchen had churned out unbelievably delicious pulled pork sandwiches, and I felt certain that my version would fall enormously short of his.

Instead, I came up with a surefire Italian American preparation, inspired by my fantasy of having had an Italian American *nonna* in whose steamy kitchen I had learned the craft.

I seared the butt on all sides in a smidge of oil in a large pot over high heat to give it a crust, then added a ton of salt and freshly cracked black pepper. Then I threw in a few chopped onions, a head of unpeeled garlic cut in half, and two chopped celery stalks. Next I added about a cup of cider vinegar, two cups of homemade chicken stock, and a small can of tomato paste that I smeared on the flesh. More salt, more pepper, enough water to submerge the meat, and then I covered the pot with a lid and placed it in the oven at two hundred degrees for a nine-hour braise, turning the meat periodically.

When I got to the restaurant two days before Christmas, as planned, I walked over to Marjorie, who was at the pass. I put down the pizza and the pot of pork and said hello.

"He'll say the pork needs more salt," I said to her.

She laughed.

"Oh, no, he won't," Marjorie said. "That's not the way he was raised!"

Matt came over.

"What's in this?" Matt asked. He looked inside the pot.

"Nice," he said. "Really nice."

He poked the meat with his fingers. Cooks cannot just look at food, they have to touch it.

"I'll put foil on it," Matt said, "and flash it for about half an hour. We'll get the fat crispy that way."

It was about an hour before the staff meal would be served, and meetings were de rigueur. Many meetings were taking place all over the restaurant. Planning, finishing touches, efforts toward refinement. Nothing was ever finished.

"What if a guest is waiting for his drink and the bartender is in the weeds?" asked Carl. He was meeting with the other GMs and Ted. "The next line of defense, if you will, will be for someone to get the guest water, attend to them, go to their table."

Bunny walked by all dolled up.

"I love Christmas!" Bunny said.

Tony turned a corner with a big box of presents for staff.

"Got to take care of the people!" Tony said. "Got to take care of the people!"

Tony went into the bar area to arrange a gift table.

Marian came up to me with a long tray of pink pork filets. Each piece had a thick ribbon of white fat.

"You should try the fat," she said. "It's so sweet, even raw."

I tasted. It just soared.

For the past five or six months, I preferred being in the restaurant long before it opened. With guests or customers, staff acted out roles.

When Tony came back to the pass, he looked at the stack of pizza boxes.

"Get those open," Tony said. "Let's eat!"

I cut the peppermint-striped strings, opened the boxes, and lifted the foil.

Matt returned with the pot containing the pork butt.

"This looks great," Tony said, "and I'm not being critical, but an easier way to do this would be to braise it, let it cool, slice it, and then go back to braising. It's easier to slice the meat when it's cold."

"Jill," he said, "cutting board."

"On it, Chef," she said.

Tony placed the meat on the board and within seconds cut it into thick, perfect slices. Then he took a few small pieces between his fingers, dunked them into the sauce, and thought about what he was eating.

"You should be proud," Tony said, after a moment that seemed for me to last an hour. He quizzed me how I had prepared it and about every single ingredient used. "It came out fucking awesome."

"Thanks," I said.

Hearing that, I knew how the cooks felt all the time: validated. It was not that I was a good person, but that my food was good, which felt even better. The chef approved of my food!

After grabbing a slice and filling a bowl, Tony shouted to the cooks: "Everyone stop what they're doing and get over to the bar area! Christmas!"

It was time for their gift exchange, which they called "Secret Santos"; they swapped grill gloves, videos of famous chefs, and bottles of whiskey, beer, and tequila.

About an hour later, when the cooks returned to their stations, the lights dimmed, candles were lit in the dining room, and Marian asked Ted to change the music back to what the cooks *really* loved: Dre, followed by Snoop. Servers and cooks started to sing and dance to the music.

Marian took a small aluminum tray of fish to her station.

"Back in the spring, before you were here," I said to her, "Tony was the only one allowed to cut the fish."

"That hasn't changed; Chef has his reasons," she said.

Drew unlocked the front door, and the first people on line started to come in, their faces expectant.

Matt was in charge, at the pass, and I marveled at how much he had grown professionally. Just about a year ago, he was downstairs working in prep, unable to pull small bones properly from fish. Tonight he was running the show. No wonder he had stuck around, through the hard days and nights, the criticism: All along he had believed in his potential.

"You look poker-faced," Bunny said to him.

"Yeah, well you know I used to be at Foxwoods three days a week playing poker," he said.

"I know," Bunny said.

She laughed.

"But then," Bunny said, "you found your true passion was working ninety hours a week cooking!"

EIGHTEEN

Bite the Big Apple

FROM THE BEGINNING, WHEN I STARTED WRITING ABOUT CRAIGIE, I HAD in mind a trip to Manhattan with Tony to meet with several of the city's chefs and owners whom I had known for many years and whose work set the national standard for the restaurant industry. Not just to compare, but to try to understand better the different narratives needed to create original restaurants, and how Tony's story fit in with what others were doing at the top.

Tony loved the idea when I proposed it, but problems arose when it came to fixing a date. "I can't commit to a time," said Tony in early December. "When did you want to go?"

"End of January," I said. "Third week. We could go down on Monday when Craigie is closed, and stay through Wednesday."

"Let's talk when we get closer to the date," he said. "Problem is my birthday is at the end of January and Karolyn might want to take me away for a night." He paused. "Though maybe we could combine my birthday with a trip to New York."

"You tell me," I said.

Tony and I had many conversations through December, but each time he was uncertain. This worried me since I knew that the New York people had schedules at least as demanding as his. Finally, just before Christmas, I e-mailed my contacts. Within two days, I had commitments from Dave Pasternack, chef at Esca; Andrew Carmellini, chef at Locanda Verde and The Dutch; Daniel Boulud; Daniel Humm, chef at 11 Madison; Drew Nieporent, owner of Nobu and Corton; and Thomas Keller.

I decided not to bring this up when I dropped by Craigie on December 31 to wish Tony well and hear him rhapsodize about his New Year's menu. Marjorie was tweeting and adding content to the restaurant's website while Karolyn and Charlie played with colorful beads set on each table.

There were two sold-out seatings. Both had the same two courses, which included an appetizer with a choice of citrus-cured *hiramasa* with oyster aioli and sturgeon roe, and an entrée with a choice between house-cured ham and crab broth or house-made squid ink spaghetti. The second seating had a third and fourth course that offered guests either house-made cotechino on lentils or crispy goose confit, followed by either an *assiette* of veal—loin, sweetbreads, tongue, and cheeks—or slow-roasted halibut.

"It's a sick menu. Sick, sick, sick!" Tony said.

Later that night, Karolyn worked beside Tony, pairing wines with the various courses, while Marjorie stayed with Charlie.

IN EARLY JANUARY, TONY ASKED, "WHEN DO YOU WANT TO GO TO NEW York?"

"I've already arranged it," I said.

He was ringside, as usual, jotting down notes for the night's menu, returning calls, tasting dollops of sauces, texting, and answering e-mails. Committing to anything outside the restaurant was contrary to his way of thinking. I understood, outside Karolyn, Charlie, and his parents: *This* was his world.

Still, he looked sad and disappointed.

"I thought you wanted me to come with you," Tony said softly.

"I do," I said, "but you couldn't commit. The New York people are prima donnas just like you. I had to get them to schedule this before it was too late."

"You still want me to come?" he asked.

He stopped what he was doing.

"Of course," I said.

"Then send me the schedule, and I'll come to all the meetings that I'm able to attend," he said.

Tony plugged into the two Monday interviews: Dave Pasternack and Andrew Carmellini.

All set, I thought, but I had forgotten what people like Tony and me are like around food. Eating, anticipated as well as experienced, takes on unreasonable depths of meaning. Thinking about where to eat was augmented, too, by the fact that Tony simply was never away from Craigie very much, and I have favorite spots in New York where I eat regularly.

I made several reservations only to cancel them because Tony was not interested: *not gutsy enough*. I prefer fish and vegetables, Italian, Japanese or French, but Tony sent me links to dumpling places in Chinatown, a gastropub in Brooklyn, and a noodle shop in the East Village: *too gutsy*. This went on for more than a week. We exchanged more than a dozen e-mails about where to eat lunch. Finally, I realized that we would be better off simply meeting at Esca. I went to Sushi Yasuda, my favorite sushi bar in Manhattan, and Tony went to ABC Kitchen.

I loved my lunch. Tony told me he sent back his entrée.

▪ ▪ ▪

WHEN I ARRIVED AT ESCA, TONY WAS SEATED AT THE BAR, IN A SWEATER and wearing a tie, checking voice mail and e-mail. He looked like a college kid on a job interview, unaccustomed to dressing up. He handed me a copy of *New York* magazine opened to a page with a paragraph on Esca in a list of New York City's 101 best restaurants.

"Have a look," Tony said.

Adam Platt, the reviewer, wrote that Esca (number fifty-seven) was not as good as it had once been because Dave Pasternack was spending more time running the fish and shellfish section at Eataly.

"I think that's silly, Tony," I said. "I come here at least six times a year and it's always great."

"Just saying," said Tony.

"I don't think Dave would leave Esca to work at Eataly if he thought it would compromise what he does here."

"Maybe," said Tony.

Tony did not believe that chefs were capable of running more than one place without the quality declining as a result. I did not want to get into this with him again since it never wound up being a discussion. In any event, Dave Pasternack emerged from the kitchen, mopping his hands on his apron, coming toward us quickly.

"Hey, how's it goin'?" said Dave.

He is burly, unshaven, cultivating a vox populi look, with a gorgeous voice that is shaped by Long Island. He looks and sounds like a fisherman.

"Good, Dave, thanks for making the time," I said.

"So, what's this all about?" he asked. "What are you doing with Daniel and Andrew?"

I told him again about the book.

"Basically," I said, "I want to find out who in their right mind would be a chef and work these long hours."

"You wanna know what it's like to be a chef?" Dave asked rhetorically. He pretended that his right hand was a gun and then pulled his index finger like a trigger. "Every fucking day I feel like blowing my fucking brains out!"

"Every day?" I asked.

"Okay, not every day," he said.

He reached down to adjust the crotch of his trousers, which was a tic he continued doing throughout our conversation.

"How long have you been working in restaurants?" I asked him.

"Thirty years," Dave said. "I'm forty-seven."

"Are you here every day?" I asked.

"It's a full-time job," he said. "I'm here five days a week. At this point, I've earned that right—I make time, always take a day off during the week. I take Sunday off. I take time off for special family events. I've come to the conclusion that I need to hire more qualified people so that I can get away from time to time."

He and Tony talked about a purveyor they had in common.

"Yeah," said Dave, "I get fish from Rod over at Browne Trading, too, but I also get product from other sources."

We were seated at the tiny bar near the kitchen. Customers drifted by us on the way to the restrooms in the back.

"We always get our fish early," said Dave. "I have my own truck for Esca."

The restaurant was moving at full tilt despite its being three in the afternoon.

"I can feel your intensity," I said to Dave, "but how do you get staff to feel it? To be motivated."

"I've got to inspire them," said Dave. "With product, passion, tenacity, and intuition."

"What if you see someone who's not getting it?" I asked.

Dave made the sign of an umpire calling an out.

"Next!" said Dave.

"What if you *want* that person to work out?" I asked. "How do you express yourself to them?"

"I take them to my other office," said Dave. "The walk-in."

He hunched his shoulders and leaned in, gangsterlike, something out of a movie.

"We have a conversation," Dave said. "'Look, you're not focused. You're distracted. Your station needs to be cleaner.' Whatever," he said. "I'll give you a perfect example: The New York City Health Department just made a big change. If you log the food that's out, you can have it out for four hours. Used to be they'd come by and we'd have to throw shit away. Now if you log it when you first put it out, and they come by to inspect you, you're good as long as it's within four hours. So if I have someone who forgot to log it, and they come by? That person just fucked up. You fuck up and you're gonna face the wrath of fucking up."

"How easy is it to find new people?" asked Tony.

"At the entry level I have two or three new guys every now and then," said Dave. "I rotate. Promote from within. Once in a while you get screwed."

"Are they all Americans?" asked Tony.

"Ninety-nine percent Americans," said Dave, "and one Haitian kid, but he grew up here and he's as American as the rest of my crew."

Dave talked like someone who grew up in the business. In a way, he did: His grandmother and her brother owned a family-style restaurant in Coney Island. "They served poor people's food: balls, hearts, lungs. Plenty of fat. It went out of style, but it's popular now."

In many ways, the food he was describing was what Tony refined and served at Craigie.

"Do you see a difference between the cooks now, kids in their twenties," Tony asked, "and ten years ago?"

"Ten years ago, we had guys who wanted to work because one

day they wanted their own place," Dave said. He reached down and yanked up. "To make a name for themselves. These days a lot of my cooks still live at home. Their mother and father still support them."

"How about as a generation?" asked Tony.

"Tremendous distractions," said Dave.

"Cells? Texting?" asked Tony.

"Exactly," said Dave. "I have a no-tolerance policy."

Tony agreed with him. Ironic, I thought, given his e-mailing and texting constantly.

"So then you have to get new people," Tony said.

"Right," said Dave. He laughed and shook his head in wonder. "I run an ad, I get a hundred resumes. Twenty people make appointments and I'm lucky if three show up," Dave said.

"Same with me," said Tony.

"So who makes it and who doesn't?" I asked.

"There's an advantage to hiring younger kids," said Dave. "I'll put people in garde manger and I can see it in their faces."

"See what?" I asked.

"Some of them? They can smell it like an animal. They want to be promoted. They'll work hard to get to that next level. They can smell that fucking piece of meat."

We sipped our glasses of water.

"How did your father discipline you as a child?" I asked Dave.

"I got 'punched' as a kid," Dave said with a big laugh. He was exaggerating, and referring back to old-school parenting: not how do you feel, but do what you're told. "Can't do that here. So, yeah, it's hard to discipline people. Next thing you know they're calling 1-800-LAWYERS. Look, in the past I'd go ballistic when someone's fucking up. Now? Now I try to stay levelheaded. Takes the fun out of it."

Tony and I laughed.

"So when you're really upset and can't express it?" I asked. "How do you feel then?"

"Lemme tell you a story," Dave said. "Christmas morning this past year, my wife hands me an envelope. 'What?' I ask her. 'You're giving me money?' 'Just open it,' she says. So I open it and it's our mortgage statement: zero, zero, zero. She paid off the mortgage! When I get pissed off, I think about that."

"Right," I said, "but when you're here, and feeling furious and overwhelmed, where is your patience?"

"I developed patience," Dave said.

He stood up and led us to a framed photograph in the back dining room that showed him and his father smiling and holding an enormous fish.

"This was my pride and joy this past summer," Dave said.

The caption read, *Mel and Dave P. 7/4/11. 51 lbs/49 inches. On the Debra.*

"Fishing is my patience," said Dave. "My father and I spend hours and hours together on the boat."

"What do you talk about?" I asked.

Dave laughed.

"Talk? We don't talk," he said. "We fish!"

Dave had literally reframed his relationship to his father. He seemed to have made some peace with that authority. At the very least, an idealized version was on display.

I had intended to walk from Esca, on Forty-third and Ninth, all the way to The Dutch, on Sullivan and Prince, but Tony wanted a second lunch. I had forgotten about the appetite of chefs.

We cabbed to the East Village and grabbed stools at Momofuku Noodle Bar. Late afternoon, pouring rain, the place was empty. Staff had the chill indifference and cool intensity characteristic of servers at Ko. They acted as if they were doing us a huge favor by serving us, and for some reason I still can't quite fathom, this was appealing. It was not like dining out, it was like dropping in at a brilliant, quirky friend's house. The only thing missing at Chang's establishments were video games to play while eating.

I had never been, but Tony was at home. He ordered pork buns for us, and we each ordered noodle dishes, and soon the food vanished.

"Screaming with flavor," I said.

"I know, right?" Tony said.

By the time we reached The Dutch, the two lunches we had enjoyed slowed our pace, but we were still in the game. Even with a full belly, Tony has far more energy than most. I was doing all I could to maintain his pace.

I had met Andrew Carmellini in November 2003 in Tokyo, on a junket led by Daniel Boulud and organized by The James Beard Foundation.

Daniel Boulud had been invited, a few weeks after *Lost in Translation* opened, to put on a few dinners at Park Hyatt Tokyo, which was where the movie had taken place. Daniel, in turn, invited me and two other writers, Adam Sachs and Adam Rapoport (current editor of *Bon Appetit*), to join him. Andrew was Daniel's executive chef at Cafe Boulud back then. Andrew was joined by Rich Torrisi, who worked with him, and Mark Fiorentino, who is still Daniel's head baker. Rich Torrisi now runs two of New York's hottest restaurants: Torrisi Italian Specialties and Parm.

None of us, except Andrew, had been to Japan before, and with Daniel in charge we wound up staying up all night, dozing during the day, and developing very close bonds with one another. One night, around four A.M., after leaving a yakitori restaurant, Andrew had stepped between me and a line cook who was about to punch me out.

The line cook had asked me where I was from, and when I told him cheerfully that I was from New Jersey but had "gotten out," his mood changed so fast it was scary. He went from laughing and joking and being pleasant to pursing his lips, turning red, balling his fists, and stepping to within inches of my face.

"What's wrong with Jersey?" he demanded to know. "My mother still lives there. What are you saying about my mother?"

I explained that I was not talking about his mother and apologized for what I had said.

"No, c'mon," he said, "you said it. You 'got out.' Got out of what?"

I kept backing away from him, but there was no place to go. The guy was wiry, eyes blazing, and committed to a course of action. I could not appeal to him.

Andrew saw what was happening and stepped between us. After he moved the line cook to a safe distance away, Andrew came back to apologize for his line cook.

"What was that about?" I asked Andrew.

"Richie doesn't get out much," Andrew said.

I would not say that Andrew is a calm person, but he has several attributes often associated with being a calm person such that when a situation he is in is chaotic, he does not react emotionally to it. It is not that he is oblivious to what is going on. Far from it. It just does not interest him. Social cues appear to him, I think, almost like notes in sheet music. He can choose to respond to them or not.

That disposition was evident when we met at The Dutch in the private cellar room that looks like a hidden gambling and hooch parlor from Prohibition days.

"I've been on grand jury duty for ten days in a row," Andrew said, after I had introduced him to Tony. "Ten cases a day. We had to watch video surveillance tapes. Rape, murder, mayhem. They don't fuck around."

"Are you stressed out?" I asked.

"Yeah," Andrew said. "The other night my wife's like, 'Let's watch CSI,' and I'm, like, I'm going to bed. On top of grand jury duty, I've got leftover food poisoning from a week in Paris."

He leaned forward. Andrew is tall, lean, and often very quiet. I do not have to draw him out, but he uses words more carefully than most. He seems precise in his thinking, which is consistent with his strong musical interests. Back when he completed parochial school in Cleveland, he chose between going to Berklee School of Music and the Culinary Institute of America, having applied to and been accepted by both schools.

"So being here must be a refuge from what you hear in court," I said.

"It is," Andrew said. "Not always. The business attracts a certain type of person not adjusted to the norms of daily life."

"Right," I said, "that's who they are not, but who are they instead?"

"Usually it's someone who doesn't see themselves on a PTA board in the suburbs," he said. "We have a lot of ADD going on, too. Look, you don't have to be talented. If you can work at Federal Express putting small boxes into big boxes, you can work in a kitchen. It's the physicality of the work that's important. Having a general work ethic, too, whatever that is."

"That may be true for cooks," I said, "but what about chefs? Who becomes a chef?"

"You have to find your cooking voice," Andrew said. "It doesn't happen for some people, but you have to try to find it. It comes from food you experience while traveling, from your family, and from training experiences."

"If you're twenty-two years old," said Tony, "and I'm not trying to sound like an old man, but expectations are different now from when we started out."

"It's true," said Andrew. "There's been a shift culturally in the world of the professional chef. I would have to say that there's been a whirlwind of interest in the profession. A lot of people are getting into the business having no idea what it is. White-collar kid families, kids who never worked in high school."

"It's a huge slap to one's ego and pocketbook," Andrew said. "Imagine being that white-collar kid making ten dollars an hour and watching a kid from Guadalajara who can do the work a lot faster than you!"

"No one tells them what it's like," said Tony.

"I paid for my school myself," said Andrew. "My dad was in the marble terrazzo business. The family was salt of the earth from Friuli. Hardworking family guys. They owned a business in south Cleveland."

"So what's your advice to someone starting out?" I asked.

"First thing," said Andrew, "get a job. Work at Applebee's for six months. I don't care what you're doing. Pick up potato skins. Go fucking wash dishes. Make artichoke dip. So you understand what the business is. My cousin, she's from Akron, Ohio, I brought her to New York. She mopped floors. She worked with whiny little bitches. She's here two years. Now she opened her own place. She's not afraid to work hard. It's not how it's portrayed in media."

"I imagine that you have situations then with young cooks who can't keep up with your demands," I said. "How do you deal with your frustration with them?"

"I've changed over the years," Andrew said. "I had an immature chef life before. Now we schedule more time training people so that they get it. Not just me. Sous chefs, chefs de cuisine, we all do the training. There are more people involved."

"And if someone still doesn't get it?" I asked.

"I'll throw people off their station and do it myself," Andrew said. "If I have to. Look, everyone has a bad day. There are a million variables. But the difference between now and when I was younger? There are more teams involved these days."

Andrew is forty-one, a year younger than Tony.

"Yelling and screaming, yelling and screaming," Andrew said. "Chefs and sous chefs? Sometimes that's all they do. There's not a lot of teamwork then. At my places, Locanda and The Dutch? There's not much yelling that goes on."

"Is that because of the teams you've built?" I asked. "That's the trend in medicine, you know. The doctor decides and writes the orders, but it is a team approach to the patient these days. The patient benefits from the observations or insights of everyone on the team."

"Here's how I see it," said Andrew. "If we're doing a lot of yelling, it is a failure on our part because we're not hiring the right people."

"If I had a fifty-seat restaurant, I might feel differently," said Andrew, "but we're busy at two restaurants and I'm opening a third in Miami. On Saturday night? Locanda did a thousand covers."

"Wow," I said.

"I can't be there every day," said Andrew. "That's why I have a team. It also allows for creativity."

"When you walk into Locanda Verde," asked Tony, "how often are you finding something wrong despite the fact that you have a top team in place?"

"Rarely," said Andrew. "My teams are heavily incentivized. I self-funded The Dutch. Look, once you get the second restaurant, it's different, man."

"In building these teams," I asked, "you must choose people who want to cook for you. How do you help them stay disciplined?"

"I help them develop a sense of responsibility," said Andrew.

"There are also emotional and psychological components," said Tony. "I mean, just because someone can cook well and then move up, it doesn't necessarily mean they can lead."

"Right," said Andrew. "And you'd better be passionate about the business. You have to live the business. Being socially awkward, I'm not part of the nine-to-five society. I don't even know what a nine-to-five job is."

"So how do you see yourself?" I asked Andrew.

"I say to my guys: 'I'm Joe Torre and we're gonna build the Yankees. That doesn't happen on Day One.' Restaurant life has kept me out of more trouble than not," said Andrew. "I got into plenty of trouble in high school. Restaurants? They give me a regimented life."

I WALKED BACK TO WHERE I WAS STAYING ON FORTY-SIXTH AND THIRD, AT a friend's apartment, and the long, solitary time gave me the opportunity to think about what was happening. The two chefs Tony had met ran operations on scales vaster than his, and I wondered how it made him feel. I knew he did not like it. Showing me an article in *New York* magazine on Esca's "decline," asking if Andrew noticed problems at Locanda Verde when he was not there. Tony would not acknowledge to me that these chefs might teach him something about decreasing stress and providing good food. He saw expansion as a step that would lead to compromise in the quality of the food and the dining experience.

I saw things differently: I felt that by building teams, establishing layers of trust in people, and delegating authority, a chef could be a facet of a restaurant's success rather than its only reason for being in business.

I recalled a conversation I had had with Tony months ago while on the floor at Craigie.

I had said, "You're lucky to have this place, it gives so much purpose to your life," and he had said, "They're lucky to have *me!*"

It wasn't a good situation, it wasn't a bad situation, it was simply how Tony chose to be a chef, and if he suffered for it, and he did, that was his choice. That suffering served some psychological purpose. It broke my heart. Every restaurant tells a story; this was his. In doing so, Tony illustrated that there is a home for each of us. Craigie was the home he built.

NINETEEN

Stars in Their Eyes

TONY HAD TO RETURN TO BOSTON THE NEXT MORNING TO WORK AT Craigie, and I went to see Daniel Boulud with my friend Sasha, who is a starstruck twenty-six-year-old eager to work in restaurants. I met Daniel sixteen years ago. Every time we get together, I learn something new from him.

"Hold on," Daniel said when he saw me walk in. "I'll be right with you. I'm with a Master!"

We were at his latest venture, Boulud Sud, off Broadway and near Lincoln Center, and Daniel was saying good-bye to Jacques Pepin at the door.

We were seated at the bar, sipping water, and when Daniel returned, he put on a very serious face and said, "Have you eaten?"

A server stood to his right.

"We're all set," I said.

"Have some hummus," Daniel said. "Or baba ghanoush."

"I don't want to get you mad," I said, "but we've eaten. Really."

"Please bring them desserts," he said to the server. "Yes? Okay?"

"Okay," I said. "Thanks."

"So tell me about the book," he said.

Daniel is a dead ringer for Jackie Chan despite being French. He moves and talks rapidly, better at anticipating than most.

"What is the book about?" Daniel asked.

"'Being in the weeds,'" I said.

"*En la merde*," he said, and then more politely he changed it to "*dans le jus*."

Daniel laughed.

"Thomas Keller and me," he said, "we're never in the weeds!"

"Oh, sure," I said.

"No, I'm joking," Daniel said. "The real motivation, the real joy of cooking, it's *when* you're entering the weeds. Then the battle starts. The high concentration, the precision."

His food arrived: a small, simple Greek salad. Our desserts were brought over as well.

"Give the young lady the grapefruit givré," Daniel said, "and give Scott the cassata."

I ate as we talked. Sasha leaned over to me and whispered, "This food is *amazing*!"

"There are clean weeds and dirty weeds," Daniel said. "Clean weeds are when you're in full control, it's exciting, exhilarating, nonstop, you can't take a breather, you're cruising."

He took a bite of the salad.

"And dirty weeds?" I asked.

"You have to redo plates," Daniel said. "A customer goes outside to smoke, but his food is ready to bring to the table. You can't get out of the weeds, there's a rush of people, you're working so fast."

"I understand how you've learned to deal with it," I said. "After all, you've been cooking for forty years."

"Forty-five," he said.

"But how do you motivate the younger cooks?" I asked.

"We teach them the proper way to do things," Daniel said. "We don't compromise on product. We use first-quality equipment in the kitchen. We give them the supervision and support they need. It starts with the chef, but it trickles down. It's all about the structure of my brigade. I have a pyramid of chefs at Restaurant Daniel. Me on top, two corporate chefs, then a chef de cuisine, and six sous chefs with four on and two off. This way I can concentrate on food and administration. Look, the hardest thing in our business is consistency. Educating young chefs: techniques, seasoning. If you can teach your cook consistency—master it—you have accomplished your duty as a mentor."

His iPhone started ringing. He handed it to me. The photo on its surface was of Alix, his daughter, with whom I spent time in Boston when she was a student at Tufts.

"Do you have one of these phones?" Daniel asked me. "How do I turn it off?"

I showed him.

"Thirty years ago, becoming a chef was different," Daniel said. "We weren't super educated. It was a job. You didn't need an education to be a chef. Kids today? Some of them come to me from the Ivy League, they're very smart, they get it."

"So you don't feel, like some chefs I've spoken to, that this generation of cooks lacks commitment?" I asked.

"Not at all," he said. "They made a choice! They are more sophisticated than we were: attentive, focused, consistent. Good people to work with and trust. My early days? You know what I call them?"

Daniel laughed.

"The Bastille days!"

"You talk about your ability to establish a workable structure," I said, "and to mentor others. What in your family background contributed to that?"

"Nothing," he said.

He turned sullen.

"Nothing?" I asked.

"Well, let's say it kept me humble," he said. "Hardworking, passionate about food, passionate about people. You have to remember I was born on a farm."

"Yes," I said. "You see, your family did shape you!"

"Maybe," he said.

Maybe not. He wished it were not true.

Plates were cleared. He insisted that we put orders in for espresso.

"You started as a cook," I said, "but you became a chef. What does a cook need to become a chef, talent aside?"

"Every cook has a chance to be a chef," said Daniel. He spoke rapidly, as usual, the tumble of words barely able to keep up with his thoughts. "How would I define a chef? You have to influence the next generation of cooks, have an impact on the industry, be an imprint in the path of the city and country where you are working, stay motivated, have good motor skills, be intelligent—very important! Be patient and elevate talent, and show loyalty."

Our espressos arrived. Daniel's was in a large cup. He tilted the cup and looked at the server.

"Is this a double espresso?" Daniel asked.

"Yes," said the server.

"Do we have smaller cups here?" he asked calmly. "But large enough for a double espresso?"

"Yes," said the server.

"So next time," Daniel said, "please serve the espresso in a smaller cup. It will stay warmer."

Daniel returned to the topic of loyalty. "Of course," said Daniel. "I have a stable now of two hundred and fifty cooks and chefs. We reward them. We have incentives."

A smaller cup arrived holding a double espresso. The larger cup was removed. A manager came over to tell Daniel that Philip Seymour Hoffman was at the bar and had wanted to say hello, but had had to run.

"He's here something like four times a week," Daniel said. "I'll try to see him next time."

"I wouldn't say that you're calm," I said, "but you don't seem too stressed these days. Not like when we first met."

"We're not the most stressful restaurant group on the planet," Daniel said. "I'm not part of the FY generation."

"The FY generation?" I asked.

His eyes twinkled and he gave me a big smile.

"You don't know what that is?" he said.

"No," I said.

"Hah!" He laughed again. "It's the 'fuck you' generation. The younger generation of chefs."

"Tattoos? Fuck this and fuck that?" I asked.

"Exactly," Daniel said.

"I suppose David Chang epitomizes that," I said.

"Right," he said. He laughed. "Every time I see David he looks more stressed than before."

Daniel mimicked Chang by moving his head side to side, twitching his hands, throwing his shoulders back and forth, and saying, "'Yeah, Daniel, it's fucking crazy these days!'"

We sipped our espressos.

"I ask myself: 'Can it last?'" said Daniel. "This attitude? This punk attitude. Is it sustainable? At the end, you have to be a successful businessman."

Daniel looked at the bottom of his cup and called the server over.

"Do you see these grounds?" he said to her. "There should not be grounds. Is it the machine? Or does the person making the coffee not know how to do it?"

"I'll check," said the server.

"Please," said Daniel.

"I have good people around me," Daniel said, "because every day I worry about something."

"Right," I said, "but you seem to manage your stress well."

"Look," he said, "I don't think cooking should be something you want to quit."

The server returned.

"I adjusted the grind on the machine," she said. "It's working better now."

"Not because she didn't clean it?" he asked.

"No," said the server.

We were finishing up, so talk turned to our daughters. Alix was in Singapore working for an investment fund; my daughter was in Brooklyn working as a consultant at Bridgespan.

"Yes," said Daniel, "Alix will probably sign a two-year extension."

"Singapore is too far," I said. "I miss having my daughter in the same city!"

He laughed.

"You have to open a restaurant, Scott," Daniel said. "That way you have a family around you."

NEXT TO DANIEL, THOMAS KELLER IS THE CHEF FROM WHOM I HAVE learned the most about the restaurant business. He is also the most intimidating: towering, speaking quickly with me, and more focused than anyone I have ever met. I always feel as if I have to be on my best game with him, and I imagine those who work for him feel the same way.

Yet for all the seriousness that he conveys, I have always found him to be earthy, an unusually good listener, and a person who brings out the best in those around him.

"Daniel tells me that he's looking for more balance in his life," I said to him.

"Daniel said that?" said Thomas. "He wants more balance in his life?"

He laughed.

"I think he's striving for it," I said. "He also said he doesn't want to be like the FY generation."

"What's the FY generation?" he asked.

I explained. Thomas laughed again.

He was in New York for ten days at Per Se. He went back and forth between Per Se and The French Laundry.

"I know Daniel pretty well," Thomas said. "I'm closer to him than anyone who works for me. The FY generation! Well, you see that. I think it comes from what they see on TV."

"Could be," I said.

"You know, my generation of chefs was the first to be considered celebrities by the media," said Thomas. "Do I seem like a celebrity to you?"

"No," I said. "You seem like a cook."

"Exactly," he said. "The FY generation of chefs is the first generation to act like celebrities."

Cooks were coming and going around Thomas as he spoke to me, but he was not distracted by them. He looked as comfortable as a chauffeur behind the wheel.

"You once told me years ago that your restaurants are your children," I said. "Do you still feel that way?"

"Sure," he said. "Of course. Now more than ever. Look, when you have just one restaurant, you're spending all your time there. Nothing happens there without your knowledge. You're in control. When you have more than one, you have to let go of that control a little bit."

I thought of my son and daughter having left home, and how I worried about them but surrendered to their independence, trying to see things from their point of view, and remembering how I had felt at their age leaving my mother and father.

"How do you do it?" I asked. "Give up that control?"

He paused to sip his coffee.

"You have to gain trust in those around you," Thomas said, "and confidence in those individuals. It's like you've been raised all your life as a chef to be in control and not necessarily trust anyone. That has to change. It takes depth and collaboration. I went from having ninety people at The French Laundry to having another one hundred and ten here at Per Se. So now I have two hundred people working for me."

"That's been good for you? Emotionally?"

"I think you have to be prepared to be the next person," Thomas said. "We grow so much stronger by changing. It's all about trust. I use a sports analogy. I run a sports franchise, right? When I was in the kitchen, I was the franchise player. But I'm fifty-six years old; I can't do what a thirty-year-old does. At some point, you have to prepare the next generation."

"How do you do it?"

"The chef is the manager and the cooks are the players. It's a big responsibility teaching, mentoring, and training the cooks. We give them the best products to work with—you know, you and I have talked about this before; I never ask what things cost. The best things these days are the rarest."

"Still, it doesn't work out for everyone who comes to work for you."

"Of course not. How many people can play pro ball? How many major league teams are there? Not many. It takes true talent. Dexterity, balance. We call it in my kitchens, 'the dance.' When I was on the line, it could be a gut-wrenching evening with the new guy struggling next to me, and I'd ask him: 'Can you really do this?' The next day, he'd be back, full force, and say, 'Yes, Chef, I can do it!' You keep training them."

"Does it ever get emotional?"

"That's not common," he said. He laughed. "I have boring kitchens. It's not good TV."

"Right, but what if you see someone failing and they still want to work for you?"

"I talk to him at the end of the night. I take him aside and ask, 'Is this something you really want to do?'"

"All young people, twenty-three or twenty-four, they want to do something new," he continued. "I was that way, too. 'Give me something new, Chef! Give me something new to do!' But that's not how you become a chef. You become a chef by doing the same thing day after day, night after night."

"Surely you lose patience with cooks who find your outlook challenging for their own developmental reasons," I said. "I mean, they may not get it because, as you said, they're in their twenties and want to do new things each day. So how do you handle your anger?"

"I play golf when I get angry," he said.

"But what about when you're in the restaurant and can't go golfing?"

It was nearly time for Per Se to open its doors for the evening.

"I'm more compassionate now," Thomas said. "What might I do? I might say, 'Get off the line,' and then find another cook to take over. It's the same as being benched in a game. No one wants to get benched! Or I might say, 'If you don't have time now to get it right, when will you have time?'"

"So there's no drama?" I asked.

"I'm not saying I'm unemotional," said Thomas, "but you know what happens when you lose it and scream at a cook? You lose out because later you have to apologize to that person. You have to ask yourself, 'Why'd I say that?' I'll tell you what really kills the kids, if I say to someone, 'You really disappointed me,'" Thomas said. "The last thing you want to do is disappoint your chef."

I RECALLED SEEING AND HEARING THOMAS THE TIME WE HAD BEEN TO-gether before this conversation. He and Daniel Boulud had invited me to hang out in the kitchen at 11 Madison to watch squadrons of cooks—under the aegis of that restaurant's chef, Daniel Humm—prepare a series of courses at a $500-per-person benefit for The Bocuse d'Or USA Foundation. I wrote down what Thomas said that night as it was happening. The cooks were making his version of Dover sole Veronique:

"Do we have all the plates we need?" Thomas said.

"*Oui*, Chef!" the cooks responded.

"Take your time. Take your time. Take your time. No rush!" said Thomas.

As the cooks prepared their stations, Thomas said, "When you're ready, let's go."

Throughout the assembly of the dish, everyone worked methodically, with a clear rhythm, and Thomas said, ten times, over the course of a few minutes, "Everyone take a breath."

Finally, as each plate was completed and carried to the expediting table, Thomas said, in a soothing voice to all the cooks, "The fish is beautiful. Beautiful job. You make us all look good." He then said, ten times, almost as if chanting, "Great job, everybody."

"I'll tell you what's weird," Thomas confided to me now. "I've met cooks who like being yelled at."

I told him about Bobby.

"Weird, huh?" Thomas said.

"So what concrete steps do you take to decrease stress in your kitchens?" I asked.

"I don't stretch it out. I don't require twelve-hour days. You have eight hours, and let's say twelve things to do for service. Get them done and leave."

"Leave?"

"Leave," he said. "I'm committed to efficiency. It can be difficult to get kids out of the kitchen, but I tell them not to worry about getting the job done. Be more efficient at what you do. Work more quickly. That way you have time to do something else."

"Is that what you did when you were starting out?"

"Exactly," Thomas said. "That way I could watch the guy next to me. That way when the chef promoted him and asked who could move up and take *his* place, I was the one who said, 'Yes, Chef! I can do it!' I could do it because I'd been watching and studying him every day for weeks! You promote the guy who knows what he's doing."

I found this line of thought inspiring. I loved how Thomas opposed passivity, and how, as for Daniel, anticipation was fundamental to his personality.

"You have always got to be thinking about tomorrow," Thomas said. "Prepare for the next job!"

"HOW OLD WERE YOU WHEN YOU STARTED COOKING?" I ASKED DANIEL Humm.

Humm was New York's latest top-rated three-star Michelin and four-star *New York Times* chef. He had joined the most elite group of chefs in the city. The only others to have been so recognized were Daniel Boulud, Thomas Keller, Jean-Georges Vongerichten, and Masa Takayama. Humm was twenty years younger than these chefs. His drive intrigued me.

"I started at fourteen," Humm said.

We were walking through the kitchen at 11 Madison. Humm was making certain that his cooks were getting their jobs done.

Before I could respond to what he had just said, Humm said: "My father is an architect."

I found it fascinating that he brought up his father in relationship to a question about when he had started cooking, and decided to store away that fascination until later.

"My father wanted me to go into his profession," he continued.

Humm's mood stayed thoughtful and cheery. We had met several times before, and I had been attracted immediately to his engaging style. He is Swiss, and like my closest friends, who are his compatriots, Humm expressed himself through observations about what went on around him rather than with opinions.

"I had summer internships at architectural firms," Humm said. "I was age eleven."

"What could you do in a firm as an eleven-year-old?" I asked.

We were passing by a huge black-and-white photograph of Miles Davis that faced the pass.

"They took me under their wing," Humm said. "Took me to construction sites. Explained to me how the plans work. But in the offices? Sitting down was the worst nightmare for me. I could not sit down. Also, I didn't want to go to bed growing up."

"Why not?" I asked.

"Because I was afraid I'd miss something," said Humm. "It's the same today."

He has an impish grin, which contrasts with his imposing height.

"Architecture was not for me," said Humm. "But I learned a very important lesson from my dad. You don't have to be a doctor. You don't have to be a lawyer. Just be the best at what you do."

We walked by a long, stainless-steel table where three pastry cooks were assembling very colorful desserts.

"I then decided to work on farms," Humm said. "I grew up outside of Zurich. I loved it. I loved working on the farm."

"But?"

"But my father said, 'You can't be a farmer because we don't have a farm.' So I thought: What do I love about the farm? The products!"

From his love of products, Humm realized that he might learn to transform and refine their essence.

"Slowly, I started falling in love with cooking," Humm said.

"Right, but was it difficult at first to make the commitment to restaurant work? You said you didn't like being confined to an office, but here in this kitchen? No windows. Most kitchens are the same."

"I'm passionate," said Humm. "You have to be. When I first started, there were brutal hours. The pay sucked. I was treated like shit. *Im seich*."

"*Im seich?*"

"In the shit. You say, in the weeds," he said. "All the time. But: Everyone was so passionate about food!"

"I understand the passion, I think," I said, "but passion can be fleeting. Paul Liebrandt talked to me once about the difference between passion and intensity. How did you develop the intensity needed to cook long hours?"

"Maybe something else you should know about me," Humm said. He stopped to watch a pair of cooks making sauces. He nodded approval. "I was on the Swiss National Mountain Bike Team. I raced from age eight until I was nineteen years old. I was one of the best in Switzerland. I trained really hard, four to five hours a day, from age ten. I loved it! I finished in the top ten; I was sponsored early on. But I was never in the top three in the top European events," he said. "I was never on the podium. And then, when I turned eighteen, I crashed. I was out three months."

"I'm so sorry to hear that, Daniel," I said. I paused. "What exactly happened to you?"

In the three years I had known him, I had never seen him look so sad.

Unlike joy, pain is the easiest thing to forget. Why else would people pay thousands of dollars to see shrinks to help them remember pain if they could do it on their own? Cooking trumps psychology. There is a *Joy of Cooking*, but there will never be a *Joy of Psychotherapy*.

"I was going downhill," Humm said, "really fast. Going all out. Anyway, I broke my right shoulder, two ribs. I had a lot of things. Blood everywhere. It took me a long time to come back."

"I'm so sorry."

"*Ja*," said Humm.

Behind us, Will Guidara, Humm's business partner and manager at 11 Madison, was interviewing a job applicant.

"How do you take criticism?" Will asked her.

Humm and I sat down.

"Working in the kitchen," he said, "I loved it. After the crash, I just focused on that. That's what I did. Cooking? Cooking for me is like a sport."

"Thomas Keller said something similar," I said.

"It's an endurance sport," Humm continued. "The way you deal with changes is what makes you a great chef."

"And when your cooks let you down?"

"When I was younger, I would lose it," said Humm. "It doesn't happen anymore. I think when I lost it was the times when it all went over my head. Today I yell, but I first think about it: 'Is this a good time?'"

"So you exercise self-control?"

"Yes," he said.

We got up to walk to the area in the kitchen closest to the dining room. Humm pointed out all the awards that the restaurant had won in the past year.

"I've been working really hard to get to this point," he said. "I run marathons. I'm still riding a mountain bike. I'm training for the Boston Marathon!"

"So you have ways to let go."

"I don't like environments where there's yelling. I'm a pretty mellow person."

He did not look like a mellow person, but I liked the fact that he wanted me to think he was.

"How do you go about creating that environment?" I asked. "With staff, I mean. How do you hire cooks?"

"I choose based on what kind of person they are," Humm said. "Not if they can cook. I don't even read résumés any more. I ask: Do I want to spend three days a week in the kitchen, fifteen hours a day, for years with that person? If the answer is yes, I can teach that person how to cook. The cooking is the easy part by a lot!"

"So it's about personalities?"

"Right."

"How do you build or organize these relationships in your kitchen?"

"I think it's important that you don't take yourself too seriously. Not think of yourself as an artist or craftsman. If you do, I think you miss the point. Cooking is a true team sport."

"Yes, and how do you do that concretely?"

"Every week, I sit down with my sous chefs," Humm said, "and we each create a different dish using the same three components. Then we take them apart, analyze them. It's not a defensive exercise. It's not a competition to see who will win."

"And that works?" I asked.

"My kitchen is truly very collaborative," Humm said. "That way . . ."

"That way?"

"That way I don't need to yell at people," he said.

Kind of Blue was playing through speakers in the kitchen.

"So why, in your opinion, do some chefs get so angry that they always are screaming at their cooks?"

"I don't think it's really anger," Humm said.

"No?"

"No," he said. "I think it's rock star behavior." He laughed. "But I don't think that works in our business. If you feel that way, I think you're in the wrong business. Look, a restaurant? My restaurant? It's like inviting people into your home."

We had strolled over to garde manger. Three cooks were cleaning up rapidly.

"One thing I learned from Danny Meyer," Humm said, "is that the food starts the fire, but then everything else has to follow. The food is less important than the whole dining experience. Danny has truly taught me hospitality." He laughed. "And when you have both great food and excellence in hospitality? Then you kill it!"

"It's not just about you."

"Look," he said, "I don't want to be tied to the stove. You can't micromanage every situation. Anyway, if you try to do that, people will stay two years and leave. They will leave because they can't influence the direction of where the restaurant is going. But if people feel that they are a part of the movement, they're not gonna want to leave."

Now we headed to the back of the kitchen, where an array of pots and pans glinted or were covered in suds. I loved the heat of the washing, the clouds of steam, and the sounds of Spanish.

"Four days," said Daniel, "every January. We brainstorm all our ideas. We honor the past. We take a giant piece of paper and write down the year's accomplishments. For two days, the managers brainstorm the direction we want to go in. We establish our goals. For two more days, the whole team gets together. We break it down and become more specific. Everyone has ideas and we incorporate them. Everyone feels embedded in the organization." Humm had one hundred fifty people working for him, seventy-five of whom were in the back of the house.

We came to the pass. Lunch service was ending, so things were calm. Humm had Leah, a cook, make me the Jack Rose cocktail.

"It's made with liquid nitrogen," Leah said, "and apple brandy."

Pomegranate foam, sorbet, and, best of all, delicious.

"I suppose your father must be proud of you," I said, "after all these years later, all the awards you've won."

"When I decided to begin my career in restaurants, my father didn't speak to me for maybe three years," Humm said. "He felt like cooks don't have a family life. He thought they all drink." He paused. "Too much. That they live above the restaurant in this little closet. *Ja*, that's how it was. There was a part of me that wanted to prove him wrong, for sure. I have a lot of respect for my father. He always held me to very high standards. He had high standards for himself. But I could not help it!"

"Help what?" I asked.

Humm looked at his big hands.

"I didn't like being in an office," he said. "I liked being in a kitchen. And my father just couldn't understand it. It was a long time, I'm talking maybe three years ago, and I've been cooking twenty-two years, to convince him that there was more to what I do than what he thought. It's a real job."

Neither of us spoke for a while. I heard the motors of the refrigerators.

It was a heartbreaking story to have heard up close, and an even sadder one to live through, I knew. I also felt that I understood that the expression of love implicit between father and son could be experienced firsthand in Humm's food.

FROM A SON TO A FATHER, IT WAS TIME TO MEET ONE OF THE MOST PATER-nalistic men in the industry. Drew Nieporent chose to work with two of the world's best, but most difficult chefs in the business: first David Bouley, and now Paul Liebrandt. What was he thinking?

"How you doing, buddy?" Drew said.

We were in the private Skylight Room of Tribeca Grill, which is one of Drew's *other* restaurants. More humble than his other properties, it is where he conducts business, sees friends, and hangs out.

His cell phone was ringing, a GM came back to speak to him, e-mails pinged. Drew chewed gum. He threw his coat onto a bare table and motioned for me to do the same. He is a big, bearded man, always in motion, and his excitement reminded me of guys I saw shooting craps in Vegas.

"Lunch?" he said.

Drew has a mellifluous voice, seductive in tone, and I suppose that it is both natural and related to his having had a mother who performed on the radio.

"My mother was a radio actress," Drew said, after we sat down. We were the only ones in the room. The restaurant itself was packed. "She was very charismatic."

"And your father?"

"My father worked for the New York State Liquor Authority," said Drew. He placed a napkin in his lap. "He was the one who got me interested in restaurants. I grew up in Peter Cooper Village in lower Manhattan, and my dad would take us out to dinner to these great places where he knew all the owners. It was brilliant theater. It was the sixties, so that the chefs were literally just off the boat. We had every possible ethnicity."

A waiter handed us menus. Drew thanked him by name, drawing out every syllable.

"So I was faced with a choice," Drew continued. "I went to Cornell; I thought I was gonna be a chef. I loved cooking, but I also loved the front of the house."

"What helped you decide?"

"Look," he said, "my mother, when she stopped acting? She became a casting director. That's pretty much what I do. I have my parents' genes, my mom's talent. I cast people to cook in and manage my restaurants. My biggest contribution to the industry is the number of people I gave opportunities to. For example, I cast David Bouley for Montrachet. I wanted Daniel Boulud, but he was heavily involved in Le Cirque, and he referred me to David."

Drew glanced at the menu and then continued talking.

"The thing is though that guys like me, restaurateurs?" he said. "We're dinosaurs. The chefs have become restaurateurs the same way that actors became directors."

The waiter came by to take our orders. Drew asked to start with bratwurst to be followed by garganelli. I got the tuna sashimi and the pappardelle. We drank tap water.

"Chefs are more marketable," said Drew.

I wondered if being a dinosaur bothered him, but then I could see that it didn't. He meant that he was the last of a species, and that no one in the future could top a *T. rex*. When giants roamed the earth.

"We have a huge family tree," Drew said, "of all the people who came out of my restaurants. I want you to see it. Hold on."

He called an assistant and asked her to bring me the diagram.

"All of us in the business have family trees," Drew said.

"What is unique about your families?"

"One, fairness," said Drew. "Two, I wanted to create my own Shangri-La. Three, I wanted my restaurants to be genuine and accessible."

The first courses arrived. We ate quickly. The tuna came with two little spools of noodles.

"Nobu, which I opened with Robert De Niro?" said Drew. "We had to make it accessible."

He began to describe the food at Nobu, and as he talked, the flavors came to mind from meals I had enjoyed there. He was rhapsodizing about Japan when a manager came over to our table with a customer in tow. The manager explained that the customer was considering renting the Skylight Room for her daughter's twenty-fifth birthday party.

Drew began to pitch.

"Dina will craft a deal for you, Amy," Drew said. "This is a great place for a party. I have had my kids' birthdays here. And this is the room where De Niro and the Weinsteins cut all their deals."

Some dinosaur, I thought. Like most of the other chefs and restaurateurs I knew, Drew was always hungry.

After the manager and customer left, Drew returned to our conversation.

"I understand your point of view," I said, "but how do you work with chefs who don't share it?"

Drew laughed.

"Paul," he said, referring to Chef Liebrandt, "he doesn't listen to me. But here's the thing: I don't worry about money."

"Oh, come on."

"No, really," he said. "There are no budget reviews. Paul and the other chefs have to self-discipline. How not to waste food. How not to overproduce. People say I'm hard to get along with. I'm not. I've had two chefs here at Tribeca Grill in twenty-two years. I must be doing something right."

"How would you describe your style?"

"I modeled myself on Joe Baum," said Drew.

Joe Baum had been one of New York's greatest restaurateurs. He opened Windows on the World and The Four Seasons, among others.

"You have to actuate your ideas," said Drew. "You have to hire talented people."

"You also opened restaurants in Tribeca back before it was a neighborhood associated with luxury," I said. "I remember when there was nothing here but warehouses."

"It's true," he said. "I helped change the landscape of New York dining. I improved it. Back when we opened Montrachet, it was the middle of no place. And now, twenty-six fucking years later, we're still here with Corton, Tribeca Grill, and Nobu."

Our entrées arrived. They looked to be the same. Drew smiled.

"This is why I have to be here all the time," he said.

We had both been served the pappardelle.

Drew told the waiter that he was fine with it but asked him to check to see that he had not gotten someone else's order by mistake.

"Ah, restaurants," I said, digging in.

"It's a challenge," he said, "but I love it."

"This is no big deal, getting an order wrong. It happens. But what breaks down in the restaurant among staff? What emotional conflicts arise?"

"There are drugs," said Drew. "Bipolar disorder. No frame of reference for problems. Problems."

"How do you handle these problems?"

"I can work with anyone," said Drew. "A-ny-one. I'm Angelo Dundee. Bill Parcells. I'm a coach. A director."

"What happens when you try to coach Paul Liebrandt?"

"He never listens," said Drew again. He laughed in wonder. "He never listens to direction. After three years at Corton, I still think: This guy is intense!"

We were offered desserts, and Drew insisted I take one.

"Carmellini is intense, too," said Drew. "You know, he opened up Locanda Verde in this neighborhood. I've been here over twenty years. He's partners with De Niro. I'm partners with De Niro. Does he say hello? No. So I send a guy over to him with a cake. Welcome to the neighborhood. Let's be friends. I say to the guy: 'Make sure you give it directly to Andrew. Don't give it to anyone else.' The guy comes back, he's given Andrew the cake. I don't hear anything. Then I hear from someone that Andrew is mad at me. Mad at *me*? I invite him here for coffee. You know, maybe he'll apologize, say he's been busy opening the restaurant. He comes in, sits down, looks at me, and says, "Well?"

"He says, 'well?' " I said.

"I can see I'm not getting an apology," Drew continued. "So then he tells me that he's from a different generation than mine. He doesn't have to say hello, he doesn't owe me that, he doesn't owe me anything. We made up, we're friends, but that's how it is."

"I love Andrew," I said, "but he doesn't always respond to social cues."

"Yeah," said Drew, "you don't have to tell me. My son has Asperger's. But no one tells Andrew? No one tells Andrew the right thing to do?"

"Why do you think chefs act that way? With anger or resentment, I mean."

"It's almost as if they're being rewarded for bad behavior," said Drew. "Take Paul. I know he *says* he doesn't get angry any more, but I've seen it. It's like you got married to someone and found out after the ceremony that the person is a wife beater."

"There are a lot of angry chefs."

"Daniel Boulud used to be like that," Drew said. "I worked with him a long time ago. He had been unbelievably mean to a waiter, and I told that waiter, 'Don't take that from him.' Daniel came over to me and said, 'Fuck you!' I said, 'No, fuck *you!*' Then Daniel said, 'No, fuck *you!*' It was crazy. Finally, Daniel apologized and defused the situation."

"You're all older now."

Our lunch was ending, but not before Drew's assistant showed up to hand me his family trees.

It was an eight-page invitation, in folds, for Drew's fiftieth-birthday celebration. On each page was an egg-shaped drawing with the name of one of his restaurants. Emanating from each shape were lines connected to the names of the people who had worked or were still working for Drew.

There were 197 names. After leaving Drew's families, people had gone on to work at Veritas, Jean-Georges, Bond Street, Capital Grille, Aureole, Felidia, The Modern, Aquavit, Masa, Redd, Picholine, Lupa, Gramercy Tavern, Spago, Slanted Door, 11 Madison, and Jardinière. Among those who had worked for him were Kerry Heffernan, Rocco DiSpirito, Don Pintabona, Traci Des Jardins, Richard Reddington, and Masaharu Morimoto.

"I try to treat people the way I want to be treated," said Drew. "We used to call it a bunker mentality. If we dig in, we can get through this together. I want to create work situations where the staff isn't killing themselves to get it right."

ON THE TRAIN RIDE BACK TO BOSTON, WITH THE GORGEOUS CONNECTICUT shoreline shrouded in darkness, I devoured the *massese* pizza I had bought at Eataly: mozzarella, tomato sauce, salami, fresh basil, and olive oil. It was shaped and produced according to the strict rules of the Verace Pizza Napoletana Association. The rules meant, among other things, that each pizza had to be baked in a wood-fired oven at nine hundred degrees, that the dough had to be kneaded by hand, that the tomatoes had to be San Marzano (preferably from Naples or Campania), that each pizza be no larger than eleven inches, and that the baking time be ninety seconds, maximum.

As I ate, I thought of what the people in New York had said to me about their work. I had heard about men and their fathers, men who compared cooking to sports and battle, men who spoke of brigades and bunkers.

The pizza really was spectacularly delicious.

To create that pizza, rules were needed. Rules were needed to make all sorts of food. That was what cooking was about. The rules came from tradition, experience, and the chef. Every kitchen was different. Some were more about rules than others. The best kitchens were the ones where chefs could use rules to make certain that their creativity was expressed consistently in their food.

It is the same as a relationship. You want the people you depend on to be consistent. A chef has a relationship to food, and the cooks who cook it and the servers who serve it, that must be consistent as well. To be consistent in food, as in any relationship, you need rules.

People often come to therapy looking for rules that will make their marriage work, solve problems more reliably, be productive, and get along with others.

To establish rules for consistency in the kitchen, a chef needed a game plan, strategies, an ability to improvise when in the weeds, passion for the work, and a willingness to be a responsible leader.

The authority implicit in being in charge stemmed from the chef's relationship to authority in the home that he or she grew up in. If the chef had an unreliable authority, the matter of trust becomes more complicated. As does the delegation of authority to others.

What struck me about Tony when I first started working with him a year and a half ago, and what was true now, I thought, was his confidence and startling ability to make things new. He was still making up his own rules, and when he had ones he could depend on, night after night, there would be no stopping him.

I knew more than ever why I had chosen to try to understand him, his devotion, and his restaurant family: He was a contender. It was like watching a guy at a gym train for a shot at the title. Few people knew him at the top, but that was where Tony was headed.

IV.

CUT

TWENTY

The Year-End Party

IN THE MIDDLE OF JANUARY, WHEN BUSINESS IS SLOW IN THE RESTAU-
rant industry, Tony holds an annual party to celebrate the year's achievements and look ahead. I was among a handful of people outside Craigie on Main employees to have been invited.

"The cooks trust you," he said, "and that's no small thing. They're not a trusting group of people."

This year the party was being held at Brick and Mortar, which was a new bar in Central Square, opened only a month ago, just down the street from Tony's restaurant. There was no sign to indicate the bar. Tony had introduced it to me a few weeks before, and I loved it immediately. The exposed bricks, darkness, and old soul music gave the place a retro, hipster feel. It felt as if we were on the set of *Hawaii Five-O*.

Each person attending the party received two tickets that could be redeemed for drinks. Servers walked around with trays of snacks.

The room was packed with the Craigie family, but the strange thing was that when people came by to say hello, I did not recognize them. I had to look twice. Without their uniforms, the women with their hair down and wearing more makeup, everyone with more expressive, happy faces, it was as if I was meeting them all for the first time.

Jill looked like a teenager out on a date. Mary's skin tone made her face appear to be made of white porcelain. Ted's posture was a slouch. Chuck kept grinning.

"So, Jill," I said, "tell me, please. Why is this the craziest kitchen you've ever worked in?"

She clutched her drink.

"I can't say," she said. She kept grinning. "I can't!"

"Tell you what," I said, "touch your left ear if the answer is yes, and touch your right eyebrow if the answer is no. Is the kitchen crazy because there are so few rules such that everything has to go through the chef?"

Jill touched her left ear.

"Is it crazy because the rule you followed on Tuesday for a dish might not be the same rule for the same dish on Thursday?"

Jill touched her left ear again.

"Is it because the rules are unique? You are not being asked to follow a tradition," I said. "You're not making a Bolognese or a Mornay sauce."

"It's all of that," Jill said, "but more, much more."

She would not elaborate.

People mingled and laughed and talked volubly for over an hour until Tony, wearing a white shirt and tie, went behind the oval-shaped bar, stood on a crate because of his stature, and shushed the crowd to make his year-end speech.

"Craigie had its best year yet," Tony said. "We made four million in sales. But we're not done yet."

People whooped and applauded.

"There have been a lot of achievements," Tony continued. "Over half of the people in the kitchen have been with us for six months!"

People cheered.

"Twenty-five people are now on the schedule to be in the kitchen," Tony said. "Check averages are now ten dollars higher per person compared to the year before." He paused, put his chin down dramatically, and then looked up again. "There have been some pretty cool things that happened this past year. *The Wall Street Journal* mentioned us. *U.S. Airways In-Flight* magazine named us one of the top fourteen restaurants in the country. We donated eight thousand dollars to Share Our Strength!"

Tony went on to list the year's highlights, and the staff positively glowed. There was a deep, true sense of belonging evident in their faces.

"We won James Beard, Best Chef Northeast," Tony said. After the shouting died down, he added, "We could coast, but we ain't coasting!"

Karolyn and I shared a shot of champagne.

"Craigie on Main," said Tony, "is family, and I really mean that. It is a family. So give it up!"

People shouted, whooped, and applauded more wildly than ever.

"Thanks to Matty O'Foley, Danny Scampoli, and the entire management team," said Tony. "And now some special awards. The wine award for excellence in sales, and for his eloquence and poetic writing . . . Chuck Sullivan!"

People were giddy and proud. There were awards for "most improved in front of the house" and "most improved for back of the house." Jill was named "Family Meal Hero" for the delicious food she cooked for staff.

"We've dealt with allergies," said Tony. "We've cleaned toilets. We make things happen. So here's to 2012!" He waited for the family to quiet down. Then he said, slowly, his voice so low that you had to listen closely, "Every year we write a new chapter."

∎ ∎ ∎

AS MY TIME INSIDE CRAIGIE WAS NEARING THE END, KAROLYN AND I AR-
ranged to meet. I invited her to my home and made us breakfast,
figuring that the intimate setting would make it easier for her to
talk openly about Tony.

"I was wondering when you'd get around to talking to me," she
said breezily.

"I didn't want to intrude," I said.

"You're not intruding!" Karolyn said.

We had fresh-squeezed orange juice, rye toast, Swiss yogurt,
Amish butter, and a pot of Vietnamese coffee. Like the cooks I had
fed before Christmas, Karolyn was grateful to have someone take
care of her for a change.

"Strong coffee," she said after taking a sip. "It has a faint taste of
chocolate." Karolyn has a wide face, and her hair was brushed back
so you could see her forehead. She looked like the kindergarten
teacher she had been: honest, kind, and nothing hidden about her.
The overall effect was calming.

"It seems the perfect combination," I said, "for a chef to be married to a kindergarten teacher. He lives in a world of madness. That
you're grounded must be very important to him."

"Tony is actually surprising," Karolyn said. "He's more prag-
matic than I am."

"You have to be practical when running a restaurant," I said.
"Still, it's not like running a kindergarten class and soothing little
kids, is it?"

"No," she said, and laughed. "Look, I can relate to his madness.
That's why I've always had a restaurant job."

Then she asked *me* a question: "Do people lose their instincts
when the chef is in charge?"

"What do you mean?" I asked.

"Do they ever learn to be in the groove?" she asked. "In the kitchen, on the floor. They don't act independently."

"Some do," I said.

"Sure," Karolyn said. "Danny is a sled dog. Orly is joyful. Matt works hard. There's lots of energy, but not a whole organization."

"That's true," I said. "I've seen it."

"It's a lament," she said, "the same lament since he opened his doors, and I wonder: Why hasn't he solved that problem? It drives him mad. I'm half-joking when I say that there should be a Craigie learning specialist. The staff doesn't know how to organize themselves. We draw in people with learning disabilities and ADD. Millennial employees! A learning specialist would teach them organizational skills."

"So you'd apply classroom techniques in the restaurant," I said.

"Right," she said. "If they don't have the organizational skills, you keep burning through guys and gals," she said. "Why continue doing things the same way? Why not create something in the kitchen that helps them organize?"

"Until that happens," I said, "the situation will continue to be deeply frustrating for Tony."

Karolyn nodded her head in agreement.

"Two different people have said to me after a couple of drinks, these were a server and a cook, that they think there must be a side to Tony they don't usually see in the restaurant," she said.

"What exactly did they say?" I asked.

"'You humanize him. We look at you and Charlie when you're with him. Seeing him with his family makes him more likable,'" she said.

"It's true, when I talk to Tony about his family, he is less intense. We're all like that to some degree, but chefs, I think, have greater intensity than most people. I'm guessing you knew this when you decided to marry a chef."

"I wish I could be in the restaurant about one day a week," Karolyn said. "And we're both well aware of the fact that most restaurant couples don't make it. So we catch ourselves once in a while, saying, 'Wait a minute: Have I told you lately that you're important to me?'"

We peeled back the foil from the little cups of Emmi yogurt. We each ate spoonfuls.

"I think it's easier for Tony than for his cooks and servers," I said. "As the owner, he has total control. He can walk away. He can take a day off. He can go to the gym any time of day."

"That's true," said Karolyn. "Just the other day I needed a break from Charlie. I called him. He came home."

"I saw that, too. Last month he went home each night to light Chanukah candles with Charlie and then came back to the restaurant."

"He did," said Karolyn. "But it's not always easy for us. I do lean on him. I'll say, 'I'm not getting what I need.'"

In the brightly lit kitchen where most of the wall surfaces were glass, there was a transparency to our conversation.

"Tony will say, 'You have no idea what I'm going through,'" she said. "At home he will roll out of bed, go on the computer, get on the phone. I have to say, 'Pay attention to Charlie. Can you spend some time unplugged?' He says, 'No, I can't, I really can't.' I'll ask him: 'Do you notice? Do you care?'"

Karolyn spoke in a matter-of-fact tone, not sad or angry, not resigned or impatient. Loving Tony for his detachment, which, by implication, was an endorsement.

"He gets single-minded. He doesn't see anything else," she said. "Tony will say, 'You don't get it. This is our lives,' and I'll say, 'I want more than a warm body.'" She paused again. "It's lonely. It is lonely."

I cleared the plates, brought them to the sink, and poured more thick, black coffee.

"How is he different at home from the way he acts in the restaurant?" I asked.

"He's awkward or clumsy," she said.

"Oh, come on. I've seen him in action. He moves like an athlete."

"Right," Karolyn said, drinking the last drop of coffee. "He could navigate the restaurant blindfolded, but at home he bumps into stuff."

"Why is that?"

"In the restaurant, as the chef, he always has the right of way," Karolyn said. "At home he doesn't always have the right of way."

TWENTY-ONE

The First Thing You See, The Last Thing You See

ONCE THROUGH THE GLASS DOORS, YOU PASS BY THE SMALL RECEPTION area and face, directly in front of you, an open kitchen. There you see the chef and the cooks behind him.

One hundred twenty-one covers were expected on what I decided would be my last night in the kitchen at Craigie. I would spend six hours beside Tony. Watching him, taking it all in, trying finally to see what it took for him to be a chef.

"I'm not angry," he said with a laugh.

I had told him once again that I thought he was, and that his anger interfered with his achievement and efforts to run the restaurant.

"*You* try getting these guys to cook," he said, gesturing over his shoulder at the cooks. "You've seen what it's like."

"I have," I said, "and I agree. It's frustrating. You're right to *feel* angry. It's how you express that anger that I wonder about. I don't think it's productive to yell at people. It doesn't make them better at their jobs."

He shook his head and wrote on a couple of tickets coming in. He was more animated than I had seen him in a long time, energetic, but focused. I thought of all that I had learned from him over the past eighteen months. Profound concentration was at the top of the list.

Tony clapped his hands.

"Okay," he said to the cooks, "let's do it!"

Doors had just opened. Casually, well-dressed people filed in. A man took a seat ringside and immediately began taking pictures of the cooks with his phone.

Katie, the server Tony had referred to as awesome at the tense staff meeting months ago, came up to the pass.

"Chef," she said, "a deuce wants a tasting with the pig's head as the final course, and the woman has allergies to curry, crab, and vanilla."

"No crab in the house," said Tony. "Curry? A curry allergy? Curry is a spice mix. Can you please find out what spices she's allergic to? Cumin? Coriander? Fennel?"

Katie returned to the guests.

"Coming up, walking a chicken," said Devon.

Devon was a new cook. He had replaced Kyle. Devon had long eyebrows like scimitars. He walked a smooth, perfect line between Matt and Marian to present the bird to Tony for inspection.

"Kyle," Tony said to me, "did not work out. Lots of attitude."

The chicken was flat-out beautiful: golden brown with dark patches, promising to be crisp and juicy, the aroma enough to make you think about it.

The man ringside, eating alone, was staring at the open kitchen where the cooks were now moving rapidly. He stroked his white beard and adjusted his old-fashioned eyeglasses. He sipped champagne from a flute. He mopped sauce from his plate with a slice of bread. He snapped more photos: Showtime!

"Okay, she's not allergic to curry," said Katie, having returned to the pass. "She says it just makes her nose itch."

"Great," said Tony. "So no crab, no vanilla. Those are the real allergies."

Matt began to plate the chicken that Devon had brought over. The teamwork was impressive.

"Move over, ya big lug," Tony said to Matt with affection.

They both laughed.

Tony got a pan of sauce from Patrick. He had moved Patrick from garde manger to saucier this week.

"What's in that sauce?" I asked Tony.

"Toasted garlic, cilantro, dashi, and a little soy," Tony said. "Just a simple little pan sauce."

Tony was handed mussels and Arctic char. He spooned the mussels into large white bowls, placed the char on top, and spooned the golden sauce over them.

"Jill," Tony said, as he was working, "put paprika on your list of things to do tonight."

"Yes, Chef," she said.

"Patrick," Tony said, "tighter on the scallops."

"Tighter on the scallops, Chef," said Patrick.

Matt set out four bowls next to Tony and ladled in soup.

"Mr. Foley," said Tony, "shave truffles on the soup."

Matt got hold of a winter black truffle the size of a Ping-Pong ball and began shaving curls. When he was done shaving, Tony took the truffle, put it to his nose, and then handed it to me.

"Amazing, huh?" Tony said. "*Tuber melanosporum.* I get these from Tennessee. Better than China, better than Oregon!"

It was early in the evening, but the kitchen was moving with consistent rhythm. The planning, anticipation, and preparation were paying off.

Bunny arrived at the pass.

"Eighty-six the burgers," she said.

Two of the by now sold-out burgers arrived at the pass. Tony was going to plate them with bacon on top. He looked unhappy, however.

"Guys," he said to Davey, Marian, and Devon, "you're being cheap on my bacon. I need more bacon."

"After all, you *are* the Prince of Pork!" shouted Davey.

I thought of how watching Tony make the burgers had changed forever the way I cook them at home. I still bought Wagyu-style beef from Snake River Farms in Idaho that Thomas Keller had introduced me to years ago, but now I pan-seared them in Amish butter, put high-end Gruyère on top of the meat under a broiler, and fried bacon from a farm in Kentucky called Father's. I cooked in steps; each product required a different technique. The result tasted so much better than what I had been doing. Tony had taught me how to think like a chef.

Tony posted a ticket: "S2 Ally to Crab/Vanilla, Pig Head Final."

Everything was scripted in the restaurant, whether it was front of the house or in the kitchen, which meant that all you needed to do to be successful was to memorize your lines and say them when prompted. Stay in character. What a relief to be someone else every day, someone with purpose, someone who fed others, someone who served, someone who could, at least for a while, forget their fears and needs.

"Jillian, I want to taste that sauce you're working on," Tony said. "Jillian, I want a veg pasta in the window!"

"Yes, Chef," said Jill.

Tony saw that Patrick was having difficulties, so he walked over to help him out. He stood next to Patrick and began to stir sauces in two small pans.

"I'm showing Patrick how to make sauce," Tony said to me.

Tony squirted juices from squeeze bottles into the pans. He dipped a finger into the boiling sauce and tasted it. He shook the pans. Then he spooned the finished sauce onto pieces of salmon that Patrick had placed in white bowls.

"Does that sauce have a name?" I asked Tony.

"Toasted garlic saffron," Tony said.

"Do you make it the same way each time?" I asked.

"Sometimes I'll add miso or yuzu," he said.

Tony then turned to Jill to help her with some scallops she was searing. When he was sure that she knew what to do, we returned to the pass.

"Jean-Georges licked the bowl when he had the mussels," Tony said. "He licked the bowl!"

"Jean-Georges Vongerichten was here?" I asked.

"He has a place downtown," Tony said. "*Market.*"

"Right," I said. "So what happened?"

"Okay," said Tony, "so I'm in a plane on the runway in Chicago and my manager calls me to say that Jean-Georges is coming in for dinner that night. I'm supposed to have dinner with Karolyn in Chinatown. Not gonna happen. I call Karolyn, ask her to meet me at the restaurant, have a chef's jacket ready. The plane gets in at five fifty-five; his party of four is getting in at six. I only missed the *amuse*, but I cooked the next nine courses for him. Great evening! Jean-Georges went through the roof!"

Tony glowed. The words had spilled out. I understood how, from his perspective, he had felt it was necessary to cook for one of the world's greatest chefs, and why there was no one on his team he could trust to take his place. I also wondered how his cooks and sous chefs felt knowing that.

"We had just moved to the new location," Tony explained.

"Jean-Georges's people called that same day! It was too important to leave to my team in several ways. I know how chefs think, for one thing: If the food had been bad, if the experience had been bad, word would get around. I've cooked for Chang twice since then. And for Wylie. Chefs talk. I wanted Jean-Georges's experience to be a good one. Just as importantly? If things fucked up, *I* wanted to be the one responsible. Not my sous chefs. Not my line cooks. You know how they feel when someone sends food back? Awful! I didn't want to let them down."

"What if you simply could not be here?" I asked.

"I would have asked that Jean-Georges come in when I could be here," Tony said.

"Do you feel the same way these days?" I asked.

"I trust my crew more now," he said. "Look, if Jean-Georges remembers Craigie on Main, we've got a fighting chance!"

Tony looked over a ticket.

"Pick up black bass," Tony said.

"Great!" said Davey.

"Go, go, go," said Tony.

Tighter organization was evident in the kitchen tonight. Davey, Marian, Patrick, and Jill were working beautifully together, anticipating one another.

"I hope it lasts all night," said Tony. "This is a good push. It's gonna define the night."

Davey was working on several orders at once. Marian and Devon began to fall behind.

"They get nervous," Tony said to me. "They need to know that the only way to do it is to go through the nervousness."

Suddenly, there was a slight turn of events. The machinery seemed to have been oiled by Tony's persistent and encouraging words.

"Coming in!" shouted Marian.

She dived down next to Tony to grab a few plates and returned to her station.

Tony asked Matt to take over at the pass. He went over to help Patrick again.

That done, Tony walked over to Marian. She was red faced, frowning, and moving slowly. She looked overwhelmed as she tried to slice a bone-in duck breast. Tony stabbed the duck with a long needle to test for rareness.

Then he returned to the pass and looked down at a VIP order: Charlie's preschool teacher was in the house!

"I need one meat *amuse* on the fly," he said to Orly. "VIP! On the fly, fly!"

"Chef," said Marian, "could you taste the duck I'm working to see if it's ready?"

Tony did not even look up.

"When it's done and rested, it's ready," said Tony, furiously. He turned to me and said, "We've been over this a dozen times."

A server walked up to the pass to put in two tasting menus, and to add, "Chef, I have an allergy. Shrimps, crab, lobster."

"Got it," said Tony.

He crossed off a completed order.

Meanwhile, Marian was standing over the piece of duck almost motionless, which is taboo in any kitchen.

Tony glanced sideways at her.

"Marian," Tony said, "you have a memory problem. I need you to remember things for at least twenty-four hours."

She did not look up. Davey went over to help her. They conferred. Tony shook his head in annoyance.

Marian was deep in the weeds. It started with not knowing when the duck was ready, continued with not slicing it right, and now she was not plating correctly.

"Why do I see three pieces of duck on each plate?" asked Tony.

He was looking over plates that Marian had brought to him at the pass. "Two! Two pieces! I thought I was clear about that."

"Yes, Chef," said Marian.

She and Davey took back the plates.

Tony's fury was growing by the minute with Marian. One thing she got wrong led to another thing she got wrong until she was getting nearly everything wrong. She could not find a way out. It was sad and terrifying to watch her predicament. The other cooks had to work harder to make up for her mistakes. They also empathized with her, and I could see resentment on Jill's face. It was bad that Marian was having problems, but worse, in her view, that Tony had lost patience with her.

"You were faster yesterday, Marian," Tony said. "You were more organized yesterday."

Marian did not say a word, but every bit of her exposed skin was now bright red.

"I need two more duck right now," said Tony. "Two duck! Two duck! Two duck! Two duck! Listen, Davey, the first time I called this it was ten minutes ago. You gotta make this happen, buddy."

"Yes, Chef," said Davey. "Now!"

Davey was hampered by his efforts to keep Devon on track and Marian focused, all the while cooking food that Tony needed, too. The situation was spiraling out of control.

The risk was this: If Marian did not manage to complete her orders, the other cooks would need to do her work. Then they would fall behind with *their* orders. Soon the entire kitchen would be cooking older orders that should have been completed. New orders coming in would not get done. Guests could find themselves waiting impatiently for food. Servers might not receive good tips. Tony's intensity and anger were fueled by the recognition that as the chef, he was the only person who had the authority and responsibility to turn things around.

"Marian," Tony said, "you're standing there doing nothing."

He stopped what he was doing and walked over to Marian. He put his hands on his hips. He glared at her.

"Marian," he said as calmly as he could, but his voice deepened and grating, "you're taking so many extra steps with the duck. Slice it right."

He took the duck breast from her and swiftly butchered it correctly.

"C'mon," Tony said, "make this happen, please."

He returned to the pass, hoping that his intervention had worked, but when Marian brought the duck over, which she had plated, Tony could not believe his eyes. He was exasperated, but struggled to speak.

"Marian!" he said, finally. "Where's the sauce?! When I tell you it needs sauce, it needs sauce!"

She took back the plate and shuffled off. Tony's anger was getting worse. All the planning, the preparation, the trials before he put a dish on the menu, the expensive product, the thought that had gone into the recipe, the efforts of the cooks . . . gone! Gone because one cook was not getting it right.

Rather than give in to his frustration, Tony chose Davey to handle the situation and decided instead to shave black truffles over a plate of veal, then a second plate, but at the third plate he stopped cold.

"Look at the veal!" he said. "What the *fuck* is this?!"

Davey, Devon, and Marian froze. The veal had come from their station.

"Where are my two sweetbreads?!" asked Tony.

They had forgotten how to assemble the dish despite having made it dozens of time. This lapse further infuriated Tony.

Then Matt stepped in and Davey got even better. The sweetbreads were added to the plate. Food started getting cooked the right way. The cooks regained their intensity.

"Awesome," Tony said almost happily to Matt when he brought over a perfectly cooked whole chicken.

"Oh," sang Davey, "oh, we're fucking doing this!"

Tony clapped his hands.

"Okay, let's go," he said.

He turned to Devon and began to shout orders in rapid succession.

"Four marrow!" said Tony.

"*Oui!*" said Devon.

"Black bass!"

"*Oui!*" said Devon.

"Chicken!"

"*Oui!*" said Devon.

Davey stood between Devon and Marian and kept them organized. He told them what to do; he took the pressure off Tony.

"Marian," said Davey, "what can I do to help you?"

Marian did not say anything, which was a terrible mistake. Cooks might be forgiven when they ask for help or welcome it, but not when they refuse to participate.

"Are you okay?" Davey asked her.

Marian did not respond. The yelling had gotten to her. She was shutting down.

Davey grabbed a chicken to sear on the grill, almost colliding with Marian, and then smiled at me and rolled his eyes.

Tony walked over to her.

"You were so different yesterday," he whispered to Marian. Now his anger was tempered by a desire to understand what was wrong. "What's different tonight?"

Being direct with people, when he did it calmly, focusing on the task rather than the individual, was one of his skills. Tony shook his head and returned to the pass. His phone timer went off.

"Tweety-bird," Tony said. "Okay, Davey, there's your pickup."

Davey got the chicken and placed it on a cutting board for Tony. Tony turned and began slicing it with a long, white-handled blade. He was faster than anyone else in the kitchen and deft with a knife. First, he cut off the thighs and legs. He put them on a plate, spun around, and put that under the salamander. Then he sliced the breasts off the bone. The juices spilled out, the aroma wafted, and by the time he was done, I was salivating.

The chicken was Marian's job, but Tony had had to step in.

Then he came back to the pass, took a ticket for a completed order, and put the paper through the spike. Another ticket came in while he was doing this.

Marian was given a chicken by Davey to cut. He placed it in front of her. She worked laboriously, pressing in, not slicing so much as pushing the knife in. She wasn't close to the bone and then she was too close to the bone.

"You know what we should do?" said Davey. He grinned exuberantly. "We should fire some pigs. Yeah, let's fire some pigs!"

He referred to pigs' faces, which were flying out of the kitchen that night, as usual.

Pigs fired, Davey walked over to Marian and whispered in her ear. She turned and thrust her hips against him, miming sex.

"That's what I want to see!" said Davey. "Some fire!"

Matt showed up at the pass with a small bowl of rye flour *casarecce* with house-cured ham and mushroom ragoût to send out. Tony had gone downstairs to check on Santos, Carlos, and the pastry chefs.

When Tony returned, it was with big strides, focused, in a hurry, trying not to fall further behind. Then he looked over at Marian.

"Marian," he said. "Marian?"

She looked back at him with a defiant expression.

"What are you doing, Marian?!" Tony asked.

She was trying to slice a duck but was doing it wrong again. She worked slowly and without precision. Tony bounded over to her station, grabbed the duck out of her hands, peeled the breast off the bone with a knife, and tossed the bloody bone into a bin next to her.

"That is how you do it!" Tony yelled. "The skin needs to stay on the meat!"

He returned to the pass. Marian just stood there looking at the duck.

Out of Tony's earshot, I heard Marian grumbling to Davey.

"What's wrong?" asked Davey.

"The skin," said Marian. She did not look up. "The skin was okay."

Davey nodded sadly.

"I understand," Davey said to her.

That was all he could say or do.

"C'mon, Jill," Tony said, "I need three things!"

"Yes, Chef," Jill said.

As Tony gave Jill orders, the chicken stuffed with sausage arrived at the pass: Vidalia onions, spinach, potato purée, chanterelle jus.

"Jill," Tony continued, "do you have sandwiches for me?"

"On it, Chef," Jill said.

Orders were not being completed again, the cooks could not keep up again, and Tony was angry again.

"Guys," he said, "are you talking to each other? You are? I don't hear it!"

Tony went back to get the char from Jill to bring it to the window. Even when the cooks were getting it right, they were too slow. Tony shaved black truffles over the fish.

"Okay," he said to Katie, handing her the char, "I need this out of here."

Tony went back to Jill again, this time to get a plate of sandwiches he had ordered and that she had just finished cooking. He gripped the plate rather than held it.

"C'mon," he said tersely, "this is a shit show!"

Then Tony picked up the phone and called downstairs.

"Can you set up a fish board for me and two Arctic char," he said to Carlos. "I'll be there in five minutes."

Downstairs, Carlos set up two big stainless-steel trays next to the vacuum sealer. He put a bed of ice on the first tray and put the second tray on top of it. Then he went to the walk-in and returned with a whole Arctic char, which was about eighteen inches long. The fish had tiny pointy teeth, translucent eyes, and glistening silver skin. Carlos wrapped the fish in a white towel that had long orange and blue stripes alongside it.

Tony showed up with two very large knives. He told Carlos to move everything to a different, larger station where he would have more room to work.

Tony sliced into the fish, just below the gills, and lopped off the head. Next he sliced it across the back.

"Grab a pair of tweezers," he said to Carlos.

"Yes, Chef," said Carlos.

"Get a scale," Tony said. "Grab something to put on it."

"Yes, Chef," said Carlos.

Tony tossed the head and spine into the garbage.

"Now go get some brine," Tony said to Carlos when he returned with the fillets and scale.

Tony continued to trim the fish. He sliced off fat.

Carlos returned with a big bucket of water. Tony portioned the fish into fillets and weighed each piece perfectly on the tiny scale Carlos had brought to him.

"Okay, so listen," Tony said to Carlos, "I want you to pinbone this so I can put it away."

"Yes, Chef," said Carlos.

"It used to be that with every bone I found, there were ten push-ups," said Tony.

"I'm fine with that," said Carlos. "Better you find it than the customer."

"Exactly," said Tony.

Carlos went to work with the tweezers.

"Not bad, Carlos," Tony said. "You have a fighting chance! Let's see if you can do other things as fast."

"Thanks, Chef," said Carlos.

"Now bring the fish up to Jill," said Tony.

Carlos ran behind him and up the narrow stairs to meet Matt at the pass.

"All apps it is!" shouted Matt.

"All apps it is!" said the cooks in unison.

Matt stepped aside. Tony took his place at the pass.

"C'mon," shouted Tony over his shoulder. "We've got to be better! We've got to be better!"

Marian was still having a hard time. Tony shook his head with frustration: He was devastated by how poorly his cooks retained what he had taught them.

"Guys," said Tony, "I'm not the only person with eyes here. C'mon, guys, let's do this right, please."

Tony took a small pot and spooned polenta into bowls. Matt ladled eggs that had been cooked bain-marie onto the polenta.

The dishes finished, Tony stared at the veal that Davey handed him. He had a look of disbelief. Nothing was going right for too long. Just when he was out of the weeds, he was back in again.

"Give me stuff on the veal!" Tony shouted to Davey. One veal dish had the correct sides and *jus*, the other didn't. "Look at this one, and look at this one!"

"Right," said Davey. "That's bullshit! That's bullshit!"

Matt yelled out: "I need an egg on the fly!"

The pace was picking up, but the focus was not there. People were running in circles.

"Listen!" yelled Tony. It was the angriest he had been all night. "LISTEN! No excuses! I don't give a shit! Pay Scott to listen to your bullshit! He's a shrink!"

Then Tony picked up his cell phone and called home. As if he had never even thought of having just been enraged at his cooks, Tony said softly and sweetly, "Hey, Charlie Maws, I just wanted to call and wish you a good night. What'd you eat for dinner? Asparagus? Cool." He listened to his son talk for a few moments. "Awesome! I miss you. Got to go. See you in the morning."

After ending the call, Tony faced the cooks.

"Easy! Easy! Easy!" he said. "Finesse! Finesse! Finesse!"

An ambulance roared by the front of the restaurant, red lights visible, but siren inaudible because of the noise surrounding us. A second ambulance followed. The ambulances were heading either to the housing projects down the street or to the emergency room at Massachusetts General Hospital across the bridge over the Charles River.

"Give me tongues!" shouted Marian. Finally, there was urgency in her voice. The night was ending. "Tongues! Tongues! Tongues!"

Then, not clearly apropos to what was happening, Tony started to tell me a story. "I had a conversation with my high school coach," Tony said. "He turned to me and he said, 'You're not gonna make the team.'"

I looked at Tony's sad face.

"Which sport?" I asked.

"Hockey," Tony said. He crossed off a ticket and put it through a spike. "Hockey was my sport. Belmont Hill. I loved being on that team."

"When was this exactly?" I asked.

"Sophomore year," said Tony. He sighed heavily as he recalled events that took place twenty-seven years ago. "Man, I cried. I just stood there and cried!"

Veal three ways arrived at the pass, and Matt squirted *jus* over the meat and dabbed the rims of the plates clean.

"Why not?" I asked. "Why didn't you make the team?"

"I wasn't tall enough," said Tony. "I wasn't big enough. I weighed one hundred and fifteen pounds: one elbow, one little elbow, and I'd go crashing down to the ice! Coach said I was spunky and a fighter, but that I didn't have the size."

Tony shook his head.

"I still remember that conversation," he said.

He leaned into the pass, slid tickets across the board so that they fanned out, and told Patrick he needed sauce for the chicken.

"That teacher/coach," said Tony, "he's a legend at Belmont Hill. A great guy. About a year ago, he ate here with his family. I hadn't known he was coming in. I missed his name on the reservations list. My jaw dropped! I almost cried. About a week later, he sends me a three-page letter, handwritten on his personal stationery. I picked up the phone and called Karolyn."

"What did you say to her?" I asked.

"'This is fucking awesome,'" he said. "'No one gets this kind of letter!'"

When I thought of what Tony had said, I wondered what it had been like to have been cut because of physical limitations he could do nothing about.

"That coach saved your life, Tony," I said.

Tony laughed.

"How's that?" he asked.

"Saved you from concussions, head injuries, lasting neurological damage," I said.

"Oh, c'mon," he said. "Hockey is a great sport!"

"It's great," I said, "but it's dangerous."

"I loved playing hockey!" he said. "What are you saying?"

"I understand that," I said, "but I'll tell you something: Charlie will never play hockey. Karolyn won't let him. Charlie? Charlie will play tennis!"

"We'll see," said Tony, crossing off another ticket. "You might be right, but we'll see."

It took me over a month before I was startled enough to realize that the story of the coach who cut him was Tony's public narrative: the one Tony believed, and the one that he was convinced I should believe with him. But that coach existed alongside other, more private experiences, much longer stories, and to appreciate Tony's anger, resilience, and ambition it was necessary to put all of these together.

No life has a single "Rosebud" moment that explains everything. What was clear instead from Tony's story was that he still felt he had something to prove to that coach who had cut him because he was too small and to his father who had belittled him for striking out. The fact that Tony could not provide that measure of validation to himself fit in well with cooking for a room of guests to gain their approval, but it was also an infuriating, repetitive exercise. He was, ultimately, angriest at himself.

"Six ducks," said Matt, "two by two by two."

Marian brought the ducks to the window.

"Listen," Tony said to Marian. "Listen, listen, listen. I can't serve this! One of these is nothing but fat! And this one?" He held up a piece of duck meat. "This one is sliced too thick!"

"Yes, Chef," said a crestfallen Marian.

She returned to her station to redo the ducks with Davey's help.

"I need . . . these . . . ducks . . . please," said Tony between clenched teeth.

At long last, the ducks arrived again.

"When I'm done with these ducks," Tony said to me, "we can have dinner together in the bar."

Tony organized the ducks. They had not been plated correctly by the cooks.

Then he walked over to Marian and, livid, he said, "Whatever you fucking did in other kitchens, I don't care where, we don't do that here. I don't cut corners. I don't cut corners! The best thing you can do when you have a shit night is to do it right. The bullshit I'm seeing tonight? It stops now. Right now!"

She was berated for a while. There was no reaction. What could she say? What could anyone say?

"Let me just check on things in prep," Tony said calmly when he was done yelling at Marian.

Tony went downstairs.

It was around midnight. The cooks were breaking down their stations, washing up the surfaces and stovetops.

"Want to go out for a drink when we're done?" Jill asked me.

"Sure," I said. "When do you think that will be?"

"About an hour and a half from now," she said.

"One thirty?" I asked.

"That's about right," she said. "That's when we get out."

I had to say no. I'm up at six with my dogs.

"It was a rough night of service," Matt said to me with a big grin.

"It wasn't unusual," Jill piped in. "I'd say it was typical. Pretty typical for this place."

"But I'm sure you've seen nights like this before in other restaurants," said Matt.

Of course, Matt was right. Chefs are allowed to display public anger, a prerogative unique to professional sports as well, and one they especially revel in early on in their careers. It sure felt better than being sad or worried, and it was glorious to be able to scream at people knowing that they had to take it.

But I also knew that chefs, no matter how great or famous, would have been more productive and had happier lives had they felt and shown less anger. Anger is debilitating, a distraction, and a weak emotion compared to the power of love to change us.

So while I could relate to their intensity, their need to create and nurture, and their passion, it was only when I got older that I understood: You have to let the anger go.

Tony did not have anything to prove to anyone.

When he came back upstairs, he walked over to me. I was standing at the pass.

"What do you feel like eating?" Tony asked.

"Surprise me," I said.

■ ACKNOWLEDGMENTS ■

I get deep pleasure from thanking Laura, my wife, who introduced me to wine, and who shows me how to savor all things
sensual. Delighted, too, to thank Jenni Ferrari-Adler, my agent
and jackal in the making; Andie Avila, my editor, for her keen
eye, honesty, and intelligence; the chefs who introduced me to
restaurant kitchens—Gordon Hamersley and Silvano Marchetto;
Darra Goldstein, who understood right away this project years
ago in *Gastronomica*; the chefs, restaurateurs, and industry folks
from whom I learn something new each time we are in contact:
Daniel Boulud, Thomas Keller, Joël Robuchon, Luca di Vita, Al-
fred Portale, Roger Berkowitz, Mark Fiorentino, Carl Fantasia,
and Jiro Takeuchi; friends who take the time to educate me about
food and dining—Yuko Enomoto, Shinji Nohara, Claude Man-
gold, Shoko Inumaru, Georgette Farkas, Kristine Kiefer, Karina
Shima, Ken Yokoyama, Ueli Buetikofer, Nancy Berliner, and
Takeshi Endo; Chalit Chawalitangkun, a true friend; Jay Cantor,
a real Krazy Kat whose kindness runs deep; Marjorie Maws,
Stewart Maws, and Karolyn Feeks; the entire, stalwart front of
the house and back of the house at Craigie on Main for allowing
me to join them—including, but not limited to, Danny, Jill, Matt,
Orly, Santos, and Ted, whose ferocity is kind of scary; to my
mother and father for picking up the tab all those years—and for

my dad who often told me about how the food he ate while we were growing up fell short of what he remembered eating as a child in Bavaria, and by telling me that introduced the idea that food could anchor memories otherwise adumbrated; and, above all, to Chef Tony Maws, a true original and man whose protean outlook and passion and skill are inspiring.